POSITIVELY
GEARED

FULLY UPDATED AND REVISED EDITION

POSITIVELY GEARED

HOW TO BUILD A MULTI-MILLION-DOLLAR PROPERTY PORTFOLIO FROM A $50K DEPOSIT

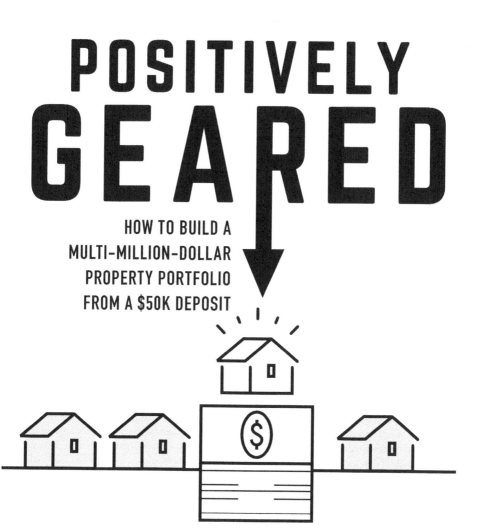

LLOYD EDGE

WILEY

First published 2025 by John Wiley & Sons Australia, Ltd

© John Wiley & Sons Australia, Ltd 2025

The right of Lloyd Edge to be identified as the author of *Positively Geared (second edition)* has been asserted in accordance with law.

ISBN: 978-1-394-29360-5

A catalogue record for this book is available from the National Library of Australia

Registered Office
John Wiley & Sons Australia, Ltd. Level 4, 600 Bourke Street, Melbourne, VIC 3000, Australia

For details of our global editorial offices, customer services, and more information about Wiley products visit us at www.wiley.com.

Wiley also publishes its books in a variety of electronic formats and by print-on-demand. Some content that appears in standard print versions of this book may not be available in other formats.

Cover design by Wiley
Cover image © Scar1984 / Getty Images
Author Photo: Cathy Tiddy, Diamond Portraits
Internal icons: © Happy Art / Shutterstock
Map images: © pingebat / Adobe Stock

Set in Garamond Premier Pro 12/15pt by Straive, Chennai, India

CONTENTS

ABOUT THE AUTHOR

Lloyd Edge was a high-school music teacher and conductor, living in a heavily mortgaged one-bedroom apartment in Sydney's St George region, when he set off on his property investment journey. Over 20 years, Lloyd accumulated a formidable cashflow-positive property portfolio worth $25 million. Today he is an award-winning buyer's agent, the founder and Managing Director of Sydney-based buyer's agency Aus Property Professionals, and author of the bestsellers *Positively Geared* and *Buy Now*.

'Property became my passion,' says Lloyd, 'when I realised it can be a vehicle to financial independence and lifestyle choices.'

One of Australia's most celebrated property investors, Lloyd has helped thousands of Australians to overcome debt and get ahead financially through property. Lloyd's expertise and strategies have made him a household name, regularly contributing to major TV and radio shows, and hosting the podcast, 'Positively Geared', where he leverages his teaching background to demystify property investment. As well as his two books on property, Lloyd has regular columns in real estate publications such as *Australian Property Investor Magazine* and *The Property Tribune*.

For Lloyd, work is now a choice. Retired from the rat race, he lives in a beautiful multi-million-dollar Sydney waterfront home with his wife Renee and two young sons, Riley and Caelen. The family home and their south coast holiday home are both mortgage free, thanks to the investment strategies in this book, which allowed him to 'manufacture' equity without ever having to wait for the market to rise.

Most of all, Lloyd loves to help other people replicate his success by following in his footsteps. This was his motivation for becoming a buyer's agent.

Lloyd has a Diploma in Property Services and holds real estate licences in NSW, QLD, VIC, SA and WA.

He has received several REINSW awards for excellence as well as Real Estate Business (REB) awards and *Your Investment Property* Top Buyer's Agent awards.

Industry accolades for Aus Property Professionals include (at time of publication):

- 2024 — Australia Prestige Awards: Aus Property Professionals, winner

- 2024 — *CEO Magazine's* Executive of the Year Awards: Lloyd Edge, finalist, Property Development and Real Estate category

- 2024 — REINSW Awards for Excellence: Lloyd Edge, winner, Buyers' Agent of the Year

- 2024, 2021, 2020, 2019, 2018, 2017 — REINSW Awards for Excellence: Lloyd Edge, finalist, Buyers' Agent of the Year

- 2024, 2021, 2020, 2019, 2018 — REINSW Awards for Excellence: Aus Property Professionals, among top three finalists in the Buyers' Agency of the Year category

- 2022 — Australian Enterprise Awards: Aus Property Professionals, Property Investment Strategists of the Year

- 2021, 2020 — Real Estate Business Awards: Aus Property Professionals, finalist

- 2021, 2020, 2019 — Real Estate Business Awards: Lloyd Edge, finalist, Buyer's Agent of the Year

- 2019 — REINSW Awards for Excellence: Renee Edge, finalist, Operational Support

- 2018 — Property Investors Awards, *Your Investment Property* magazine: Lloyd Edge, Buyers' Agent, ranked first in NSW, third in Australia

- 2018 — REINSW Awards for Excellence: Renee Edge, winner, Operational Support

ACKNOWLEDGEMENTS

I would first like to thank my wife Renee, with love and gratitude. Renee has been an amazing support for me in everything I do. From the start she encouraged me to follow my dreams and was a major catalyst in getting my business going. I love her more than life itself. Thank you, honey, for all your amazing love and support, and for being such a fantastic mum to Riley and Caelen.

To my gorgeous boys Riley and Caelen, you are the inspiration for everything I do.

To my parents, although they are no longer with us, much respect and gratitude. You made me who I am today. I have always aspired to be as good a parent to my kids as you were to me.

To Anna Warwick, my amazing developmental editor. None of this would have been possible without you. I truly appreciate the tremendous task you took on with me, and I thank you from the bottom of my heart.

To my staff at Aus Property Professionals. You are an amazing team and we are building something special. Thank you each and every one of you for everything you do.

Thank you to all the staff at Wiley for your wonderful support.

PREFACE
LET'S GET POSITIVELY GEARED

Why I wrote this book and why I'm excited you're reading it.

 I'm Lloyd Edge, Australia's leading equity growth strategist. Thanks for picking up this book. Let's get into positive gear and tap a rich vein of the Australian property markets together.

First-time investor? Or just tired of waiting for capital growth on your investment? This book offers a step-by-step guide, presenting the same information you would receive if you hired me as your buyer's agent.

So you're already ahead by more than $10 000 — you're welcome!

In this book you will learn to 'work smarter' in the Australian property markets, taking stress-free steps towards your financial goals by employing my proven strategy of finding high-growth properties, then adding equity and enjoying cashflow every step of the way.

It's what I call my property trifecta: instant equity plus cashflow and capital growth!

THE PROPERTY TRIFECTA

EQUITY + **CASHFLOW** + **GROWTH**

I *won't* promise you'll be buying your dream house this year, or even next year. I *will* show you how to achieve a positively geared portfolio of rental properties that will more than pay for itself — and pay you a nice annual salary as well — so you can quit the 'nine-to-five grind', starting with a deposit as low as $50 000.

My wife Renee and I bought our dream house, a six-bedroom waterfront property in Sydney, New South Wales, in 2018, and only four years later, in 2022, we had paid it off. But in 2008 I was a full-time music teacher earning less than $70 000 per annum, still paying off my first property — a negatively geared one-bedroom unit in Rockdale — when I finally realised *I was never going to get that dream house if I kept doing what I was doing.*

Now I have a property portfolio worth $25 million and a thriving business doing what I love — which is helping people to become financially free, to make better lifestyle choices and to live the life of their dreams, like me.

Every day I help people like you to build wealth through property investment so they can work less and have more time to enjoy life. My clients are paying off their mortgages, getting on top of their debts and achieving financial goals so they no longer need to stress over money or their retirement savings.

I wrote this book so you, too, can find financial freedom by:

- setting a clear, personalised strategy to build a property portfolio that guides you towards your long-term lifestyle goals

- ensuring you buy the *right* property at the *right* price and under the *right* terms

- making money whenever you buy a property, through 'equity creation' (adding value), so you don't have to wait for the long term to see your profits.

SURMOUNTING HURDLES TO SMART PROPERTY INVESTING

Are you a first-time property investor? What's the biggest hurdle preventing you from purchasing a property?

There are six main reasons people become stuck in the nine-to-five grind and are unable to achieve their financial goals:

- They lack the confidence to begin investing in property.

- They don't know where to start.

- They don't have the time to do research and due diligence.

- They don't know how to negotiate on matters related to property and construction.

- They feel trapped into going to work each day to pay off debt.

- They imagine it is too difficult to build wealth through property.

If you feel stuck, you've picked up the right book, because I aim to take the stress out of investing for you. I won't drown you in jargon and complicated investment stuff. I'm not here to show off my hard-won expertise, but to share it! Since the first edition of *Positively Geared* (PG) was published, in 2020, thousands of people have told me they found this book easy to follow. I run free workshops for high-school students, and even these kids love it. Hopefully, so will you.

Do you want to build wealth?

When I was younger I decided I didn't want to wait until I was 65 to retire and finally live life on my own terms. I retired from the nine-to-five at age 40. I can help you too to enjoy life now, to live life on your own terms while you're still in your prime.

Everyone wants to be financially secure and not have to stress over money. You already know that investing, making your savings work for you, is the key to achieving your financial goals. But are you wondering how you can actually make this happen?

Most people buy and hold property for the long term and forgo the opportunities that can be seized in the short term. The problem is most people don't understand that the key to property investing is to *make your money when you BUY, not just when you sell.*

Lose that debt and achieve financial freedom as fast as I did

If you're ready to take the next step, you will love the equity creation strategies I'm going to share with you in this book. I'll detail exactly what you need to be doing to get ahead with your property investing, including:

- how to get that deposit started
- how to read property market cycles
- how to locate areas ripe for capital growth
- how to find off-market purchase opportunities
- how to negotiate effectively on price
- how to manufacture equity in a property.

Once you have devised strategies to suit your starting budget, circumstances and goals, you'll learn about every aspect of implementing these strategies, from securing financing to choosing the right property; from winning at auction to developing properties, becoming a landlord and more.

I have some mind-blowing real-life case studies from my own and my clients' successful investments to share with you as well.

The *huge* benefit of what I'm going to teach you is that you get to reap the rewards of your investment in the short term, so you can use your gains to grow your portfolio. This means you can pay off your mortgage faster, retire earlier and buy your dream home sooner, just as I did. And you'll no longer need to stress about money.

Are you ready to create equity through property so you can achieve your lifestyle goals?

Let's do this!

Lloyd Edge

INTRODUCTION
MY ROAD TO FINANCIAL FREEDOM

How life shaped me to be a successful property investor.

I'm not trying to sell you a hypothetical dream. It's true that I had enough income from my property portfolio to retire by the age of 38, and I did just that at 40, but I wasn't born with a silver spoon in my mouth. I was 28 when I bought my first property. At that time I had a successful career as a musician and music teacher, but I wasn't earning a lot of money.

How did I become a financially independent property investor within 10 years? I'd say it all started with who I was brought up to be. In this introduction I'll share with you something of my journey and the essential qualities and roles, both personal and professional, that helped me create the life I enjoy today.

RESILIENCE

I grew up on a 100-acre (40-hectare) property surrounded by bushland on the outskirts of Orange in the Central West of New South Wales. My dad, Jack, ran a truck springs and chassis repair business he inherited from his father, who had started out repairing wagons and horse-drawn carts. My mother, Barbara, had a side business breeding chickens, Murray Grey cattle and Palomino horses.

We were a very happy family. My younger brother Robert and I spent much of our time riding horses and motorbikes. If I wanted to go camping with my friends, we'd take a tent out the back paddock.

Mum and Dad never had any investment properties. Their only properties were the ones they lived in. Dad sold his house in town to Mum's parents at way under market value, when he moved in with her on the stud farm we grew up on.

Back then you could buy a house for $20 000 — and Mum and Dad were of the mindset that if you couldn't afford to pay the $20 000 in cash, you couldn't afford that house. There's no lending in my family, so they never had any debt.

We were brought up to work hard and to save. My first business venture was a pizza shop, which Dad built for me on the farm. Mum bought the ingredients, then I made and sold the pizzas to my parents for three bucks each: 100 per cent profit! I was eight years old!

Around that time I was knocked unconscious by a cricket bat at a Scouts meeting. I began to suffer from chronic migraines during which I couldn't walk or talk; I was paralytic, overcome by nausea. Mum and Dad spent a fortune on doctors. The migraines happened nearly every day until I was put on medication, and even then I still got them every couple of weeks.

I soon realised this was going to be a part of my life, and I've managed it as best I can ever since. Sure, there have been times in my life when I've been depressed about it, but I haven't let it get me down too much because as soon as I get over being sick, I'm happy and back at it again. I inherited this resilience and love of life from both parents.

A COMPETITOR

When I was nine I joined the local band, playing the baritone, a brass instrument like a small tuba. Despite experiencing a migraine after every band practice, I loved music. Harry, my teacher, started to enter me in local eisteddfods, then regional eisteddfods. But I didn't start winning until I really began to practise. Before the first state championship I entered I practised for hours each day, and sure enough I won for the very first time. I was 13 years old when I learned that if I worked hard enough at something, I would be successful at it.

This was a valuable lesson indeed, because in fact nothing I have achieved in my life has come naturally or easily to me, and I have never succeeded at any venture at the start. But whenever I have developed the passion for something, persisted and worked on the goals, I have won.

Through high school and beyond I won several state and national solo competitions, playing trombone, euphonium and baritone. I sometimes helped my music teacher by mentoring some of his younger students, and I enjoyed that as well.

I also played golf competitively while in high school. I was a member of all three local golf clubs and regularly won Saturday morning competitions around Orange, touring to compete in Bathurst, Wellington and Dubbo. I played off a handicap of 12 by the time I was 15 and I thought about becoming a professional golfer, but I gave it all up because of the migraines and decided to focus on music.

At high school, economics was actually my best subject, but I had my heart set on getting into the prestigious Sydney Conservatorium of Music. I did well in the HSC and in my audition, but I only got a place in the Bachelor of Education program, as 'the Con' didn't accept euphonium players in its Performance course.

Teaching was not my goal, so I went elsewhere. I studied at the ANU School of Music in Canberra and the Illawarra Institute in Goulburn, where I could play my euphonium and work on the trombone. Two years later I reapplied for the Con and got into the Bachelor of Music (Performance) program, majoring in the trombone. I'd auditioned for several other music universities around the country and was offered a place in all of them. My hard work had paid off again!

At last I moved to Sydney to study music. I was living close to the water and as a country boy I appreciated the convenience of walking to the shops. I would go to see orchestras play at the Sydney Opera House and walk around Circular Quay, soaking up the atmosphere. Several of my classmates at the Con were former 'rivals' from music competitions I'd entered growing up, so it was a lot of fun, and we had excellent teachers and mentors.

At university, funds were tight. I often lived in share accommodation with several other students. I was on limited fortnightly Austudy payments from Centrelink. Once I had paid my rent, electricity, train fares and maybe a little petrol for my car — a lovely old petrol-guzzling 1979 Ford Falcon with more kilometres on the clock than I spend on a property these days — I didn't have a lot left over.

Sometimes my old flatmates, who are now very successful musicians, like to remind me of those times, back in the day, when all I could afford was a 30-cent ice-cream cone from McDonald's for lunch and I often had to go without dinner. I guess I have come a fair way in the past 30 years!

I was loving life though, but then in 1995, while in my first year at the Con, my dad got cancer. I knew he was 26 years older than Mum — he'd fought in World War II — but I was young and still believed my parents were going to be there forever.

The day my father died Mum came down to Sydney to watch me play in a recital. She broke the news to me afterwards. It hit me hard. I was devastated. I had to take time off my studies and repeat a couple of subjects as I'd slipped so far behind.

A TEACHER

At last I graduated from the Con and was playing professionally in bands and orchestras: the Sydney Brass Ensemble, the Sydney Youth Orchestra and the Willoughby Symphony Orchestra. I even played at the Sydney Opera House quite a few times over the years.

I was very happy as a musician but the work was inconsistent, so with a bit of reluctance I started picking up some instrumental teaching jobs. I loved helping the students play the best they could on their instruments, the way I had done when I helped Harry back in high school. That's when I realised that teaching was actually something I would enjoy. Soon I started to love teaching more than playing.

Even now I can't stop teaching. A desire to educate people about property is the reason I wrote this book. So my passion for teaching has never died.

A SAVER

As soon as I was earning money, I started to save as much as I could. I was renting in poorer areas of Sydney because that's what I could afford. I never had a credit card, I didn't go overseas on a 'gap year' holiday and I still drove old cars. I just put my money away for the future.

I am still very frugal. My wife Renee often urges me to buy new clothes. We have a running joke between us that I'll spend hundreds of thousands on an investment but won't fork out $20 for a new shirt from Kmart. The way I see it, that shirt will not yield a financial return so it's not a good investment!

A HOMEOWNER

I was fortunate to be teaching at schools in quite wealthy areas on Sydney's North Shore and in the Eastern Suburbs. I'd go around to give a kid a private music lesson at their harbourfront home with their parents' BMW convertibles parked in the driveway and I'd think, geez, how do these people afford to live like this? I'm a struggling musician here, renting a cheap unit. How I'd love to be in this position one day!

In 2004 my grandma passed away, and my mother moved off the farm and into the house in Orange that originally belonged to Dad's parents almost 100 years ago. She gave the farm to my brother and me as 'a start'. Rob bought out my share; he's still got the farm and lives there to this day.

With this small family inheritance and the money I'd been saving, I had a good deposit to buy my own property. But how was I going to get a mortgage, as a self-employed music teacher earning less than $50 000 a year?

I found a very good mortgage broker who got me a 'low-doc' (low-documentation) home loan from a non-bank lender, where I didn't need to produce payslips. I would have struggled without that first loan, so I was lucky.

With my pre-approved budget, the choice came down to an older two-bedroom apartment or a brand-new one-bedroom apartment. I decided to go with the new apartment in Rockdale: a shoebox of less than 50 square metres that cost me $250 000.

When I first moved in, Rockdale felt small to me, but it was close to the water and, while I had no clue that I'd be a serious property investor one day, I knew this was just a start for me in the property market.

It was the start of my travels as well. Six months later I took my first trip overseas: a whirlwind 16-countries-in-three-weeks Contiki tour of Europe. At 30 years old I was the second-oldest person there, but I didn't care.

A STRATEGIST

Since 2003 I'd been working at Moriah College — a private Orthodox Jewish school in Sydney's Eastern Suburbs — first just one day a week, but by 2005 I was there four days a week, teaching brass and conducting.

In 2006 I was appointed the Head of Brass and Percussion at Moriah. Now a full-time teacher, I was still playing gigs and conducting with the Willoughby Symphony Orchestra and the NSW Fire Brigades Brass Band, with whom I went on tour to Austria and Germany. Competitive as ever, I joined several of Australia's leading brass bands — I continue to play with them to this day — and win national band championships.

I was now drawing a pretty good teaching salary for a job that didn't involve classroom teaching. But I knew there was a limit to how much I could earn as a teacher, and superannuation wasn't going to pay me enough to retire on.

Rockdale, my 'buy and hold' property and home, wasn't worth any more than I'd paid for it in 2003. I was thinking, what have I done? I've got property in a good location, just like you're supposed to, but I'm not making money.

Of course, I'd bought Rockdale at the wrong time: after the Sydney Olympics 2000 spike, when the property market was declining. But the fact that the property hadn't performed yet made me think there had to be a better way of doing this, because there were people out there making a lot of money from property.

I started reading books and articles about wealth creation every night after work. I realised that trading your time for money your whole life doesn't get you anywhere. I was inspired by people who had used their success with property to achieve financial independence. That's when I decided that if I was ever going to retire from teaching, property would be the vehicle.

AN INVESTOR

I thought, okay, I want to start expanding. I need a second property. I looked at some of the cheaper areas in Sydney and in 2008 bought a three-bedroom villa in Ingleburn for $262 000. I moved into Ingleburn and rented out my Rockdale property straight away. I was now officially a property investor, but Rockdale was negatively geared.

I was living in a working-class suburb and everyone at school was bagging me out. It was frustrating being so far out, 50 kilometres from the Sydney CBD, but now I was focused on the bigger picture. I knew the first few years would be hard, but I had the end in sight. I wanted financial independence, and then I bought my third property — and I knew I could get there.

Two months after buying my property in Ingleburn I looked into how much I was going to have to borrow to buy another. I realised that if I was to keep moving forward I needed 'cashflow-positive' properties. But I didn't yet understand that *creating growth* is more important than high rental yield.

While educating myself, I enlisted the help of a buyer's agent. I told him I wanted cash in the bank at the end of the week. The property he found me was a house in a regional mining town called Blackwater in Central Queensland. It cost $260 000 but it was returning about $800 a week, so it had a good yield, and for the first few years it was getting a lot of growth.

Then the mining sector collapsed, and in towns like Blackwater rents and values tumbled. Some people had 10 of these properties. Fortunately, I'd taken a calculated risk and bought only one. In hindsight the buyer's agent should not have recommended that property. More about that later when we discuss locations and investment-grade properties.

After Blackwater, I really started to get the bug. I became a lot savvier about my purchases. I was pretty single-minded. Colleagues at work were saying, 'Four or five properties — aren't you worried about debt?' But I was just getting started, and to my mind they were too wary of the risks.

A ROMANTIC

In 2009 another passion was ignited in my life. I was conducting the Sutherland Police Citizens Youth Club band and one day we welcomed a new clarinetist: a beautiful and brilliant brunette who immediately caught my eye.

Renee was a chartered accountant working for Ernst & Young. It took more than a year for me to ask her out. I imagined she saw me only as the conductor at the front of the band. She's 12 years younger than me, yet this was half the age difference that had existed between my parents. Dad had always thought the age gap would be too big between them, which meant Mum had to chase him for four years before he finally decided to go out with her.

Luckily, I shared my mother's romanticism and patience, because I had to chase Renee for a while. I started organising parties at my place in Ingleburn. Renee didn't realise I was having 20 people over every couple of weeks just so I could get to know her more. I was forever dropping hints like, 'You don't know what you've got till it's gone ...'

Then we went on a couple of band trips and in Tasmania, at the 2010 Australian National Band Championships, we got quite close. After that, we started to spend time together, and she would come for rides on the back of the motorbike with me. She had no fear, which I thought was pretty cool. We had a lot of fun.

Three months after we started dating, I thought, this feels right. Let's set up a life together ... and we bought an $800 000 house in Sydney's Inner West. Buying a house with a mortgage on it is a bigger commitment than an engagement ring, but the risk was on me because it was my $200 000 deposit. Maybe Renee would have felt differently if she had put down money! Then she went and bought all the furniture, so I knew she was on board. Three months after we moved in together, we were engaged.

Meeting Renee changed my life in many ways. I know she helped me dress better and was always taking me shopping, but she inspired me in many ways — and ultimately it was Renee's idea that I start a business in property on top of my investments.

AN OPTIMIST

In 2010 I was appointed as director of Moriah's Symphonic Wind Ensemble. I took them on a tour of America and Israel in 2011 and again in 2014. We did 20 concerts in 21 days, including performances at Disneyland. I also conducted them to victory at the NSW state championships and in the Sydney Eisteddfod in 2012.

It was a great experience for the kids in the ensemble, but it took up a lot of time, as we rehearsed every Sunday and all school holidays for the whole year. I was also getting up at 5:30 every day to conduct an early-morning band rehearsal. I didn't get paid overtime, and every time I conducted I was rewarded with a migraine.

After a while that lifestyle took its toll. I thought, you only live once. That's a cliché only because it's true. I've always felt strongly that when you're not passionate any more, you should start looking for a change. There were teachers at the school in their sixties who said they wished they'd retired and done something else 30 years ago. I thought, well it's not very fair to the kids if you're just here because you don't know what else to do.

I already knew exactly what I wanted to do: I wanted to create the financial freedom to live life on my own terms. Since I was a kid entering those first music competitions, I'd known that if I worked hard enough, I could achieve anything. When I got serious about property investing, I adopted the mindset that I would succeed no matter what. So I made the difficult decision to step down as director of the Symphonic Wind Ensemble.

A DEVELOPER

I had a good property portfolio, but it still wasn't returning enough to cover my salary and make me financially independent. So I was doing lots of reading and attending seminars on ways to make money quickly by *developing properties instead of waiting for capital growth.*

In 2012 I bought a corner block in the best area of Armidale in NSW's Northern Tablelands for $159 000. I built a duplex on it and the whole development project, including construction, council costs, stamp duty and legals, came to $629 000. And when it was completed, it was subdivided into two separate properties.

Here's the kicker: I had the two separate properties valued and they came back at $380 000 and $390 000 respectively. This left me with $141 000 in equity — twice as much money as I was making in a whole year of teaching.

And that's when the light bulb went off in my head. I thought, well, I'm onto something here. The two properties rented easily. Now I had positive cashflow *and* I was able to borrow off the equity.

Renee and I got married and I was on top of the world. Best of all, the Armidale subdivision really got Renee interested in property as well. She said, 'Let's do it again!'

In 2013 alone I bought five properties in New South Wales and Queensland using mainly the equity achieved from that first subdivision. I'd come home and say, 'Honey, I bought another property today!' and Renee would say, 'Oh yeah? Where?'

The Armidale duplex was my 'aha moment'. As I repeated the process in 2013 and 2014, I had some good developments where I made $200 000 profit — and from there the profits increased exponentially. Now I was creating equity, and my life turned around. And I'm thinking, okay, now I know how I'm going to achieve my goal.

The idea of starting my own business crept in when Renee started saying things like, 'When you're meeting clients in cafés you can talk to them about your duplexes!'

Knowing I had a few good investments, family and friends started asking me whether I'd recommend the suburb they wanted to buy in, how contracts worked and whether I would recommend builders I'd used. It got to the point where Renee said, 'Why don't you just start writing blogs and getting it out there, so I don't have to listen to you talking about property at home all the time?'

So I started a blog called Aus Property Powwow, posting all kinds of free information on property development as well as some of my own investing insights and my thoughts on the markets in general. People were reading the blog and commenting, then some started to approach me directly, asking if I could help them with some property searches, but I wasn't yet qualified to give such advice.

By the time I was 38 years old, my passive income from my property portfolio had topped $100 000 annually, which was higher than the best salary I'd ever earned as a teacher. But I wasn't going to leave teaching and just do nothing, so I made a decision. I resolved to become a buyer's agent and help people navigate the world of property.

A GOAL-SETTER

I enrolled in a three-year Diploma in Property Services. The kids at school knew about the blog and used to ask me about property, but none of the teachers at Moriah knew what I was doing or that I'd soon be retiring from work.

I was on a mission. I'd get up at 5:30 am, start work at 7:00, teach all day then study until about two o'clock every morning. I ended up getting my diploma in three months and obtained my full real estate licence in multiple states.

One of the perks of my new passive income was that when I had free time, I could afford to travel. So in April 2015 I decided to climb to Mount Everest Base Camp to celebrate my graduation.

My previous travels to Europe and the Middle East had been about experiencing different cultures in modern cities, but going to Nepal and seeing first-hand how people lived — on virtually nothing — changed my perspective in a few ways.

Many Nepalese lived in houses that were only half built or were built of straw. They didn't even have clean drinking water. Yet they seemed so happy, despite having so little, because they knew no other life. The kids ran around and played in the streets and were happy just to be alive.

Back home we all worry about how big our houses are and getting the latest sophisticated toys for our kids, yet people in developing countries who lack our advantages can still live full and happy lives.

But what I also saw is that these kids were missing out on a decent education. It made me realise how lucky we are in the developed world, and it made me want to help change this situation in the future.

I was thinking, I build duplexes back home so maybe I can build something for these people here someday. Maybe we can contribute to building a school or community housing? This new big dream made me see how developing my wealth and growing investments and my business might give me the opportunity to do something significant for others. I was more motivated than ever to succeed.

A PROPERTY PROFESSIONAL

When I got back from the 17-day hike to the Everest Base Camp, I saw some missed calls and emails from the Moriah College rabbi's wife. I thought, am I in trouble? But she knew I was an investor—and she became my first client. I started popping in on my way to school to give her property advice.

To make it official, Renee had registered my business name, Aus Property Professionals, while I was away in Nepal. My initial thought was, well, if I can help 10 clients a year, that'll be a good business. I wasn't planning on having anyone else work for me. I thought, if I can earn enough money to replace my teaching salary, while maintaining my property portfolio (which had also replaced my teaching salary), I'll be happy.

But then things really took off. I was featured in various property podcasts, on radio and in magazines, and I started getting a profile as a property investor, especially for my duplex developments. The media were calling me 'the duplex guy'.

I had people contacting me even before I had a website up, wanting to know about what I'd done and how I'd done it, and whether I could help them. Many of them could really relate to my story: that I had not always been doing property; that I was a teacher, on a fairly ordinary income, when I started investing, and I grew my portfolio from there.

I was getting multiple enquiries a week. I was already used to getting by without much sleep after cramming for my real-estate qualifications. I'd start work very early in the morning, teach all day, deal with clients by email over the lunch break, then deal with more clients at night, and at weekends. I did two full-time jobs for a year.

I'm sure some of the other teaching staff saw that I was becoming less motivated than I had been, and I can freely admit now that I was struggling to be there every day. So I took long-service leave and used the three months to make sure that I could run the business successfully full-time. Failure just wasn't an option.

While on leave in January 2016, I summited Mount Kilimanjaro in Tanzania. I was the only climber from all the groups that day who elected to stay up on the freezing summit, despite the thin oxygen, to view the spectacular craters for five hours before descending.

Yes, that was risky. Leaving a full-time job could be perceived as risky too, but you need to take some risks if you're going to achieve your maximum potential in life. I am a firm believer that there is no such thing as job security. This is why we all need to invest and take control of our future. It was also a main catalyst for my decision to write this book.

AN ENTREPRENEUR

I was 40 years old when I retired from teaching so I could get out there and give it a go for myself in business.

Renee and I had a mortgage together. I think a lot of spouses would have said, 'Oh, you shouldn't give up the security of your job,' but she totally supported my decision to quit that job and follow my passion in property.

A couple of days before I finally resigned from my job at Moriah, I went to a park, sat by myself and worked it through in my mind. Okay, is starting a business the right decision? Should I do it now? Is this really the right move? I concluded I had a very clear decision to make. And what I did was I backed myself. I knew I would succeed; I was confident that I had the knowledge and the work ethic to grow the business. Plan B was to make sure plan A worked.

People asked, 'Are you at least going to have a holiday after you retire from teaching?' But that Friday afternoon, the last day of my teaching career, I got into my car and took a call from a developer. As I drove out through the school gates for the last time, I realised it was the end of an era.

And on Monday morning I went straight into my business full-time.

I definitely felt a sense of freedom, because I wasn't tied down to a job routine any more, and great satisfaction that I was no longer answerable to a boss. And I didn't have to sit in peak-hour traffic to get to work every morning. It was fantastic. This had been my dream. I was living life on my own terms, building the life I wanted, creating my own destiny.

I already had years of successful investing behind me, so in no time new clients were coming to me. They were impressed that I had grasped the nettle and retired early to live the dream, and that I was doing something a bit different, which was creating equity.

Very soon I had 10 clients in a month. I learned so much. I got involved with a lot of other entrepreneurs and business owners. I started a group on Facebook called Base Camp Property Group, which is where I mentor people entering the property market. I employed more people — and pretty soon we had so much on the go, I could scale the business.

A SUCCESS

I have some big clients who've done multiple properties through us over the years, and some bigger properties. We've got expat clients in the UAE, Hong Kong and Singapore, who we get to meet with when we're travelling.

I'm not all about just helping people with massive property portfolios, though. I love helping people on low incomes who are trying to get ahead. Those are the people I really enjoy helping to grow their portfolios, build larger incomes and improve their lifestyles, because I started where they are, I get all that.

Renee came on board in September 2017. I didn't really have a job for her, but she pushed her way in! As a chartered accountant with a Bachelor of Economics who then did her Certificate in Real Estate, Renee was highly qualified.

Soon she was sourcing properties, finding property managers and organising insurance for clients. She turned out to be pretty good at writing blogs herself. Renee has won awards from the Real Estate

Institute of New South Wales for the successful work she's been doing, to add to the wall of top buyer's agent awards in my office.

Today I have a property portfolio worth $25 million, a beautiful waterfront home, nice cars and a boat. Renee and I don't need to work but we both love what we do. And when you love what you do, it's true that you don't work a day in your life. I started with that one-bedroom shoebox apartment and worked up to this, so I still look back on where I used to be and really appreciate where I am at the moment.

A FATHER

Renee, Lloyd, Caelen and Riley

Along with our dream jobs, our dream home, dream cars and a dream boat (you get the picture), in 2019 we welcomed a son, Riley. His second name's Jack, after my dad. Then, in 2021, our second son, Caelen, was born. His middle name is Danny, after Renee's dad. As my own boss, I was able to get to every single one of Renee's prenatal appointments and Riley and Caelen's baby appointments, and I can take the boys to swimming lessons, martial arts or to the park during the week. It's all about creating lifestyle choices so you can actually do things like that.

I want my sons to grow up well-grounded and with integrity, as I did. I also want them to have empathy for those without their advantages and a real understanding of their own good fortune. When they are old enough, Renee and I will bring Riley and Caelen with us to volunteer in Africa or Nepal. That's one of my big life dreams, and it's one of the reasons I am still in the game and growing my business. It's not just about becoming a multi-millionaire, but about what I can do for others and the legacy I mean to create.

I still do something for myself, as well. I haven't given up my music and I play in Australia's premier brass band, the Sydney City Brass. We've been the state champions and the Australian champions a couple of times over the past few years, which satisfies my competitive drive as well as my creative drive.

These days I know a lot of people who live life on their own terms. Every day I deal with successful business owners, entrepreneurs and property investors — and I can tell you there are plenty of people out there who began where you did, then really gave it a go, doing much of what this book recommends to achieve financial freedom.

If they can do it, and if I can do it, I promise you, so can you.

BEFORE WE GET STARTED

My advice to ordinary Australians is that Australia is still the 'lucky country'; if you work hard and smart, you can make your own luck. You need to dream big.

Perhaps you're on an average income and have limited savings. I have discovered that a deposit of as little as $50 000 is a viable starting point to building a property investment portfolio and achieving financial independence. What's more, *you will never have to save for a deposit again.*

The truth is, the premise that holding down a nine-to-five job will guarantee our security or wealth, as we were led to believe when we were young, can no longer be counted on. Which is why we should all be investing.

I want to reach out to those mums and dads (or grandmas and grandpas) who are looking to retire and downsize, and show them how the freedom of self-reliance and a passive income for the rest of their lives is within their grasp.

This book offers a lifeline to young families who are stuck in a rut and can't see a way out of their mortgage worries and restrictive nine-to-five jobs. I also offer practical, achievable options for those who want to buy a second and a third property as stepping stones on their journey towards their lifetime goals.

Most of all, I write for those who feel they can't afford to enter the Australian property markets. If you are among those low-income Aussies, I can help you achieve a lifestyle you never dreamed possible.

Most of my clients in their twenties have expressed a desire to change their job or their lifestyle by the time they're 40. They may have a family on the horizon and want to set themselves up so one partner need not work any longer and can look after and be with their kids. If they're renting a property, they long to have a home of their own. I can show them how to achieve these goals because I have done it myself, starting from a very low base.

The worst thing you can do is to do nothing.

So let's get started!

CHAPTER 1

KNOW YOUR WHY

Set your big-picture lifestyle goals for wealth creation.

Welcome to my office! For every client who walks through my door, the process starts with goal-setting. This is a vital first step to creating their *property investment strategy*.

In this chapter, we'll work on helping you to determine your long-term lifestyle goals, then look at how you can achieve these goals using property as your vehicle. So, have you thought about where you would like to be in 10- or 15-years' time?

WHY HAVE A GOAL?

Because at the end of the day you need a reason for investing, and whether you do it in property or in shares or futures or art works, you need a vehicle that motivates you to stick to your chosen investment strategy.

We'll begin by looking at the bigger picture of what you're trying to achieve, and work backwards to figure out how much money you're going to need to get there. Then we'll look at the different types of property acquisition strategies that could enable you to achieve those goals.

Strategy is really important when you're buying an investment property. You can't just 'buy blind'. I see this all the time. People post on social media, asking me, 'What do you think about this house?' or saying, 'This house looks good!', but there's no rationale behind it.

A lot of people will buy a property solely because they think it's a good area to buy in, without really knowing what that property can do for them. Others buy close to where they live because they think that way they can easily keep an eye on the property. That's also not a good thing to do. You don't want to buy close to where you live unless where you live happens to be the best investment spot in the country. But even if it is a good area to buy in, you need to understand *why* that's going to be good for your goals.

DOING WHAT YOU'RE SUPPOSED TO DO IS A FLAWED STRATEGY

I want you to recognise that you really can do anything you want if you put your mind to it. You can be an entrepreneur, a business owner or a successful property investor (or all three). You can create your own lifestyle choices — if you set about devising a strategy to achieve it.

I believe that a lot of what we're taught in school is flawed. School is about getting good marks in the standard curriculum. It doesn't teach you enough about finances or investing. Tertiary education sets you on a single career path, so you can buy a house and pay off a mortgage for 30 years.

I did what I was 'supposed' to do, and by the age of 30 I was working for a boss six days a week, for little reward and no real recognition, and with someone else taking the glory. I realised I didn't want to be in that situation any more; I wanted to create my own destiny.

At that time I was also buying my first properties in the way that everyone has historically bought properties — by negatively gearing them. And I quickly realised that it's a flawed strategy as well. If you negatively gear your properties, you'll be stuck in that job forever. The whole idea of investing is to get yourself *out* of the rut so you can start to live the life you choose.

Most people are too scared to leave a secure job to follow their dream. But if you build up property investments that are positively geared and look after themselves, then you no longer need to rely on another source of income because *the investments are paying you an income.*

That's what I did, and now I have a business as well. These two income streams offer me far more security than being in a job where at any point the boss can say, 'We don't need you any more.'

In my case, I lost my passion for teaching music and made the decision to change my life. I set myself the goal of retiring by age 40, by which time I'd no longer need to rely on my super or pension to get by.

At the time I was on $70k. I had four properties. I lived in my Ingleburn property and had investment properties in Rockdale, Blackwater and Toowoomba. My mortgage payments, less my income from work and rent, meant I was *losing* money each week. Apart from Blackwater, I was negatively geared on all the properties, meaning the rent I received each week was less than my outgoings (mortgages, plus bills and repairs).

If I had just waited for capital growth, it would have been a very slow journey to building my wealth and each property would need to have been bought years apart. So I started to visualise how I could *manufacture growth*, and the types of properties that would work for me. After I did my first duplex development I knew this was going to work, because I was creating equity. I made twice as much money in my first duplex development as I earned in a whole year in a nine-to-five job.

CREATING EQUITY MEANS ADDING VALUE

The problem with relying on a portfolio of properties with only organic capital growth — that is, growth that occurs naturally by way of market movements — is that it can be very slow. And there is no guarantee of how much growth you will get, so typically you need to wait a long time to make a profit. I don't know about you, but I'd rather make my profit in the short term. Having said that, I still advocate that you hold your properties for the long term so you can reap the rewards of positive cashflow, which is needed to help you attain your goals. You will achieve the trifecta if you get instant equity, organic capital growth and positive cashflow.

The way to achieve your goals faster is to take control of your portfolio and actually *manufacture that growth*. This is what I mean by *creating equity* in your portfolio.

Equity is the 'fair market value' of a property based on a bank valuation, minus how much you owe on the property. So if you have a property that is valued at $400 000 and you have a loan of $300 000 on it, then you have $100 000 in equity. This would mean that your loan-to-value ratio (LVR) is 75 per cent, meaning you have 25 per cent equity in the property.

Rental yield is the return on your property investment. To figure this out, use the monthly rent to calculate the annual rental income, then divide it by the property's purchase price and then multiply it by 100. You will get a percentage that will be the gross rental yield. Net rental yield is what's left after costs are taken out.

The big difference with what I do is that, where you traditionally get 4 to 5 per cent rental yields and maybe an average of 6 to 7 per cent growth on properties (depending on the market and where it sits in the property cycle) when I focus on building duplexes or buying houses to renovate, we get a lot more growth than that. And we're looking at 7 per cent plus, for yields as well.

On top of yields you get instant equity — by which I mean within 12 months or less — which can mean 20 to 25 per cent in capital gains. Compare 25 per cent capital growth through instant equity to 6 per cent through organic capital growth over a longer period, and you can see that developing and renovating properties is a no-brainer — and a much quicker way to reach your financial and lifestyle goals.

Going back to the $400 000 property example, if you increase the equity by doing something clever with the property, such as a subdivision or renovation, you've added value to the property (from $400 000 to

$500 000). Your loan is still $300 000, assuming you haven't added to it, and suddenly you've got $200 000 equity in the property.

Now you can use that equity you've created to go and buy another property straight away, then another and another. This is how you attain your goals more quickly.

We can afford to do all of these things if we invest in the right type of properties.

MORE MONEY MEANS MORE CHOICES

People say, 'Money doesn't create happiness' and even 'Money is the root of all evil.' I don't believe this, but what money does is create choices.

You should be setting yourself up for the future, and ultimately for retirement. You've got the pension and you've got super, but they don't pay very well. And you should not have to work your whole life. If I was still teaching, I wouldn't be in a position to retire until I was 70, and even then I'd be close to broke! Far better to retire early and, ideally, leave something for your kids if you have them.

This book isn't about becoming a multi-millionaire; it's about creating the life you want to live. Without money, your choices are limited — you can only live according to your means.

As a teacher, I got to a certain level and realised, well, I couldn't progress any further. I couldn't drive a nicer car or live in a better house, because I couldn't afford it. I've always wanted to live in a waterfront home and drive a nice car. Property investing allowed me to achieve these lifestyle goals even on a teacher's salary. My salary was used to obtain the loans, but I invested strategically to create equity and cashflow, allowing me to achieve my goals and to continue investing.

Certainly, retiring from a nine-to-five job with my property portfolio has already given me great freedom. And people often ask me why I choose to keep working and running a business. Personally, I always need something to do — goals to achieve, contributions to make. Sitting on the beach all day is something I do only on holiday! I can't just do nothing. When I'm 90 years old I'll still be working, and it will be my choice.

This book is about creating freedom. Freedom is about creating choices. There are teachers out there who love their work so much, they would never willingly retire. I'm not saying everyone quit their job, because society needs dedicated teachers and firefighters and nurses and doctors, but if they build a property portfolio on the side, they can create financial opportunities to create a happier life in the present or the future. The life they deserve.

For me, there is one big reason for me to keep building and expanding Aus Property Professionals.

Building an incredible team at Aus Property Professionals has given me the freedom to take time off to go and do the volunteering activities that are so important to me. I enjoy helping people in the local community. And as we build the business, more of my funds will be directed this way.

I've participated in the Vinnies CEO Sleepout, where my clients and I have raised thousands for the homeless. I'm a regular donor to the Cancer Council of Australia, a cause that has been close to my heart since losing my dad to the disease. I donated a fair bit to the 2020 bushfire appeals. I also donate two instrumental scholarships every year to the Orange Eisteddfod, where I got my start as a musician, to encourage young talent whose families lack the means to pay for tuition fees. I offer workshops for high schools, to teach kids how to understand the property market and to start budgeting and saving from a young age so they can invest wisely.

It takes time and money, and living your life free from the nine-to-five grind, to contribute in a practical way, and my business and investments allow me and my family to do that.

Money's looking pretty good, right?

SUCCESS STORY
Using equity to buy a dream home in Sydney

My clients achieved massive growth with their Northern NSW duplex build.

I helped my clients, 30-something new parents Alex and Sam, to buy their dream home in Sydney, where they could raise their three-year-old daughter. Hardworking couple, Alex and Sam already owned a unit each in Sydney, which added up to a $3.3 million portfolio between them, when they came to Aus Property Professionals.

THE STRATEGY

Our strategy session revealed their long-term goal: to purchase a four-bedroom home in Sydney's Northern Beaches. Despite their existing portfolio, the couple's current income was a single income, as they had a small child to care for. This was not enough to give them the borrowing power to buy in the suburbs they wanted. With a budget of $2 million, they needed to create more deposit through equity if they were ever going to buy their dream home.

The strategy for their next investment was to gain significant equity in a short period of time, and we needed to find a development that we could complete for around $1 million, which would then leave room for a potential second development.

In a booming market, we decided that a duplex development on the east coast of Australia was the fastest way to build equity plus positive cashflow from day one. One duplex block would not be enough, though. They would need to use the equity to build a second development. They could then sell both developments, and sell down one of the units in their existing portfolio, to achieve the funds for their dream home.

THE LOCATION

We were drawn to Lennox Head in Northern Rivers, a town on the north coast of NSW, because we could see that the current market was undervalued, with excellent potential for future growth.

(continued)

SUCCESS STORY (*cont'd*)
Using equity to buy a dream home in Sydney

The area was ideal due to a competitive rental market, with vacancies below 1 per cent, and 10-year rental trends were on an upward trajectory. Average annual capital growth in property values had been consistently above 10 per cent over the past decade.

To meet the growing population, plenty of facilities were being developed by the local government, with $100 million committed for infrastructure projects in the area, along with over $300 million for hospital upgrades and over $350 million to improve local amenities.

THE BUILD

When sourcing land, we chose a block with a suitable coastal water aspect so we could do a design that would utilise the views. This would increase the potential return for both equity and rental. The block was in a quiet location, but close to amenities.

The contours of the land and the slope of the block, which declined away from the road towards the water, did affect the build costs, making it a bit more expensive.

Since these properties had an exit strategy, as a part of their long-term goal to buy a dream home, Alex and Sam wanted them to be as premium as possible within the $800000 build budget. Each duplex would have three bedrooms and two bathrooms, plus a two-car garage. The floorplan was designed so each duplex would enjoy water views from most rooms. They included high-end specifications, including 2.7m high ceilings, floor-to-ceiling tiles in the bathrooms, and 40mm benchtops as well as 900mm appliances in the kitchen.

The build came in within budget, all inclusive, and total time for the build to completion was eight months after the development approval (DA) came from council.

THE RESULTS

The units were then Torrens titled. The valuation of each unit at end of build was $1.1 million, or $2.2 million total. This, less the build costs, meant Alex and Sam had made $986 910 in instant equity.

Both units were rented out before handover for $880 per week per unit. This gave them a total cashflow of $1760 per week. The rental yield on the Lennox Head duplex development is 7.5 per cent.

Duplex development costs

 Land price: $400 000

 Construction price (inc. council and strata titling costs): $800 000

 Stamp duty (payable on land only): $12 735

 Other purchase costs and holding costs during construction: $30 000

 Total project costs: $ 1 242 735

Independent valuation (after strata titling)

 Unit 1: $1 100 000

 Unit 2: $1 100 000

 Total value: $2 200 000

Instant equity: $957 265

Current rental yield: 7.5 per cent

WHAT'S NEXT?

Alex and Sam are refinancing the equity in this project so they can repeat the process. In about five years they will sell these Lennox Head duplexes and one of their Sydney apartments to be able to buy their dream home. With growth the way it is currently, there is a chance they will more than double their equity during that time, leaving them with plenty of leverage. With this kind of equity and cashflow, they will not need to sell the next duplex development, but keep them rented out (to become assets for their child in the future).

GOAL-SETTING

So let's get down to it. *Where do you want to be in five, 10 or 15 years' time* with your financial and lifestyle goals?

My clients come from many different backgrounds. Some are single young professionals; some have young families; some are older mums and dads looking to retire and downsize. Some don't want to sit on just one property; they're savvy enough to want to buy a second and a third property and move towards their goals.

Everyone is different, but most of my clients in their twenties or early thirties aspire to a change in career or lifestyle by the time they're 40. There might be kids on the horizon; they may want to get to the point where they and their partners don't need to work any more. If they're renting property, they may look forward to living in their own home — perhaps their dream home.

You may not have thought it through yet, but if I give you a bit of a nudge, you will probably have a fairly clear idea of what you want to achieve. You just might not know how to get there.

Let me start by asking what kind of work/life balance you want. Would you like to:

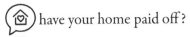 have your home paid off?

be able to retire on a comfortable income?

semi-retire?

work part-time?

change jobs?

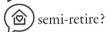 work for yourself?

If you have a family, do you want to be able to:

 put your kids through private schools?

live comfortably on one income?

go on family holidays?

build a property portfolio to secure your family's long-term future?

What else is on your wish list? Would you like to:

buy your dream home?

take a round-the-world cruise?

buy a yacht?

help underprivileged communities?

You get where I'm coming from! Start with your end goal in mind because once you know your goal, then you can turn that dream into a concrete number and begin working on your strategy and finance.

BUYING YOUR DREAM HOME

You may have bought this book because you've set your sights on buying your dream home. As part of a long-term strategy, owning a home of your own in a beautiful location is something most of us strive for.

Bad news first: if this is your goal — whether a waterfront mansion, a beach house or one next to a lovely park — and you don't have the funds to do that now, then you might need to build up to it.

The good news is you *can* actually build up to that, if you're patient. I can help you find a way to realise that dream. And you know I'm walking the talk, because Renee and I have done it ourselves only recently.

Living on the water had always been part of my plan for the future. When I lived all the way out at Ingleburn, I used to walk past waterfront properties in the eastern suburbs where I was teaching and think, I want to own a place like this one day. And yeah, it took me many years to get there.

When I was making good money as a senior teacher, and Renee was too as a chartered accountant, and I had cashflow coming in from Rockdale, Ingleburn, Blackwater and a house in Newcastle, we bought a nice house in Lewisham in Sydney's inner west. While it was nothing like the home we have now, it was still a good house, and back then we were all about that inner-city lifestyle. I paid Lewisham off while we were living there, and then sold it to help us get to where we are now.

You can see how all my homes have been stepping stones, building up to the dream. That was our strategy. This is why every property purchase needs a purpose and its own strategy.

A common issue with goal-setting is that people *kind of* want to buy a home, but they're not sure whether they should buy an investment property instead. I strongly suggest that building up a *property portfolio* is the best way to achieve that long-term goal — and acquire financial freedom at the same time. A bit of hard work and dedication now will help you to reap big rewards later on.

PLANNING TO PAY YOURSELF

Finance plays an integral part in your investment strategy. Perhaps you've never had a financial goal. Maybe, so far, all your goals have been around career, relationships, family, travel and so on. You may have some doubts about creating a goal around wealth. Rather than coming up with a big number, as though you've won Lotto, the better way to set a monetary goal is to think of a salary you'd like to be drawing.

When I first started at Moriah I was on $51 000 a year. My salary rose incrementally, while my goal was to replace that salary with the passive income from properties.

Let's crunch the numbers and get an idea of how this works. Generally, $50 000 is not enough for people to retire and live comfortably on, while to achieve $200 000 a year in passive income you have to buy a lot of properties over a lot of years. You may be different, but $100 000 annually is what many of my clients strive for. So let's use $100 000 as our sample figure.

There are a few expenses involved in being a landlord — and yes, you will be a landlord if you become a property investor. Expenses such as rates, strata fees and repairs can account for 20 per cent of your rental income. And rent is a form of income, so it gets taxed like a regular job.

If you want to clear $100 000 passive income *after* tax and property expenses, you'll need around $180 000 in rental income before tax. Based on an average of 5 per cent rental returns on your properties, that means you're looking at a property portfolio worth about $3.6 million.

But if you have mortgages to pay off, you don't get to keep that money because you have to pay it back to the bank. If you want that $100k *in your pocket*, you'll have to pay off that $3.6 million property portfolio. And to do that, you'll need to double your portfolio value — which means you're looking at building up a portfolio that's valued at more than $7 million, and ensuring they are all in good locations ripe for growth (as well as adding value yourself when you can).

Here's the kicker. As part of what is called an 'exit strategy', you can then sell half of those properties to pay down your debt and create a *paid-off portfolio* worth $3.6 million that will pay you $180 000 per annum in rent, which will allow you to clear $100 000 in passive income every year for the rest of your life.

If you have dual-income properties or commercial properties, you may get a lot more than that, so you could clear $100k with fewer properties.

Each person's strategy, and what we achieve with each client, is different. *Your* goal might be to achieve $50 000 or $80 000 in passive income. I cannot overstate, you need to buy in good locations and also manufacture equity as this won't work if your properties do not increase in value. It's the increased equity that will allow you to pay down your debts and achieve your financial goals.

But if your current plan is to settle for second-best and buy a property without a strategy but that you can afford, and to pay it off from your nine-to-five salary for decades to come, let me stop you right there. I know you're going to want to hear more about my equity-creation strategies and think about what might work better for you.

So let's dig deeper into strategy.

Chapter 2
STRATEGY SESSION

Create a property investment strategy to achieve your goals.

A lack of careful thought and planning can cost you big-time. You now know what your end-goal is and what you are trying to achieve. From here you can formulate an investment strategy and then decide whether building a duplex, renovating a property, buying a blue-chip property for long-term growth or some other move will best suit your needs.

In this chapter I'll show you where to begin in creating a clear investment strategy to help you achieve your goals, using property as the vehicle.

If you're keen to fund your lifestyle goals, property is one of the best long-term investments money can buy. If you feel like it's out of reach and everyone is investing in property except you, you couldn't be more wrong.

According to data released in June 2023 by the Australian Taxation Office (ATO), approximately 2 245 539 Australians, which is only around 20 per cent of the nation's 11.4 million taxpayers, owned an investment property in 2020–21. This means only 8.42 per cent of the Australian population could classify themselves as property investors. Most adult Australians were not investing in property at all.

These 2.24 million property investors collectively own 3.25 million investment properties. It's time for that stat to change.

AUSTRALIA NEEDS MORE LANDLORDS

Nearly a third of Australians live in rental accommodation — that's about seven million people. But only 2.1 million Australians provide 91 per cent of the rental accommodations across the country.

Australia has some of the least affordable housing in the world, with Sydney and Melbourne among the top 10 most expensive cities globally for housing.

The high cost of housing, coupled with rising interest rates and inflation, has exacerbated the affordability crisis. This has led to a situation where a median-income household in Australia can now afford only 13 per cent of homes sold across the country, the lowest share since records began in 1995.

The current housing affordability crisis is not just a statistic; it's a reality that affects millions of Australians every day. Amid these challenges, however, lie significant opportunities for innovative solutions and investments.

The housing crisis presents opportunities for investors, as well as first-time buyers, through government schemes that assist in purchasing homes with smaller deposits, or to building and investing in affordable housing.

WHY PROPERTY IS STILL THE BEST INVESTMENT

Like most clichés, 'as safe as houses' has good factual foundations. Here's why property is the most trusted investment by 'mum-and-dad investors' and major corporations alike:

 Real estate. Property is called real estate because you can see and touch it. Even if you buy 'off the plan', the land and drawings exist — and the building soon will too!

Simplicity. As investments go, property markets are easy to understand. There isn't a lot of jargon to confuse the average buyer.

 Long-term growth. Australian property has increased in value at an average of 11 per cent per annum since the early 1900s. That's comparable to the growth rate of the stock market, but historically property has been even more stable than blue-chip stocks. And unlike companies, land can't go broke in an economic downturn or through poor management. There will always be demand for land and housing in well-located areas, where people actually want to live and work. The fact that property takes longer than shares to sell, even by auction, makes it a less volatile form of investment as well.

 Lenders' favourite. Banks and other financial institutions lend more money for property purchases than for any other type of investment. Property loans are the biggest component of every bank's profit, because property has proven to be the safest type of investment, and interest rates are lower for buying properties than they are for purchasing other types of assets. Property is also ideal for 'leveraging', taking advantage of your portfolio's rising capital value to obtain more loans, increasing your holdings even faster!

 Multiple strategies. Property is a more flexible form of investment than many people realise. Different strategies can be used for different financial situations and property types. These include long-term capital growth, cashflow, renovating for profit and developing. Banks offer different types of loans to suit different strategies, too. When it comes to types of properties, the sky's the limit! Houses, duplexes, villas, townhouses, apartments — and that's just the residential market. Locations and prices range from 'exclusive' inner-city at the top end, to property in regional and rural towns that can offer great value for the canny buyer.

 Tax benefits. Property is an essential commodity in the community, so governments encourage 'bricks-and-mortar'

investment and development. Tax benefits include deductible expenses such as the interest on loans, the costs of repairs and maintenance, and management fees. Depreciation on buildings up to 40 years old is another benefit.

 Government assistance. First home owners are eligible for special one-off grants in most Australian states and territories. There are also incentives for off-the-plan properties and new constructions. Home builder grants vary from state to state and only apply to first home builders, not investors.

 Supply and demand. This is the key driver of house price growth. Demand for rental accommodation is increasing as Australia's population continues to grow faster than the supply of new housing. That puts pressure on property values and rental prices, forcing them higher.

The message for anyone with the ability to invest in the property market is clear: *BUY NOW!* I wrote a whole book based on this message, which you might want to read next.

A SOLID ASSET BASE

The first investment property will always form the cornerstone of a portfolio and drive future investment purchases. The problem with the traditional method of investing in property is that you must wait years for capital growth, and this is a very slow way to achieve your goals.

I'm going to show you how you make your money when you buy, not just when you sell, and how you can add value to properties to fast-track your goals. The huge benefit of the strategies I'll share is that you get to reap the benefits of your investments in the short term, so you can continue investing and moving towards your financial and lifestyle goals.

The first step is to get the fundamentals right for your first property purchase.

Market conditions don't play as large a part as people think. It's a matter of putting the right strategy in place that will work for the current market conditions and mitigate problems that might accompany future market changes.

KNOW WHY, WHERE, WHEN AND WHAT TO BUY

The major hurdle people face in buying investment property is *not knowing why, where, when and what to buy* — because there's so much conflicting information out there in the property markets.

Some say you should buy in Queensland, others in Victoria. Someone tells you to buy in Perth, while someone else insists you shouldn't even consider Perth. Someone says you should buy only in capital cities, while others advocate regional cities. Someone urges you to buy units; someone else says you should buy only houses, and so on. It can be very confusing.

Depending on your strategy, it might work for you to buy in the city *and* in regional areas. Different areas perform in different ways when it comes to growth and rental yields. *What is important is that all the properties you buy complement each other* to help you attain your goals.

What is *not* going to work for you is merely buying a property in one location and waiting for growth. That's what I did when I started out, and while my very first property in Rockdale is now worth three times as much as it was when I bought it, it took me quite a few years to make that gain, for three reasons:

- I didn't have a strategy.

- I bought the property at the wrong time — just when prices were declining in that market.

- Because it was a 'buy and hold' purchase, it took me a long time to achieve that growth. I was not manufacturing equity.

In the previous chapter I introduced the concept of equity. I explained how the difference between what I do and what most buyer's agents do is that I have a clear strategy in place for my clients, so they can *create equity* in properties and *create cashflow* to get to their goals, rather than sinking all their investment money into a single property that offers them no substantial financial reward for years to come.

THE FINANCING HURDLE

The other major hurdle most people face is finance. Everyone's strategy will be based on their individual circumstances, but I can find a solution for almost anyone, whether you can borrow just $200 000 or you have a million or more at your disposal.

So the first thing to ascertain is your 'financial perimeter'.

Some people come to me knowing exactly what their borrowing capacity is. If you already invest in property, your existing holdings can be incorporated into your new strategy. If you have no idea what you can borrow, speaking with a reputable mortgage broker — one who can help you to work out exactly what your numbers are — is crucial.

Even if the broker comes back and says, 'You can borrow one and a half million dollars', I wouldn't encourage you to use those funds to buy a five-bedroom house in your favourite suburb right away, as that probably wouldn't help you towards your goals.

Instead, what we do is ascertain how you can buy a series of properties, and how each property can get you into the next property, and the next. Eventually, once you've achieved your financial goals, you can target that five-bedroom dream home.

If you have a borrowing capacity of $1 million, I might be looking towards a strategy based on buying a couple of properties at a cheaper price point — perhaps homes where we can add value through cosmetic renovation.

Or we could start with a bigger strategy, for example a duplex development that will generate more than $200 000 in profit. Your borrowing capacity will likely increase once you have bought properties and have tenants paying you rent, as long as those properties are positively geared.

Alternatively, if you start by spending $1 million on a duplex development and make over $200 000 profit in a year, you can repeat that process again and again. You might then purchase a 'buy and hold' property in a capital city that will achieve a lot of growth over the long term. And you might end up with 12 properties that are valued at just as much or even more than the 18 lower-end properties.

If you can borrow only $400 000, your strategy might be to buy an older property, renovate it, sell at a profit and repeat, until you build up the money to invest in a bigger development strategy.

Each person's circumstances will be different; each will have different goals and a different starting point, and that's where the strategy session comes in.

AIM HIGH FOR POSITIVE GEARING

Having a negatively geared portfolio and claiming the difference on tax is not really a strategy. To lose money on a property in the hope that you will get some back in the future has never made much sense to me.

With a negatively geared property, where the money you owe each month (on the mortgage, rates, repairs and so on) is greater than the rent that's coming in, you have to use some of your own income to fund the shortfall. You're basically losing money so you can claim a bit back on your tax, in the hope that the long-term growth on your property will offset those short-term losses.

Of course, the danger with that, depending on where your property is located and on market fluctuations, is that quite often you won't get the long-term gains you've counted on.

Banks will also limit the amount of property you can buy if you have a negatively geared portfolio.

But the biggest issue I have with negative gearing is that it traps you in your job, because you've got to keep working to pay the mortgages, so it undermines your goal of retiring from the nine-to-five.

What we're aiming for is to build up a positively geared or positive cashflow portfolio over time. But that doesn't mean that every property you buy must be positively geared. Not every property I've bought has been positively geared from the start. Most have become positively geared over time.

Buying properties in different ways in different locations helps you build a portfolio that sustains itself. Some regional markets will have better cashflow and that offsets the negative cashflow from capital city markets, which is what we want. We want to make sure that you can build on that portfolio. If you focus only on positive cashflow properties, then you may not be getting the best asset because you're focusing on only one thing. You want to focus on the long-term gain of that property as well.

POSITIVE GEARING AND CASHFLOW

On the other hand, you do need good cashflow so the property becomes self-sustaining, and that comes from rent.

If you want to build a sustainable portfolio with a large number of properties, you really need properties that give you good cashflow, for a couple of reasons.

The main reason I call the 'sleep-at-night factor'. With a property portfolio of five, 10 or 15 properties that are paying for themselves, you know that if you lose your job or your position becomes insecure, you don't need to worry, because the rents coming in from your tenants will more than cover any outgoings you have on the properties.

If you lose your job and have a negatively geared portfolio, you might have to sell your properties — and that's not a good outcome. You want *a portfolio that sustains itself,* regardless of your work situation.

Secondly, if you have a positively geared portfolio, you won't have to work forever because your portfolio will end up working for you.

But just because it's not 100 per cent positive cashflow from day one doesn't mean it's not the right property for you. Some people who come to me want a positive cashflow property from day one. And it's not necessarily right for them, but they've read it in this book, so they think it's the right thing to do.

Again, your cashflow can build over time. You can have a good yield on a property that may be costing you a little to own. But there's a difference between having something that's giving you, say, 4.5 per cent yield (annual rent ÷ purchase price × 100 = yield) or having something that's giving 2 per cent yield. You're never going to buy something with a really bad yield.

CAPITAL GROWTH AND MARKET GROWTH CYCLES

When it comes to building up a sustainable portfolio with positive cashflow, it's important to buy in areas that have all the fundamentals of good growth.

Your properties need to be in areas where there's a rising population, good employment opportunities and proper infrastructure, with good amenities and transport links. They should be near shops and cafés where people go and hang out. They've got to be in school catchment zones. And these areas need very low vacancy rates.

Basically, your investment properties need to be where people want to live. Any properties located in those kinds of areas are going to be good growth properties in the long term.

As I've mentioned, capital growth is generally slow, because most property cycles last for between seven and 13 years, and most growth tends to occur over the latter two or three years of that cycle; the rest of the time the markets will sit flat. This is why the traditional 'buy and hold' strategy doesn't help most people achieve their goals in a reasonable time frame.

So what can we do to speed up the process of growth in a flat market? We must control the market ourselves. That means we're not simply going to buy a property in a good growth area, then stop there and hold it. We're going to try to do something with that property that will increase its overall value and its rental income.

This doesn't mean capital growth won't have a place in your strategy. If acquiring a blue-chip property in Sydney is part of your plan, I would still recommend it, as Sydney is the highest growth market in Australia. But you wouldn't build a duplex in Sydney to begin with, because the minimum spend on that would be about $3 million — not an intelligent investment, even if you have the money.

I'd recommend you start in other locations. I share some examples of good locations and how to find them in chapter 4 and in my case studies. Once you have a couple of properties under your belt and you've been creating equity via duplexes and renovations, you'll be well on your way to breaking into the Sydney market — without getting in over your head.

LLOYD'S STRATEGY

Adding value to every property is one thing I do differently from most people in the industry. Remember my 'property trifecta':

THE PROPERTY TRIFECTA

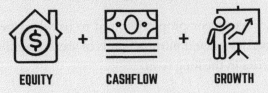

| EQUITY | CASHFLOW | GROWTH |

Because even if you're buying a cheaper property — for, say, $300 000 or $400 000 — thinking, they've told me it's sure to see capital growth over the next few years, no-one has a crystal ball. Maybe that area *won't* grow, or the growth will be very slow in coming.

That's where you need to make sure you're buying something you can subdivide and/or update, adding value to your property. Regardless of what the market does, you've created your own capital growth. And you can borrow against that new equity for your next investment. This is essentially what duplexes enable you to do, and renovations offer the same benefit.

I'll say it again. The worst thing you can do is *nothing at all*. So if you're considering investing, the first step is actually to take the plunge.

Equity is a superpower

If you ask 100 people what's the most difficult thing about buying a home or investment property, 99 will say it's saving up for the deposit. After reading this book, you'll discover that scraping together the deposit for your first property is the only time you will ever need to save up to buy a property. Welcome to the world of equity!

WHAT IS EQUITY?

Think of equity as the difference between the market value of your property (as determined by a bank valuation) and the amount of the mortgage loan owing on it. As your property increases in value over time, so does your equity, without your lifting a finger!

HOW TO USE IT

You can make the most of your equity gains by refinancing your mortgage, then using your equity as a deposit for another property. This gives you the power to start an investment property portfolio.

DUPLICATION

Another equity superpower is *duplication*. It's a favourite word of mine when it comes to building a property portfolio. If you buy one property, the capital growth will give you the equity to buy a second property. Once you have two properties, you will be generating two lots of capital growth, so you can buy two more properties. Now you have four properties! Then four properties become eight properties, and so on—all starting with that one deposit! This is why I call equity a superpower.

AVOID OVERCAPITALISING: THE RULES

The following are my five favourite strategies for *manufacturing equity in a property* to achieve uplift in the short term. All of these strategies have a place in your portfolio, helping you to move towards your long-term goals. Of course, there are rules you need to follow to ensure you never overcapitalise.

1. BUY BELOW MARKET VALUE

I define 'market value' as *whatever a property will actually sell for on that particular day*. So if you buy something below last week's selling price for the same kind of property in the same market, then you're setting the market value for this week. You're not really buying below market value.

I know it's an interesting thing to talk about, and people talk about it a lot, but market value is only a perception. Whatever you pay for the property is the market value for that property on that day.

Now we've cleared that up, I know several ways to buy below *perceived* market value. These include buying in a 'soft' market and pursuing 'off-market' opportunities such as deceased estates and mortgagee sales.

SOFT MARKET

When markets have slowed down a bit, you can get really good value if you buy at the right moment; then, perhaps 12 months later, the value of these properties will start to increase as the market turns and starts its next cycle. You've created instant equity by successfully buying under market value.

DECEASED ESTATE

Often surviving family members just want to sell the property as fast as possible. They will accept lower offers than they might under normal circumstances. Again, you've achieved greater equity in the property simply by buying it at under market value.

Mortgagee resale

This is a property that has been repossessed by the bank because the owners couldn't pay their mortgage on it. Banks don't like to own property; they just like to lend money for others to do so. If the property is worth $400 000 and has an 80 per cent LVR on it — that is, a loan of $320 000 — the bank won't necessarily sell the property for $400 000. They'll look for the quickest sale possible, and may well end up selling it for, say, $320 000 just to cover their costs.

Now this property can be sold again for $400 000 — market value in this example. Again, instant equity is created by buying under market value. Be careful when considering mortgagee sales as many are likely to be in lower socioeconomic areas, so you need to consider whether a property in that suburb still has all the fundamentals you're looking for in an investment.

2. Negotiate

On every single purchase I make, I negotiate. A property might be advertised for $600 000, but I won't offer $600 000. The listing price doesn't mean anything to me. I research comparable sales — what has sold in that market in the past six months — and base my numbers on that. After several property inspections, I ascertain what I think would be a reasonable offer.

If, after my research, I think the property is worth only $570 000, I go in low and offer, say, $540 000. Then I begin to negotiate back and forth with the selling agent, until we arrive at a satisfactory result for my client, which ideally will be somewhat less than what I believe the property is really worth.

When buying an established or second-hand property I always get a building and pest inspection done to check its true condition. If the report comes back identifying the kinds of issues that would scare a lot of people, such as structural damage or termite problems, it doesn't scare me.

I simply consult various professionals to find out how much it will cost to fix the problems. If they say it's going to cost $8000, then I'll go back to the agent and try to negotiate another $15 000 off the sale price. If that agent agrees to the price reduction, you're getting a better deal for the property — under market value yet again.

If we're doing a duplex build, I negotiate on the land, then on the build contract and get the best inclusions thrown in. I also negotiate for terms that are most advantageous to my client — such as, say, a fixed-price contract and late-completion damages. More about those in chapter 9.

You may be intimidated by the idea of negotiating around property, especially in a competitive 'seller's market'. This is where having a good buyer's agent can help you. It's not just about finding a property and saying, 'Yeah, I think this is the house for you.' The key is to *buy a property for less than you can sell it for*. It's about making sure it's the property that best suits your strategy, then getting it at the best price and contract terms.

3. Look for properties that need some TLC

I'm always looking to manufacture growth through buying cheaper properties where we can renovate for an 'equity uplift'. A cosmetic renovation — not a major gut and overhaul — will also increase the amount of rent you can earn. If you were to paint the property, replace the floor coverings, add new blinds and update the kitchen, that much alone could add significant value to it.

Lloyd's Strategy

Every dollar you spend on renovation should return three dollars in value. You can then take out an equity loan against the increased value of the property to help you get into another property. Or you might sell the property and take the profits, if that is the better strategy for you. But keep in mind the capital gains tax (CGT) when selling, and always get advice from your accountant.

4. Focus on Bite-sized Developments

Subdividing micro-developments, such as duplexes and triplexes, is a great source of equity uplift. I mean actually building them, not just buying a ready-made development on which someone else has already made the profit.

For first-time developers, a duplex is the simplest form of development. We're not talking about a multi-storey apartment building; we're talking about building a property on a block of land then subdividing that property so it becomes two homes on separate titles.

Once it has two separate titles, it gets two valuations — and that's where you create equity. Although you built them as a single property, the units can also be sold separately. And if you can build that duplex for less than you can sell the two units for, then you're creating equity. Simple!

 ## 5. Buy or Create Dual-income Properties

With a duplex you've got two streams of rental income coming in, which makes it positively geared. That rent is paying all the property's expenses, plus you'll have a bit of money left over at the end of the month.

A dual-income property can also be a house with a granny flat out the back, or any place where you have two lots of rent coming in, creating positive cashflow.

 ## SUCCESS STORY
My strategy for financial freedom

You already know that when I built my first duplex in Armidale I had $141000 in instant equity on completion plus a dual rental income. At the time I was earning about $70000 a year as a

(continued)

SUCCESS STORY
My strategy for financial freedom (*cont'd*)

teacher, and I made twice that annual salary just on the equity from that duplex. I'll tell you exactly how I developed that duplex later in the book.

In 2013 I used that equity to go straight into another duplex, as well as buying a blue-chip property in the inner-city suburb of Newstead in Brisbane. I also bought a house in Newcastle, NSW, where my strategy was to do a cosmetic renovation and add a granny flat in the backyard for a dual income.

I sold my Ingleburn property in 2013 as well and used the profit I made to go into other property deals. I came to see this as one of my biggest mistakes, though, as Sydney went through several years of high growth following 2013. But in the end, I still achieved my goals, and lessons like that are important to learn along the way!

My last year as a teacher was in 2015. For the next five years, most of my strategies involved either building duplexes or buying dual-income properties. This form of 'equity generation' allowed me to pay off our home in Lewisham in 2016.

I also bought some more properties in Sydney to keep as long-term investments. My one-bedroom apartment in Alexandria, purchased for Riley in 2019, is just three kilometres from the Sydney CBD and will be a great long-term hold.

Rockdale also became a long-term hold; it is paid off and I get around two grand a month rent from it.

All my investment properties are rented out and most have always been rented, because I *always buy in locales where there is high demand and low vacancy rates.* I've only occasionally had trouble renting out a property, and whenever that's happened it's because I didn't get the fundamentals right when I did my due diligence. I can now share these lessons with you, so you don't make the same mistakes.

I have occasionally sold properties that weren't performing well, or weren't a good fit for my portfolio, or if I was 'maxed out' from

(continued)

SUCCESS STORY
My strategy for financial freedom (*cont'd*)

the lender's perspective and needed to free up some borrowing power. A smart strategy in this situation is to sell one of your duplex units and keep the other. This is another good thing about duplexes: if you have to sell one, you can still hold on to a unit in that prime location.

I went on to adopt other strategies, including buying blocks of land and subdividing; and keeping and renovating an existing house, then building a duplex on the back of the block. I have also bought a block of land in Newcastle, secured a development approval (DA) on it and then sold it, making equity without even building.

MY STRATEGY FOR HOME OWNERSHIP

I had always planned to work my way up to buying a dream home someday. My strategy involved the following steps:

1. Rockdale (1-bed unit): leased out

2. Ingleburn (3-bed villa): leased out

3. Lewisham (3-bed house in a good location near the city): sold

4. Lilli Pilli (dream home): bought.

To help fund Lilli Pilli, our house on the water in southern Sydney, I sold one of our investment properties in Newcastle as well as our home in Lewisham. That put us in a very good position to buy our dream home, which I won at a heavily contested auction.

I like to control the scene at auctions. I like to be the first bidder, start the process and be close to the auctioneer. I had a fair idea of what the property would sell for and what we would need to pay. I always have my strategy in place and keep my cards close to my chest, so on the day even Renee didn't know our budget for the Lilli Pilli purchase. She told me after the auction how nervous she was, as I started the bidding where she thought I should finish.

We ended up in a fierce contest with the next-door neighbours, who wanted the block so they could do their own extensions. But this was our dream home; I knew how much Renee loved it and I was determined we'd win it. I didn't back down, and the bidding went up another million before the hammer finally fell. I felt incredible, although a little nervous at how much money I had just spent. But that was what I had been working and investing for all these years!

So we bought it in 2018 for $4 million and it is now our family home. We absolutely love it. And every day since we bought it I wake up and appreciate the dream. I can't believe we've got this beautiful waterfront house. So that's something I'm very appreciative of.

We've now renovated the ensuite upstairs and the pool, and we've just had an architect design a full plan for the backyard.

I am big on paying off your mortgage faster, and we paid Lilli Pilli off in 2022, so we're now mortgage-free on our dream home. I paid off the mortgage quickly, using more investment strategies, such as building and selling duplexes, and selling other properties. I also used money from my offset accounts, which I will talk about later.

Lilli Pilli is now worth close to $7 million, based on comparable sales in the area that are all being sold at between $6 million and $10 million. And those properties are not even renovated to the same extent as ours. So we've enjoyed some capital growth on the property, and obviously being right on the waterfront—the aspect that we've got is amazing, looking over to the National Park—we can't be built out. These sorts of properties always have that opportunity for good growth.

Now, if you have the patience for the long game, as I did, let's get started and have a look at your financing.

CHAPTER 3
MONEY, MONEY, MONEY

Secure financing and save for the only deposit you'll ever pay.

 In this chapter, we talk about improving your serviceability—your ability to make loan repayments so lenders will be champing at the bit to offer you mortgages. Prepare to scrutinise your financial habits, and be warned: this chapter may make you flinch.

A lot of people are under the impression that you need millions of dollars and a huge borrowing capacity to invest, but this is far from the truth. There are some great opportunities in the current Australian markets, with excellent rental returns in areas ripe for growth, from as little as $400 000 (or a $40 000 deposit plus closing costs).

But getting a mortgage is not a simple thing. You may need to overcome problems such as debt and bad credit ratings. You may also find it difficult if you have a new business or a new job.

I'm going to share with you how to overcome these obstacles to securing a mortgage, and how having positively geared properties will increase your loan serviceability.

IS IT HARDER THAN EVER TO GET A LOAN?

I've said more than once that you too can achieve what I have achieved in my property portfolio, but I admit that when I started out, in 2003, it was a lot easier to get a mortgage. In recent years lending has changed dramatically and borrowing money has become a more tedious process.

The Australian Prudential Regulation Authority (APRA) is an independent statutory body that supervises financial institutions and imposes credit conditions to promote 'financial system stability' in Australia. APRA has been monitoring the increase in investor loans and has introduced more prudent regulations and monitoring of the banking sector to prevent any market collapse driven by the loan sector.

APRA's goal is to protect Australian property markets from a US-style crash. Lending in the US was simply too easy in the mid 2000s leading up to the global financial crisis (GFC). The GFC was triggered in 2007 by a 'credit crunch', when a loss of confidence by US investors in the value of subprime mortgages (given to people with less-than-desirable credit histories) caused a 'liquidity crisis'. That is, virtually no-one would lend money and almost no-one could get access to credit.

This, in turn, resulted in the US Federal Reserve ('the Fed') injecting a large amount of capital into financial markets to boost liquidity and stimulate bank lending. By September 2008, the crisis had worsened as stock markets around the globe crashed and became highly volatile. Consumer confidence hit rock bottom as many investors tightened their belts in fear of what could lie ahead.

The housing market in the United States suffered enormously, as many homeowners who had taken out subprime loans found themselves unable to make their mortgage repayments. As the value of homes plummeted, a large number of borrowers found themselves with negative equity.

With these borrowers defaulting on loans, banks were faced with a situation in which repossessed houses and land were worth less on the market than they had loaned out originally to enable people to buy them.

What APRA has done in Australia has made it more difficult to get a loan these days, but it is for the good of all of us and for the nation's economy.

This is actually good news for investors.

I believe the banks have good intentions and want to ensure they are lending funds to capable borrowers. I am of the opinion that homeowners themselves should take responsibility if they've leveraged themselves too high with mortgages.

It is up to us, as borrowers, to be aware of banks' current expectations so we can get the results we want. If we want to continue to make progress with our investments, a requirement for larger deposits and stronger financials is not a bad thing. And these new, tighter rules around lending, I believe, will help prevent a future market crash.

But don't think you *can't* get loans these days. You can still achieve your dreams if you're willing to do the work, as the next success story illustrates.

Interestingly, now the markets are booming despite higher interest rates. Almost all of the Australian markets boomed during COVID and interest rates dropped to all-time lows. Now they have come back up, but there is still plenty of demand for property, mainly because of an overall shortage of supply across the country. High demand for low supply.

THE SERVICEABILITY BUFFER

These days borrowers are not only assessed on their ability to pay back a loan at today's interest rates, but they are also required to factor in a serviceability buffer, which sits around 2 to 3 per cent higher than the lender's current variable interest rate. This serviceability buffer is a contingency that a lender is expected to apply in the loan application process to give borrowers a chance to continue to make repayments if their financial circumstances change or interest rates rise.

So if a home buyer wants to take out a home loan with a 5 per cent interest rate, they will have to actually be able to manage a loan with a 7.5 per cent interest rate, for example. This protects both the bank and the lender. But for home buyers it effectively means you can borrow less money.

In recent years we've seen mortgage rates jump from as low as 2 per cent to around 6 per cent, which is exactly why the serviceability buffer was introduced. The assessment rates were introduced by the Australian Prudential Regulation Authority (APRA) in December 2014 as part of its efforts to reinforce sound residential lending standards.

Notably, property prices have still managed to rise during this period, which shows us that demand driven by the rapidly rising population is easily outpacing supply and the higher level of interest rates.

SUCCESS STORY
I helped a client achieve the same goal I did

As you know, I made double my $70 000 income in profit on my first duplex project. Later I helped my client Dan to do even better.

THE BRIEF
Dan, in his early forties, told me his dream was to work four days a week and take Fridays off. He too was on an income of $70 000 and had a buying potential of only $400 000.

THE LOCATION
The first property we bought was quite a large block of 1000m² in northern NSW for about $380 000, so it was under budget. It already had a house on it with a positive cashflow, returning about $500 a week. So that automatically put Dan in a better position because the rental on it was quite good. Dan had $20 000 borrowing power left over from this purchase.

We then subdivided the block (which is called a one-into-two subdivision), leaving enough space on the back block of the property to build a duplex.

CHALLENGES

Because $20 000 wasn't enough leverage for a development, I helped Dan find a joint venture partner, who assisted in developing the duplex on the back block. Dan and his JV partner signed a legal contract stipulating that each of them would keep one of the duplex units. One was a money partner and the other had the borrowing capacity.

On completion, the duplexes were individually valued at $490 000. Dan kept the main house on the block of land, for cashflow and growth, but he sold his duplex unit and made a significant profit there, which allowed him to go into another property deal, a renovation project on a $450 000 house in Brisbane.

FURTHER ACQUISITIONS

I helped Dan organise a cosmetic reno on the property and he earned $3 for every $1 spent. So he spent $20 000 on the reno and ended up making $60 000 equity on the completed property. This property was now also cashflow positive, returning about $590 a week in rent. Not bad, given it is also in a good market for capital growth — Brisbane.

With the extra funds Dan was able to go into a third deal, building a lower-priced duplex in the Hunter Valley in New South Wales, where he created about $130 000 in profit. That has allowed him to do a fourth deal — another duplex development.

RESULTS

When Dan started out he could raise no more than a $50 000 or $60 000 deposit, and needed a JV partner for his first development because he didn't have the funds to do a duplex by himself. Now, just a few years later, he's built a couple more duplexes, and they've all been returning profits of well over $100 000.

I've done this for a lot of people on low incomes, but I've got other clients on higher incomes who have done more expensive developments and of course have made lots more money.

(continued)

SUCCESS STORY
I helped a client achieve the same goal I did (*cont'd*)

Now in his late forties, Dan didn't start out when he was particularly young, but he's already leaning towards early retirement. He's managed to build his portfolio, he's changed jobs to something that pays more, and he's achieved his dream of being able to go to the pub and tell everyone, 'I don't work Fridays', so he's in a pretty good position.

Convinced?

Let's look at what you need to show lenders these days in order to get that mortgage.

1. WHO ARE YOU?

Firstly, you need to be at least 18 years of age to be approved for a home loan. If you're older than 55, you'll need to provide a written exit plan demonstrating your ability to repay the loan, and lenders may only offer you mortgages with shorter loan terms.

Secondly, lenders will want to know whether or not you are a permanent resident of Australia. For non-residents, if you are in a de facto relationship with, or married to, an Australian citizen or permanent resident, your application will be assessed in the same way as any other resident. In other circumstances, lenders may place limits on the loan amount, and you may need a larger deposit. In some cases you'll need the approval of the Foreign Investment Review Board (FIRB).

Thirdly, what kind of buying entity are you? Lenders allow you to borrow as an individual, a company or the trustee of a trust, but they require specific documentation and will likely have different lending criteria in place in each case.

2. WHAT AREA ARE YOU BUYING IN?

The property you intend to buy will be security for your home loan, so if you default on the loan, your lenders will sell it to retrieve their money; lenders are therefore choosy and will carefully examine the type of property you're considering.

Some have restrictions on which postcodes they will lend in and may not approve loans to people seeking to buy in rural areas, 'undesirable' areas or areas of oversupply. Even some suburbs in our capital cities can be on lenders' blacklists.

When building a portfolio of properties, you always need to be thinking, if I buy this property, how's it going to help me get into the next property?

The last thing you want to do is to buy in an undesirable location and then be unable to purchase another property because the banks don't like the property you've already bought — or, worse still, discover it has decreased in value or you can't find a tenant for it.

All that's very important, and we'll spend more time covering *where* you should be buying in chapter 4.

3. WHAT TYPE OF PROPERTY ARE YOU BUYING?

Lenders will want to know the type of property you're considering, and particularly whether you're buying a house or a unit. Typically, you'll find the lending criteria stricter for funding units, with most lenders, for example, requiring the unit size to be at least 45 square metres.

Lenders will prefer to fund the purchase of a property that has running water and electricity, is zoned for residential or commercial use, and can be accessed without driving through someone else's property. The property will need to have a freehold or strata title without encumbrances, so your lender can sell it without restrictions if you default on loan repayments. We cover zoning and titles in chapter 8.

4. WHY ARE YOU BUYING THE PROPERTY?

Lenders will also want to know why you're purchasing the property, as this dictates the type of loan you can get and how much you can borrow.

If you're buying as an owner-occupier, you are likely to face fewer restrictions and to be offered a home loan with a lower interest rate. However, your serviceability with banks improves when you're buying investment properties. If you're buying a home to live in, this can adversely affect your serviceability — that is, your ability to service new loans to purchase further investment properties.

This is because your home is considered a liability, not an income-producing asset. You don't typically have rent coming in for a property that is your principal place of residence; hence you can't claim the same tax deductions for it.

As an investor, you will face tighter lending criteria and higher interest rates than you would as a home buyer. On the plus side, if you have positively geared properties, you can sometimes borrow larger amounts because lenders assume the higher rental income will help you service your home loan. This does vary depending on the lender and they will still assess your earned income.

Banks will want to see proof that your existing property is rented out or see a rental appraisal when assessing you for another loan.

If your investment properties don't have good rental cashflow, you will reach your ceiling — or serviceability limit — sooner, and once you do, the banks won't lend you any more money. This is bad news for your portfolio.

Many people get stuck with only a couple of properties that are negatively geared, because they've got to dip into their own pockets every week to pay the difference. Getting a new loan then becomes too reliant on your actual earned income, which is limited by the salary you draw.

If you have a modest income and negatively geared properties, you'll hit your ceiling with the banks pretty quickly. If you focus on positively geared properties, the banks will like you more and will increase your serviceability.

You can purchase cashflow-positive properties even on a modest income and build a considerable portfolio, as I did on my teacher's salary.

With positively geared properties, the rents coming in more than cover the mortgages you have to pay on them, so the banks often approve refinancing loans on your properties again and again. In this way, you can end up buying many properties, doing multiple duplexes and really building your portfolio, as you have good cashflow from the rentals to cover the loans. This does vary depending on the lender, and they will still assess your earned income.

It comes back to having a sound strategy in place, but that strategy starts with your initial borrowing power.

5. HOW MUCH DO YOU NEED TO BORROW?

The size of the loan you're seeking affects how lenders assess your application.

When you set about securing a loan, you're applying for a particular loan-to-value ratio (LVR). For example, if you go for an 80 per cent LVR, your deposit will be 20 per cent of the price of the property and you're asking the bank to lend you the other 80 per cent.

Different banks have different terms and conditions for their loans. This is where a good broker comes in handy and can advise which lenders will give you the best loan.

Bear the following in mind when it comes to deciding on your loan amount:

1. Make sure the amount you propose falls between the minimum and maximum loan limits imposed by the lender.

2. Ensure the amount you wish to borrow does not exceed the loan's maximum LVR. In other words, you'll need to have the minimum deposit saved — commonly, 20 per cent of the property's purchase price.

3. If you have less than 20 per cent as a deposit, you will have to pay for lender's mortgage insurance (LMI), a policy that covers your lender in the event that you default on the loan. This can add thousands of dollars to the total cost of your home loan — and it doesn't cover you; it covers the bank.

It is always advisable to have a strong buffer for costs when purchasing property, as it's easy to underestimate all the costs involved. Saving enough to just cover your deposit will only lead to financial strife.

Typical costs in purchasing a property include:

- the deposit
- stamp duty
- solicitor's/conveyancer's fees
- building and pest inspection
- property insurance
- holding costs until a tenant moves in
- minor maintenance costs to ensure the property is in a condition fit for rental.

For example, if you're applying for a home loan on a $600 000 property and paying a 20 per cent deposit, you'll be paying $120 000 plus around $20 000 in costs — so all up you'll need to find $140 000. If you've saved only $120 000, you'll run into strife.

THE BEAUTY OF BROKERS

It pays to get professional advice early in your planning to help you clarify what you're aiming for and exactly what you'll need to do to get there. A mortgage broker helped me get my first, low-doc home loan when I was a casual music teacher, and I use a mortgage broker to this day.

Just as important as finding the right property for your investment portfolio is ensuring you have the right finance structure for each of your investment purchases. An experienced mortgage broker understands investment financing and will ensure your long-term investment strategy is at the heart of every financial decision you make.

A good mortgage broker can:

- assess your financial position and explain to you how banks will see it

- explain the different types of interest rates

- ascertain what loans are likely to best suit your strategy and needs

- determine which banks offer the best packages

- outline any changes you'll need to make before applying for your home loan of choice.

Getting professional financial advice has two major benefits. You save time, effort and money because you know you're working towards your goal the right way. You also protect your credit rating by ensuring you're fully prepared when you make a property loan application, so it won't be rejected, hurting your financial reputation. You don't want to be shopping around or applying for multiple loans, as all these will show up on your credit rating and make it more difficult for you to gain approval for any subsequent loan applications.

Not all mortgage brokers have the same skill set and you need to find one who will work in your best interests. Your broker should be an expert in the type of loan you're aiming to secure. For example, residential investment, construction and commercial loans have different requirements, and different lenders approach them differently.

Also be aware that some mortgage brokers are less knowledgeable than they should be. A broker whose only experience is with basic residential home loans may try to set up a client to apply, say, for a construction loan with a bank that doesn't do them, or for a loan at a 90 per cent LVR when the bank in question will only approve loans of up to 70 per cent.

A good mortgage broker should be finding you the best loan that meets your needs based on your income and goals.

Finding the right loan

Engaging an unbiased mortgage broker is a smart way to narrow down a wide field of loan options. A good mortgage broker will:

- have access to a range of lenders and loans

- be able to recommend the best lenders to suit your circumstances

- know which loans have the features you want, such as offset accounts, redraw facilities, variable and fixed rates

- be able to offer special deals from lenders wanting to get extra business

- be able to help you obtain a loan even if banks regard you as 'risky' — if you're self-employed or a first home buyer, or you have a poor credit rating

- often be able to get your loan approved more quickly than a bank can by chasing it up

- provide excellent customer service because they're less bureaucratic than large banks.

TYPES OF HOME LOANS

A wide range of types of property loans are available in Australia, including the following:

 Variable (principal and interest) loans. A variable interest rate loan is a loan in which the interest rate charged on the outstanding balance (and therefore your payments) will vary as market interest rates change.

 Fixed loans. A fixed interest rate is an unchanging rate charged on your mortgage. It might apply during the entire term of the loan or for a part of the term, but it remains the same throughout the set period.

Split-rate (principal and interest) loans. In a split-rate loan, the loan is divided into multiple parts. You can nominate a portion of the loan to have a fixed interest rate, with the remainder having a variable interest rate.

 Interest-only loans. In this type of loan you pay only the interest on the mortgage (via monthly or fortnightly payments) for a fixed term. After that term is over, you can choose to refinance the loan, make a lump-sum payment or begin paying off the principal of the loan.

 Development finance. These loans are used to support the costs of a residential or commercial development project. Unlike long-term property mortgages, development financing is short term, with lifecycles in the range of six to 24 months. Loans can be used to buy land and pay for construction costs, and are suitable for ground-up new builds, conversions or refurbishments of existing properties. A lender will usually lend up to 75 per cent of the GRV (gross realised value) of the project. So a feasibility needs to be submitted with the application. This loan doesn't affect your borrowing capacity. On completion the property needs to be sold, though. These loans are not for 'buy and hold'.

 Construction loans. A construction loan is a mortgage agreement designed specifically for someone who is building a new home. Having a builder on board is crucial to your funding, as securing this type of loan depends on having a signed building contract with a licensed builder. Bottom line: no builder, no loan. With a construction loan, the lender considers the total amount required to pay the builder to complete construction. This amount is then broken down into 'progress draws': separate payments that come out of your mortgage-available funds and are made to the builder at each phase of the building process. The lender will require you to pay only the interest due on the amounts drawn.

Introductory loans. An introductory loan is charged during the initial stages at an interest rate that may be as low as 0 per cent. This rate is not permanent, and after it expires a normal or higher-than-normal rate will apply. This is also called a 'teaser' rate.

 Bridging loans. A bridging loan is secured by the current property to pay off the mortgage on a new one, and goes towards closing costs, fees and a deposit on the new home. It is a short-term loan, usually for a period of no more than six months. Usually a bridging loan comes with two payment options. Note that these are offered only to those buying homes, not investment properties.

 Line of credit loans. A 'line of credit' loan allows you to borrow in increments, repay the money, then borrow again as long as the line remains open. Typically, you will be required to pay interest on the borrowed balance while the line is open for borrowing, which makes it different from a conventional loan, which is repaid in fixed instalments.

 Low-doc loans. Typically, a low-doc home loan is offered to a potential borrower who is self-employed, or a small business owner, and doesn't have the documents required to obtain a traditional mortgage. This is for when you can't provide pay-as-you-go (PAYG) payslips or financial statements and tax returns.

 Non-conforming loans. A non-conforming home loan is a loan offered to potential borrowers who don't meet the standard lending criteria of their bank or major lender. These may include applicants who have poor credit histories, have previously declared bankruptcy or are self-employed.

REFINANCING

Refinancing can be done in order to get a loan on your property with better interest rates than your original mortgage, or to change to a different lender. Refinancing is important for drawing equity from your developments and is key to all my strategies of investing that equity in more properties.

It's important to check whether the loan agreement allows your bank to use money from the sale of any of your properties to pay back other loans. If it does, this can prevent you from using the sale proceeds as you see fit — for example, to obtain more property loans.

You can refinance and take out a second loan on a property, but if you have too many loans with the same lender you risk damaging your serviceability through overexposure, so it's best to spread them out over several lenders.

THINKING OUTSIDE THE 'BIG FOUR' BOX

A lot of brokers work consistently with one or other of the 'big four' banks — Westpac, National Australia Bank (NAB), the Commonwealth Bank of Australia (CBA) and the Australia and New Zealand Banking Group (ANZ) — because this way, they can get loans put through faster and can market that as 'platinum service' to their clients. Sticking with one bank is not in your best interest, however, because you won't be able to borrow as much from the 'big four' as you often can through smaller, 'non-bank' lenders such as La Trobe Financial Services, Pepper Money Australia or Liberty.

For example, a big bank might suggest that on your income you can borrow only $600 000, whereas with a smaller lender your serviceability might be $700 000. The big bank will say no to you if you want a $700 000 property loan, but the smaller bank will say yes.

Often interest rates are lower with the non-bank lenders, but they can be higher. It all comes back to engaging a broker who can find the best deal for *you*. Most brokers have access to a panel of at least 30 lenders, so they should be able to provide you with a number of loan options.

MORTGAGE PACKAGES

Interest rates are not the most important element in finding a loan that suits your needs. Usually a package gives you the option to bundle several products and offers much more than favourable interest rates, such as:

- a standard variable mortgage, potentially at a lower discounted interest rate than a no-frills mortgage

- a mortgage offset account, where the account's balance (or part of that balance) is 'offset' daily against your home loan balance, and as a result you're charged interest only on the difference between the total loan balance and the amount offset

- a transaction account or savings account

- a credit card

- discounted general insurance options (for example, home and contents insurance, landlord insurance and car insurance)

- discounted risk insurance options (such as life insurance, total permanent disability cover, trauma cover and income protection insurance)

- discounted financial planning and share trading.

Of course, you don't need to choose all of these and I don't advocate them all. I don't recommend the credit card option, for example. Nonetheless, there is a lot more to a mortgage/home loan than many people realise.

HOW LIKELY ARE YOU TO PAY BACK YOUR LOAN?

Obviously, the main thing lenders want to ascertain before they approve a loan is your serviceability — that is, your ability to pay back the loan. As well as your property investments, potential lenders will scrutinise your spending habits, any other loans you have and your capacity to pay them back, any debts you have and so on. They need to be absolutely confident of receiving your mortgage payments plus interest.

Let's look at the main factors that come into play when a prospective lender assesses your serviceability.

EMPLOYMENT

Lenders will examine your work situation carefully to determine whether you have a stable source of income.

If you are a PAYG employee, you should have a relatively easy time proving your income through payslips from your employer. Lenders prefer borrowers who have been employed in the same job for at least three months (past probation) and in the same industry for a minimum of two years.

If you're a casual or seasonal employee, you could find securing a loan more of a challenge, but some lenders are willing to consider potential borrowers with this type of employment record on a case-by-case basis. Again, we need to think outside the box here and consider approaching some of the smaller lenders.

It is sometimes more difficult for self-employed borrowers to provide income documentation, although there are lenders who specialise in providing low-doc loans to this type of borrower. You will need to provide recent Business Activity Statements and tax returns, or a letter from your accountant, or perhaps bank statements showing regular income. You'll usually require a larger deposit as well. Banks will lend you only 80 per cent LVR in this situation, meaning you'll need to put down a 20 per cent deposit.

I needed a low-doc home loan to buy my Rockdale property because I was getting paid by the hour to tutor music students and had no real proof of income. The broker presented me with three lenders who did low-doc loans, all with different terms and packages and interest rates, and explained what each offered. I borrowed less than my approved limit, so I remained within my comfort zone and didn't overextend myself.

Banks consider low-doc loans high-risk, so the interest rates are a bit higher. After I got my full-time teaching job at Moriah, I refinanced my low-doc loan to a full-doc loan in order to obtain a lower interest rate.

That's how I got started. I would have struggled if I hadn't been able to get that initial loan, so I was lucky. Now, as a business owner, I still use low-doc loans.

INCOME

Your income helps a lender calculate the size of the home-loan payments you will likely be able to manage. Obviously the higher your income, the better your serviceability and the higher your ceiling.

Each lender has its own system. Most, however, are likely to ask about your total regular salary from one or more jobs, or from your business if you're self-employed. They'll ask about commissions and bonuses; and rental income from investment properties.

By providing your latest three payslips (if you're a PAYG employee), you enable your prospective lender to determine your average pay.

Other acceptable sources of income include:

 overtime pay, documented over the past two years

 rental income; typically, banks allow 60 to 70 per cent of this income to be used in calculating your serviceability

 certain Centrelink benefits, such as child support payments

 up to 80 per cent of any fringe benefits you receive, such as stipends, living allowances and car allowances

 share dividends; some lenders accept a portion of these as income

 assets, including any shares you hold, your superannuation and any other properties you own.

SAVINGS AND EXPENDITURE

If you are able to save a decent deposit — and remember, you are aiming for at least a 10 per cent deposit plus a 10 per cent buffer — it will demonstrate to lenders that you have financial discipline.

Part of your deposit can come from sources such as gifts, financial windfalls and inheritances, but most lenders will want to see at least 5 per cent of it originating from genuine savings — funds you've held in your account for at least three months. This shows you're disciplined about money, rather than simply having been gifted the money.

LLOYD'S STRATEGY

Put 15 per cent of your weekly earnings into a separate account from your everyday one, then don't touch that money.

I find that many people earning reasonable money don't understand why they're struggling to save. Often it's because they don't have a budget in place, so they have no idea where their money's going each week.

Even if you already have a deposit saved, it's crucial to *prepare a budget* so you know where your money is going, because when you're applying for a loan, lenders will look at your three most recent monthly bank statements to verify your living expenses against what you have declared. If the bank decides you have 'bad' spending patterns, your loan application may be declined.

To work out how much you're spending, create a budget spreadsheet like the one shown in table 3.1 (overleaf). Write down all your incoming payments and outgoing expenses over a month, such as those for your home and utilities; insurance and financial; groceries; personal and medical; entertainment, including eating out; transport and automotive; and children (as every parent knows, they cost money, and the banks count them as a liability!).

The following table enables you to set a clear budget and work out where all your money is going.

Table 3.1: budget planner

View: Annual			
Income	**$**	**Frequency**	**$**
Your take-home pay		Fortnightly	
Income from savings/investments		Monthly	
Other income		Monthly	
Home and utilities	**$**	**Frequency**	**$**
Mortgage or rent		Monthly	
Council rates		Quarterly	
Electricity, gas and water		Quarterly	
Internet, pay TV, phone		Monthly	
Other		Monthly	
Insurance and financial	**$**	**Frequency**	**$**
Car insurance		Monthly	
Home and contents insurance		Monthly	
Personal, life and health insurance		Monthly	
Loans		Monthly	
Other		Monthly	
Groceries and personal	**$**	**Frequency**	**$**
Supermarket		Weekly	
Education and school fees		Quarterly	
Sports and fitness		Weekly	
Entertainment and eating out		Weekly	
Other		Weekly	
Transport and auto	**$**	**Frequency**	**$**
Bus, train, ferry or taxi		Weekly	
Petrol		Weekly	
Road tolls and parking		Weekly	
Rego and licence		Yearly	
Other		Weekly	

Summary

	Monthly totals	
	Home and utilities	$
	Insurance and financial	$
	Groceries and personal	$
	Transport and auto	$

When you add up the totals in your budget, you may be amazed how much you spend on things (like going to the movies) that aren't as important as saving for your home deposit!

Some bank assessors go through your bank statements line by line, so it is a good idea to curtail your spending and even reduce online and card payments during the three months prior to applying for a loan.

The banks look at two main categories of expenditure:

- *basic living expenses* — the necessary expenses of day-to-day living, such as utilities, groceries and transport

- *discretionary living expenses* — the nonessentials you could cut back on, such as eating out, recreation, entertainment and incidental shopping.

The bank sees discretionary living expenses, or anything that can't be defined as basic living expenses, as *disposable income*. They want to see that you've been putting that disposable income towards saving for a deposit, not spending it frivolously.

LLOYD'S STRATEGY

Go back to 'old-school' cash payments before applying for a loan, because it means you'll accrue fewer transactions on your bank statements for loan assessors to query. That means fewer hassles for you and the likelihood that your loan application gets through faster.

To achieve that budget surplus at the end of each month and to save that 15 per cent, you obviously have to *spend less than you're earning*. A lot of people who come to see me aren't actually doing that. When they crunch the numbers, it turns out they're spending their entire pay cheque, or sometimes more, and they're unwilling to give up their credit cards.

LIABILITIES

Lenders look at any *debts* you have, including those on your credit cards, personal loans, car loans and student HECS/HELP debts.

They also look at your *credit score* to assess your debt repayment history. You can obtain a credit score from a credit bureau. Credit scores obtainable from Experian range from 0 to 1000, while those from Equifax range from 0 to 1200. A good credit score is 700 or above.

Some lenders specialise in helping borrowers with bad credit histories and low credit scores. They will offer home loans to a borrower who has defaulted or been served with a writ or a judgement against them, or even a discharged bankruptcy; however, interest rates are usually higher on these loans.

LLOYD'S STRATEGY

I was brought up to believe that all debt is bad, but there is such a thing as *good debt*. Good debt is debt that you take out to buy assets that increase in value, such as property.

I've always avoided bad debt — which is a loan on something that depreciates in value, such as a car, a TV or a great entertainment system from Harvey Norman — because even if it's only a $1000 loan, you'll have that two-years interest-free loan on your credit card, and on your credit file, so the bank will question that.

A car loan by itself is not a bad thing, as long as you're paying it back on time. But if you get out a couple of payments and then you're a month late and maxed out on your credit card, you'll get stung when the bank declines your loan application.

You may believe having an extra credit card is a good idea. But even if you haven't spent a cent on that card, it counts against you when you're trying to get a loan.

Potential credit-card debt

As part of the credit-card debt assessment, lenders look at the *combined credit limit* of all your cards rather than what you owe on them. So if you have a credit card with a limit of up to $20 000, the bank sees you as having a $20 000 debt to the credit-card company. And if your combined limit is $40 000 or $50 000, that's a red flag to the bank.

Generally, they assess this assuming a repayment of just 3 per cent of the total card limit. For example, if you have a credit card with a $10 000 limit but you pay the whole amount owing every month, your lender will still calculate your repayments at $300 per month. So unless you *need* a high credit card limit, minimising it will increase your loan serviceability.

I recommend you pay off your credit card(s) or at least stop using them and pay cash.

I was 35 years old before I had a credit card, and I only got one then for things like booking hotels online, paying for flights and that kind of stuff.

My mother and father drummed it into me that *if you can't afford to buy something with your own money, don't buy it.* I still believe this, so I recommend that you don't spend money on anything unless you can actually afford to pay for it now.

There's no magic trick to paying off your credit card. You just need to *know where your money's going.* You're in debt for a simple reason: you've been spending too much.

Look at your budget and stop buying extras.

LLOYD'S STRATEGY

If you go out for dinner three times a week, cut it down to once a week. Put the money you save from not buying those extras onto your credit card to start paying it off.

Pay off more than the minimum monthly repayment amount, because that covers only the interest, so you're throwing your hard-earned money at the bank. If your minimum payment is $100 a month, you have to find a way to put in $150 or $200 a month so you're paying off some of that principal.

MAKING A LIFESTYLE MINDSHIFT

If you do your budget and realise that without credit you can't cover your basic living expenses, you might need to find somewhere cheaper to live or a way to increase your income. Can you get a promotion at work or take on a second job?

Maybe your 'currency' has been a lifestyle of rich cultural and spiritual experiences. That's fine and looks great in selfies, but if you're always on the back foot financially because you're chasing those short-term gains, you'll have nothing to fall back on in 10 or 20 years' time.

Can you delay your lifestyle gratification, shelve the travel plans and rent a room in a share house somewhere you can afford while you save for a deposit? The middle of nowhere is not a convenient place to live (trust me, I lived in Ingleburn), but perhaps you can find somewhere easy to commute from, maybe with a vibrant immigrant community so you can still get a 'culture fix', then once a week have coffee where you'd *like* to be living.

If you have generous parents, they might let you move back in and pay minimal rent while you save for that first deposit.

Even if you really can't save a cent, there are ways to get a home loan without a deposit. Close family members may agree to act as *guarantors*, offering their home or other assets as security for your home loan, eliminating the need for you to save. But putting the hard word on Mum and Dad to put their retirement savings at risk can affect family relationships later on. To me, that's something to avoid at all costs.

The fact that you're reading this book means you're ready to educate yourself on finance and investment, so there's a light at the end of the tunnel.

I achieved financial freedom but that's not my currency. I'm all about lifestyle choices, and I now travel the world and live every day exactly as I please while helping others achieve the life of their dreams.

I wouldn't be here if I hadn't budgeted, driven a car from 1979, and dealt with some short-term location pain for long-term, positively geared property-portfolio gains.

PAY OFF THAT LOAN!

Once you've got yourself a mortgage, if you need added incentive to make those repayments on time, remember that you can build equity even faster by paying more than your standard mortgage repayments, and that every dollar you pay is another dollar in equity you can use!

Capital growth, when combined with paying off your mortgage ahead of schedule, has a superpower effect.

CHAPTER 4
LOCATION, LOCATION, LOCATION

Finding an investment-grade property.

Before you enter the market and start your property portfolio, you need to do your due diligence and ensure you buy a solid investment-grade property. In this chapter I'll teach you what to look for as well as how to identify locations with genuinely good growth potential.

What we're looking for is *the trifecta: instant equity, cashflow and growth.* That's the investor's dream, and it's how I have structured and modelled my entire property portfolio.

THE PROPERTY TRIFECTA

EQUITY   CASHFLOW   GROWTH

Choosing sound investment locations means your portfolio will be sustainable. You will see growth long after you've added the initial equity, and owning prime-location properties 'recession-proofs' you against major market downturns.

THE FIRST INVESTMENT PROPERTY

Your first property will be the cornerstone of your portfolio and drive future investment purchases. Start with a solid investment, then ensure that subsequent properties in your portfolio complement one another — that is, each property you buy contributes to the growth of the overall portfolio, helping you to achieve financial freedom in the long term.

If you purchase the wrong initial investment property it can cause you to become stuck there. According to data by the ATO, 14.57 per cent of Australian property investors own just one investment property, and only 3.85 per cent of Australian property investors own two investment properties.

Aussie property investors who have more than six properties (that's me!) make up a mere 0.89 per cent (or 19 920 Australians). That's a very small percentage of the population who are actually helping themselves to achieve financial independence through property.

According to data released by the ATO in June 2023, 2 245 539 Australians, which is only around 20 per cent of the nation's 11.4 million taxpayers, owned an investment property in 2020–21. This means only 8.42 per cent of the Australian population could classify themselves as property investors. Most adult Australians were not investing in property at all:

- 71.48 per cent of those investors held just one investment property

- 18.86 per cent of investors held two investment properties

- 5.81 per cent of investors owned three investment properties

- 2.11 per cent of investors owned four investment properties

- 0.87 per cent of investors owned five investment properties

- 0.89 per cent of investors held six or more investment properties.

Buy the wrong kind of property first up and you'll be unable to refinance your mortgage and move on to a second property purchase. Moreover, the cost of offloading that first 'bad buy' can be high, undermining what you're trying to achieve.

I was lucky that Rockdale, my first property, was in a good location. Although I had no strategy yet, I still managed to choose a good property. It was slow to perform at first as I bought at the wrong time, but it ended up performing well, which allowed me to build up good equity along the way.

This is why it's important that you understand where you're heading, and have a clear and precise investment strategy. You won't be doing it alone. You will convene a 'dream team' of experts to help you work towards your goal, and we'll get to each dream team member in the following chapters.

The important thing is that you don't waiver from your strategy or lose sight of the long-term portfolio focus as this will be detrimental to your success. In other words, take your time when searching for your property.

LLOYD'S STRATEGY

When investing, 'less is more' is a wise approach. Although the prospect of owning a lot of affordable properties may seem attractive, you'll be able to gain much more in the long term by owning one solidly performing investment rather than several poor investments.

EVERYONE'S AN EXPERT

Everyone seems to have an opinion on property, so it's crucial you seek advice from someone with proven success.

Your mates at the Sunday-arvo barbecue may love talking about property, and even think themselves experts, but avoid at all costs making an investment based on 'backyard barbie advice'. Clients come to me saying, 'My sister told me this, but Dad told me that.' Friends and family mean well and want the best for you, but unless your dad's a successful investor who has made a lot of money out of property, he's not the right person to be giving you advice.

You need to seek independent property advice from a buyer's agent or property investment adviser.

A mortgage broker and an accountant should be part of your dream team, but unless they're also qualified in the property space, they should stick to advising you on the numbers.

Also be careful about taking advice from real estate agents, as they won't necessarily have your best interests at heart. Real estate agents are selling property on behalf of vendors, so they're going to tell you how good their property is, but the property may not be what you're looking for.

BEWARE THE NAYSAYERS

There are people who love a doom-and-gloom story because it makes them feel better about the fact that they haven't got themselves into a better position financially by investing in property. Instead of being comfortable with the fact that they're risk-averse, they'll pass on dire warnings about the money to be lost from investing in property. In fact, some of the wealthiest people in the world have made their money through property.

I'm not suggesting everyone should aim to become a millionaire; it's about setting yourself up properly for the future. Most people would like to better their position. Unfortunately, many don't work to put themselves in that position. To my mind, these people should stop complaining and *make some changes* if they're not happy with where they are.

PROPERTY MARKET CYCLES – WILL IT CRASH?

Quite often the media hypes up property market downturns in certain areas, promoting the kind of doom-and-gloom market-crash stories that naysayers thrive on. Don't let them put you off.

For example, in September 2018, *60 Minutes* broadcast a story called 'Bricks and Slaughter', predicting that property owners could expect to lose up to 40 per cent of their home's value over the following 12 months. It didn't happen, and nor was it ever likely to. A nationwide fall of 40 per cent in property prices would have coincided with rising unemployment rates, rising interest rates, mortgage stress and increased bank repossessions.

But it wasn't the first time some 'guru' from another country had decided to talk about how Australian property is overpriced and everything's going to collapse. The media leapt on this angle and ran sensationalist headlines. But it wasn't the whole story.

Firstly, *Australia is not a singular property market*. It is composed of numerous different markets, each of which moves in a cycle. There are even 'micro-markets' within the suburbs of capital cities.

Secondly, *a downturn in the market is not necessarily a bad or unnatural thing*. Consistently increasing house prices are unsustainable and unhealthy for the wider economy. There needs to be an occasional levelling out in house prices in any property market. This allows first home buyers to get into the market as well.

The next day I wrote a blog that set out a counterargument to the *60 Minutes* story. I got more hits on my website that day than I'd ever had.

In my blog post I explained that much of the scaremongering segment had focused on the western suburbs of Sydney and Melbourne, not on the whole country, and that *60 Minutes* interviewed only a few families, who were under significant mortgage stress because they'd bought their properties during the peak, had overextended themselves and were now struggling to pay off those mortgages. These homeowners spoke about how hard it was to pay their mortgages and how they saw their homes as overvalued and prices as about to crash. The one-sided segment featured no experts to balance the argument and explain why the market was unlikely to crash in the immediate future.

As I saw it, the problem was that the Western Sydney market had been highly spruiked over the previous five years as 'the next boom area', so investors rushed in. This resulted in inflated property prices and created a false sense of security for owner-occupiers; a belief that their properties would grow continually in value.

The problem was that house prices in Western Sydney did rise — higher than many of the area's property-owning residents could sustain. This is why *I recommend buying in an owner-occupied area, not one driven by investors, even when you are buying an investment property.*

The Western Sydney price rise was not a true reflection of the state of the nation's property markets. Of course, *60 Minutes* did not mention that; nor did it touch on the technicalities and skill involved in buying a robustly performing property.

In my blog, I explained that as a buyer's advocate and property investor, I spent my days focusing on market data, market trends and cycles, and I believed Sydney was going through a 'market correction', but that there would be no 'market crash' because Sydney's western suburbs are home to multiple growth drivers including The Children's Hospital at Westmead, Western Sydney University and the new multi-billion-dollar Western Sydney Airport at Badgerys Creek, which will create thousands of job for the area — and, of course, this is great for the economy.

I agreed that Western Sydney was overvalued and not sustainable relative to average household incomes in the area. However, it was not 40 per cent overvalued; I predicted that a decline of 10 to 15 per cent was more likely in Sydney as a whole, and that we should be focusing on the whole city and not just on one micro-market.

And prices did decline, by about 15 per cent in Sydney and about 13 per cent in Melbourne — which they had to, given the fact that by 2018 prices had increased by about 80 per cent in Sydney over a six- or seven-year period. So I was spot on with my predictions.

Sure, there were some properties that lost a bit more value than that, and you might have been able to pick them up at a good price, especially as mortgagee sales, but *nothing* fell by 40 per cent in Sydney or Melbourne. And simultaneously, markets outside of these capital cities were experiencing growth.

A year later, prices were on their way up again in Australia's capital cities because there was (and is) way too much infrastructure, jobs, growth and lifestyle opportunities in these cities for property prices ever to continually fall. Simply put, people continue to want to live in these areas.

In mining towns, you will occasionally see legitimately huge property market collapses. But that's not indicative of the Australian property market as a whole; it's indicative of what can happen in an area that is dependent on one growth driver.

Two years after my blog post, during the pandemic, the naysayers thought the market was going to crash again, and people stopped buying property again. But those who did buy property during the pandemic ended up doing very well because, as you know, the market grew so much from 2020 onwards. For those who were prepared to take a bit of a risk, things worked out really well.

CAPITAL GROWTH VERSUS RENTAL YIELD

While capital growth is a good long-term strategy, I'm all about short-term equity so you don't need to hold a property for 15 years to get some growth on it.

Properties in capital cities, particularly the larger ones such as Sydney, Brisbane and Melbourne, have the highest growth rates and deliver better returns through capital growth over the long term. But generally, higher levels of growth result in lower rental yields and no immediate cashflow, and vice versa.

So if you go to a regional town — say, Ballarat in Victoria or Bathurst in New South Wales — you might not get quite as much capital growth as you would in a capital city, but you could get very good rental yields.

Though good rental yields will pay off your mortgage faster, they do not make you wealthy. Focus on rental yields and you're relying on one source of income in a location that's unlikely to get much growth. If you've got 10 properties today and in 10 years' time they're all worth the same as when you started, you're only breaking even; it's just not worth it. Worse still, property values could decline in some of those regions.

To create growth and get ahead in your investment, *you need to increase the value of your property*, whether that's by capital growth in the market or by creating equity.

The way I overcome the capital-growth-versus-rental-yield conundrum is by having a dual-income property, such as a duplex, in an area that is expected to get some capital growth. What I am achieving here is *the trifecta — growth, instant equity and cashflow*.

THE PROPERTY TRIFECTA

EQUITY   CASHFLOW   GROWTH

INVESTMENT-GRADE LOCATIONS

Fewer than 5 per cent of properties available for sale are investment grade. So how do you find an investment-grade property in a region that is ripe for growth?

A lot of things go into finding an investment property; it's about far more than just liking what you see. This is the stage at which doing your due diligence pays off, so put time and effort into researching where and what to buy.

If you find a property that meets your budget requirements, aligns with your strategy and fits the key criteria I recommend, I encourage you to invest.

Shortlist suitable property locations based on the following factors:

- good regional growth drivers

- the presence of several different industries in the area

- approved development plans

- approved increased government spending in the area

- excellent transport links

- low local unemployment

- increasing jobs prospects

- low vacancy rates

- proximity to education and childcare facilities

- a desirable area for both families and workers.

GROWTH POTENTIAL

When looking for investment properties, you need to focus on areas where there's a strong local economy with several industries thriving. Industry drives regional growth, creating jobs and increasing the population as well as improving local residents' standard of living.

Education's a big growth driver so it's very good to be near universities, where there are thousands of students. It's also good to be near hospitals, where there's employment for nurses, doctors and ancillary staff.

There needs to be different industries, depending on the area. If you're looking at a regional town, there'll be primary producers — wool and cotton growers, for example. In the city you're looking at industries in the manufacturing sector, such as biotechnology, food processing and electronics. Major manufacturing companies might include Arnott's, Coca-Cola Amatil and Rheem.

The benefit of having several industries is that if one doesn't go so well, there are other drivers to keep the region's economy afloat. If a major manufacturer closed in Sydney, for example, the city would keep functioning because so many other industries would keep it alive. On the other hand, if you buy property in a mining town, and the mining industry collapses, as it did in 2013, miners will lose their jobs and vacate the area, leaving thousands of empty properties and no-one to tenant them. This leads to big declines in property values. Indeed, former mining towns often become ghost towns.

The property I purchased in the mining town of Blackwater is an example of buying in the wrong location because the town relied on a single industry. Luckily, by the time the mining industry collapsed, I didn't have to offload my Blackwater property as I could rely on the other properties in my portfolio for equity and cashflow to keep moving forward. I still hold that property in my portfolio and it's not doing much. Lesson learned.

INCREASED GOVERNMENT SPENDING

Government spending in a geographical area creates jobs — both in the short term, while the infrastructure is being built, and in the long term, through the new retail businesses, hospitals and education facilities developed to service those workers. This further increases demand for workers in that area and eventually puts upward pressure on house pricing.

Ideally, you also want to be buying in areas where there's some positive new development, such as a suburb that's undergoing 'gentrification' or is slated to get some beautification or new amenities.

APPROVED DEVELOPMENT PLANS

When buying a property, you certainly don't want to find out that someone's about to build a massive 10-storey apartment building across the road. Part of your due diligence should be calling the local council to find out about any new developments in the pipeline that might impact your property, and any zoning changes planned or scheduled.

Municipal or local government zoning laws dictate how property can and cannot be used in certain areas, for example limiting commercial use of land. Zoning laws can determine whether or not you can build a duplex on a piece of land.

Zoning changes also mean that an area zoned for one type of development, such as residential-only, can become zoned for multi-use dwellings such as apartment buildings or commercial property. This can affect local property values positively or negatively, depending on the circumstances.

LOW VACANCY RATES

To attract good tenants, your location needs to have a vibrant population. I look for property in suburbs with tenancy vacancy rates of below 3 per cent, which is considered equilibrium. Often, however, I buy in areas where the vacancy rate is 1 per cent or less, so I rarely have any issues renting out my properties.

I also like to look for properties in suburbs with a ratio of about 75 per cent owner-occupied to 25 per cent rented properties. Having at least 20 to 25 per cent renters in the area is important so you can be confident there is enough demand to get your property leased.

Being in an owner-occupied area really pushes up the value of your property because it's surrounded by proud homeowners. These are also the kinds of people you'll eventually want to sell to, as they're typically 'emotional' buyers and will thus pay more for your property.

It's also important to look at statistics for capital growth in the suburb or area over recent years. Check historic area-growth figures, especially market cycles over the past 20 years.

To get this kind of information, it does help to engage the help of a professional, such as a buyer's agent, who'll likely have access to some great up-to-date data that's not available free online.

TENANT DEMAND

Do your research to understand the demographics of the area and the likely demand for the type of property in which you're looking to invest.

You may want to get the most bang for your buck, but buying a large family home in an area dominated by student accommodation would not be an ideal investment. You'll have mainly student applicants and end up dealing with a high turnover of tenants and a lot of maintenance to your property. Likewise, there's no point buying a one-bedroom unit in an area where virtually all the residents are larger families, because your one-bedroom unit won't rent easily and is unlikely to see any capital growth.

 ## GOOD TRANSPORT LINKS

Within a reasonable distance of the property you need to have transport links to trains, buses — even an airport, if possible. Properties that are close to amenities, with fast and easy access to commuter transport, have proven to be more fruitful investments. As most people still need to commute to work, there's always demand for properties near transport links.

Transport infrastructure differs from place to place. In cities such as Brisbane and Adelaide, buses are prevalent. In Melbourne and Sydney, trains, buses and light rail (trams) are all used. Sydney makes extensive use of ferry services. All major cities have roads and freeways connecting their CBDs with industrial and residential hubs.

In regional cities, commuters might use bus services or cars. Buying close to a train station, if trains are infrequent, may not be such a smart move.

Ask around or go online and get to know the transport options in an area in which you're looking to invest.

 ## THE PERFECT POSITION

Once you've got the suburb right, drill down into that suburb, as in some suburbs certain areas are not investment grade. You have to know the right streets: those that are close to the amenities you want and not too close to undesirable features such as flight paths and flood zones. You can find much of this information on council websites.

Investment-grade properties enjoy factors such as being some distance from main roads, so look for quieter streets and cul-de-sacs. Sometimes one side of a street is better than the other; often the 'higher side' is preferred and consequently sees more growth over time.

NEIGHBOURS, FLOOR PLANS AND SALES HISTORY

Look out for noisy neighbours. You might inspect the property in the morning, when all looks fine, but I like to go back in the afternoon or evening and sit outside for a while. Are any of the neighbours playing loud music? Check they're not running a drug lab next door! I consider such careful advance scouting part of my due diligence.

The other thing that has to work in order for an investment property to deliver is the floor plan. A good investment property requires minimal or no structural work. Placing the bathroom at the opposite end of the house from the bedrooms is impractical.

I also like to find out how old the property is, when it was last sold, whether it was by auction or private treaty, and how much it sold for. This gives me an indication of how much growth the property has had since and whether that's in line with the growth rate of the suburb.

LLOYD'S STRATEGY

If possible, when I'm considering a property for myself or for my clients, I'll sit outside it at different times of the day to do reconnaissance. It's good to know, for example, which way the sun comes into the property's living areas, and which parts face north and get full sun.

Buying off the plan

Buying 'off the plan' means buying a property that hasn't yet been built. It could be a unit in a big apartment building. The developer usually needs to sell about 75 per cent of the property before they'll get the finance to actually build. Ideally, they'll finish it in three years or so, but it can take even longer.

People buy off the plan for a couple of reasons.

(continued)

Buying off the plan (*cont'd*)

The first is that they're looking for a new apartment to live in, so they're buying a future home, which they're planning to settle on later, because they only have to pay a 10 per cent deposit and don't have to pay the rest until settlement. The problem is they don't know when the property is going to be finished. Also, they can't get finance for an unbuilt property today; they get finance on settlement. If their job situation changes, there's no guarantee they'll get finance in three years' time. So it's a risky thing to do.

The second reason people buy off the plan is, as investors, to get into a market with upswing in the hope the property, when it's settled, will be worth more than the contract price they're paying for it. However, that very rarely works and certainly hasn't worked in Brisbane or Melbourne, where there was an influx of apartments around 2018–19, because when there's no scarcity of supply, values don't go up — they go down. In Melbourne, apartment prices have stagnated and only the large population influx has stopped the Brisbane apartment market from doing the same.

For example, if you buy a property off the plan for $500 000 and find in three years' time it's valued at only $450 000, the banks are only going to lend to you based on a $450 000 purchase price, so you'll have to make up the $50 000 shortfall. That can become a real problem. Quite often people can't settle on the property because they lack the funds and, as a result, those properties 'fall over', then the developer has to resell at cheaper prices and people lose their deposits. Off-the-plan buyers also run the risk of being sued for not being able to settle on the property.

And when properties like that are built, with hundreds of apartments coming onto the market and being rented at the same time, you get bigger vacancy rates too.

Buying off the plan is therefore fraught with risk.

SUCCESS STORY
Location — Brisbane, QLD

This area definitely hits the investment property trifecta: equity, high rental yields and good long-term growth.

THE PROPERTY TRIFECTA

EQUITY   CASHFLOW   GROWTH

(continued)

SUCCESS STORY
Location — Brisbane, QLD
(*cont'd*)

In recent years, Brisbane has rapidly emerged as one of the country's prime investment locations.

The capital city had certainly been on my radar for many years, and I have owned multiple investment properties including units, duplexes and standalone houses. I've bought these for clients too. I've also bought boarding houses for clients. Brisbane is much smaller than Melbourne and Sydney still, and it's a funny market because it's had subdued growth in the years since the 2008 GFC and the 2011 floods.

RIDING THE WAVE

This slowly started to change as we saw large numbers of people from the southern states, particularly from Sydney and Melbourne, head north. This was already happening prior to 2020, with many retirees choosing sunny Queensland as the perfect sea change location.

Since COVID, however, the Brisbane market has evolved very quickly, and the trend has not only continued but has even started to ramp up. I agree with other property experts who see a lot of potential for long-term future growth leading as a result of the 2032 Olympics.

There's a lot of excitement there now, so I think it's definitely the right time to be looking at Brisbane and the investment opportunities. But there's also a lot of competition, and it's starting to heat up. So it comes down to finding the right property at the right price and the right time. I suggest small townhouse developments and 'buy and hold' investments are the best strategies here.

FAMILY-FRIENDLY MOVE

In the year to September 2023, Queensland's population climbed by about 144 000 people. This is a huge increase for a modest-sized city. Given that the entire country can barely build 200 000 homes per year, the impact this demographic shift will have on the housing supply and property values will be significant.

The big driver for many of these people has been the fact that Brisbane property prices have remained more affordable than those in Sydney and, to some degree, Melbourne too.

The rental yields are not too bad, and the property price points are still about 65 per cent below what you can get in Sydney for something similar. But more importantly, it's possible for a working couple to afford a house in Brisbane for the same money as a small two-bedroom unit in Sydney.

Naturally, this has led to a huge influx of families to the Sunshine State as housing affordability has been dramatically falling in recent years, with ever-higher prices and interest rates that have increased at one of the fastest rates on record.

In 2024 I bought a five-bed, two-bath, double-storey, two-car-garage house with a $1.3 million price tag in Manly, a bayside suburb of Brisbane, to add to my own portfolio. It's a good family home in a major growth area. I have bought a lot for my clients in Brisbane, so I know a lot of real estate agents in the area, and I got that one off-market. My strategy was to buy something that had already been renovated and to hold a good asset in a blue-chip suburb for long-term growth, to continue to build wealth in my portfolio. I plan to pass the house down to my boys.

WHY I INVEST IN BRISBANE

So Brisbane is much more affordable, and that means there's scope for a lot of further growth there. But affordability isn't its only appeal. The city is undergoing a transformation on a range of different levels.

Desirable for families and workers

Brisbane is celebrated for its enviable lifestyle attributes, including a subtropical climate, outdoor recreational spaces and vibrant cultural scene. The city's diverse neighbourhoods cater to varying preferences, from bustling urban hubs to tranquil suburban enclaves, accommodating the lifestyle needs of families and workers alike. Affordable housing options, coupled with a thriving job market and community amenities, reinforce Brisbane's status as a desirable place to live, work and invest.

(continued)

SUCCESS STORY
Location — Brisbane, QLD
(cont'd)

Population growth

One of Brisbane's compelling attributes is its growing population, which underpins demand for housing and infrastructure development. Along with a natural increase of 23 010 individuals, the 144 000 newcomers in 2023 included 88 000 people from overseas and 32 625 people from interstate, highlighting Brisbane's appeal as a preferred destination for both Australians and international migrants.

Property market dynamics

The Brisbane property market has been on a strong trajectory, with steady price growth over the past few years and strong rental yields. By July 2024 the median house price had soared to $953 028, with annual growth reaching 15.2 per cent according to CoreLogic. Similarly, unit prices have experienced significant gains, underscoring Brisbane's attractiveness across both residential segments.

Investors are increasingly drawn to Brisbane for its comparative affordability coupled with attractive rental yields. The city's rental market remains buoyant, driven by steady tenant demand from a growing population and an influx of students and professionals attracted to Brisbane's educational institutions and employment opportunities.

Low vacancy rates

Brisbane's property market benefits from consistently low vacancy rates, particularly in sought-after residential and commercial precincts.

The overall state vacancy rate is 0.9 per cent, with similar figures in the greater Brisbane area (0.9 per cent), on the Gold Coast (1 per cent) and on the Sunshine Coast (1.1 per cent). Markets were extremely tight throughout the rest of Queensland, including Bundaberg (0.9 per cent), Mackay (0.6 per cent), Rockhampton (0.7 per cent), Toowoomba (0.8 per cent), Cairns (0.7 per cent) and

Townsville (1 per cent). From a property investment perspective, tight vacancy rates will only continue to drive up rents.

Low local unemployment

The city maintains a low unemployment rate of 3.5 per cent, which is lower than the national average, indicating a resilient labour market. Brisbane's economy continues to attract skilled professionals seeking career advancement and a better quality of life, further bolstering its reputation as a favourable destination for job seekers and employers alike.

Good regional growth drivers

One of Brisbane's key strengths is the diversity of industries driving its economy. Beyond its traditional sectors, like resources and agriculture, Brisbane has diversified into advanced manufacturing, biotechnology and digital innovation. The city benefits from Queensland's overall economic resilience and diversification, with sectors such as tourism, education, construction and healthcare playing pivotal roles in its growth trajectory. The presence of major companies and research institutions fosters innovation and entrepreneurship, creating a dynamic business environment that helps drive sustained economic growth.

Development plans

Brisbane is poised for significant development with numerous approved projects set to reshape its skyline and infrastructure. These include commercial precincts, residential developments, and mixed-use spaces designed to meet the demands of a growing population and enhance urban liveability. Several key development plans in Brisbane, such as Queen's Wharf, Brisbane Metro, Cross River Rail, Howard Smith Wharves and Northshore Hamilton, aim to enhance infrastructure and urban connectivity while meeting the city's evolving needs. These developments will not only inject vitality into the local economy but also provide ample opportunities for property investment across various segments.

The upcoming 2032 Olympic Games in Brisbane represents a monumental opportunity for the city's growth trajectory. The Queensland government's preparations for the Olympics entail substantial investments in infrastructure, accommodation, and

(*continued*)

SUCCESS STORY
Location — Brisbane, QLD
(*cont'd*)

recreational facilities like the Gateway Upgrade North, inland rail, Bruce Highway upgrades, and ongoing road and bridge maintenance. This mega-event is expected to inject billions into the local economy, create thousands of jobs, and elevate Brisbane's global profile as a desirable place to live, work and invest.

We only have to remember what happened in Sydney when the 2000 Olympics came to town and look at how values boomed during those years.

Increased government spending

The Queensland government has committed substantial funds to bolster Brisbane's infrastructure, healthcare and education sectors. Recent budget allocations earmarked for key projects such as hospital expansions, school upgrades and transport infrastructure enhancements underscore the government's commitment to driving economic growth and improving the quality of life in Brisbane and its surrounds.

SUCCESS STORY
Four strategy sessions led this client to a prestige home in The Gap

Joe returned to Aus Property Professionals five months after buying his first investment property with us, excited to purchase his next property and grow his portfolio. Joe wanted to buy another investment property in Brisbane. After arranging finance, Joe's budget was around $1.2 million.

THE STRATEGY

Soon Joe's circumstances changed and he decided to scrap the investment property purchase strategy and search for a primary residence instead. We ran a second strategy session, and after running new numbers through the broker Joe was ready to start looking for a new home with a budget of $1.15 million.

Then Joe's personal situation changed again. Six months later, Joe and his girlfriend decided they wanted to purchase the home together, so we ran a third strategy session, and the broker ran through new numbers for this purchase. Now, armed with a budget of up to $2.7 million, Joe started the search again, but this time to find the perfect home for them as a couple. When none of the prospective properties ticked all their boxes, they were able to extend their budget to $2.9 million to open up some more options.

One of the challenges with this brief was that Joe and his girlfriend wanted different things in a home. They had conflicting ideas, and so there was a lot of back and forth. However, we were able to help them focus on and prioritise the essentials, compromising on the smaller things.

At the start of the new year Joe's partner went on an overseas holiday, which made inspections and signing any purchase contract together quite difficult. We inspected and shortlisted properties in Brisbane for Joe to view. When February came Joe decided he wanted to put the search on hold, with no further explanation. But we knew we could find the right home for them, so we maintained our search.

Finally, after three weeks of trying to get in touch with Joe, we received a new update: his personal situation had changed again, and he would be purchasing the home in his own name!

Back to the drawing board, and a fourth strategy session for Joe. The new strategy included Joe selling his original property and place of residence, and using the equity from the investment property we helped him purchase. The mortgage broker went through the new numbers for Joe's revised budget of $1.8 million.

THE LOCATION

Joe wanted to find a new primary residence somewhere away from the city where he could live in peace and quiet.

(continued)

SUCCESS STORY
Four strategy sessions led this client to a prestige home in The Gap (*cont'd*)

With this new brief in hand, it took us only four weeks to find a great property in the leafy and secluded community of The Gap, 15 minutes away from Brisbane CBD. The prestige home was going to auction in a week's time. The property was popular, with its wooden slats, sustainability-focused architecture and open-plan design. There were at least four interested parties, but Joe was really interested in this property so we wanted to secure it for him prior to auction, before the other bidders could get a chance.

We arranged for an inspection right away, and the price guide was for the high $1 millions. The agent informed us that the vendor really wanted to sell for as close to $2 million as possible.

Source: Jorma from Prime Pixels

THE RESULTS: STRATEGY PAYS OFF

We put in a strong offer of $1.7 million cash, under the same conditions as an auction, while strongly affirming that if the sellers did not accept, we would move on and would not attend the auction. The vendor countered the offer with $1.8 million, the top of Joe's budget. So, we countered back at $1.75 million with our ultimatum that we were prepared to walk away. This got them over the line.

The contracts were reviewed immediately on an expedited level. Due to our relationship with conveyancers we could ensure this was prioritised, and Joe was able to pay the deposit by Wednesday morning, getting ahead of the other interested parties and cancelling the auction.

To our surprise, due to luck and good fortune, we secured the property right before the home was featured in News.com.au real estate. A week later this article would have driven up far more interest in the property.

Joe is now living in his dream home, which is solely in his name, and still has an investment property that pays him cash.

CHAPTER 5

PROPERTY MARKET CYCLE MYTH BUSTING

Insulate yourself against market cycle downturns.

Once you learn to identify the way Australia's property cycles move, you'll understand the hype and be able to assess accurately where a particular location or property is in the cycle and what's likely to happen next. Better yet, you'll know how to buy in a stable or rising market before you add equity to safeguard your properties against a bust.

My team of buyer's agents is constantly researching and evaluating the property markets for the buyer. We are dedicated to analysing market movements and the economic reactions from government spending and Reserve Bank interest rate decisions.

So we know what to look for. Whether you are a homeowner, home seeker or investor, or just like to keep a keen eye on the market, this chapter will give you an insider's insights into market indicators that shape the Australian real estate landscape.

In recent years there has been much confusion and misinformation around, which has prompted economic experts to warn of property market crashes, yet the doomsday predictions never eventuated.

The growth in housing prices since before the pandemic (February 2020) until now (August 2024) has been approximately 34 per cent, indicating that property has proven its resilience as an investment vehicle and is now entering the next property cycle.

With rising interest rates, inflation and the high cost of living, economists are (once again) predicting a property market 'crash', but this too is an unlikely scenario.

My personal outlook on the Australian property markets is very optimistic. We should see most markets go from strength to strength, thanks to strict government controls and monitoring of the lending markets.

AUSSIE CITIES AND THEIR CYCLES

Property market commentators often refer to the 'seven-year property cycle' when talking about house price movements passing through the phases of boom, bust, bottoming out and recovery. But in Australia's cities, property cycles typically vary between seven and 10 years, and none are set in concrete. Cycles don't necessarily fall into line simply because a certain number of years have passed (see table 5.1).

Table 5.1: movement in median prices in Australian capitals, 2010 to 2024

City	Jan 2010 median price	Jan 2010 – Jan 2015 median price	% change	Jan 2010 – Jan 2020 median price	% change	Jan 2020 – June 2024 median price	% change
Sydney	$558 500	$794 000	42	$846 200	52	$1 170 152	109
Melbourne	$474 000	$599 800	27	$668 900	41	$783 205	65
Brisbane	$458 300	$479 000	5	$510 000	11	$859 240	87
Adelaide	$410 500	$443 000	8	$465 000	13	$767 974	87
Perth	$503 800	$568 400	13	$440 000	–13	$757 399	50
Darwin	$555 000	$612 000	10	$463 600	–16	$504 687	–9
Hobart	$340 000	$355 200	4	$466 800	37	$645 850	90
Canberra	$485 500	$565 000	16	$614 000	26	$870 071	79

Source: CoreLogic

The *length* of a property market cycle depends on a combination of macro- and micro-economic factors and the interplay of several social and political issues, including growth (or shrinkage) in population, infrastructure and employment.

In fact, *average Australian capital city prices have experienced multiple cycles over the past 17 years,* with booms around 2003, 2007 and 2010, in 2016–2017, and during COVID in 2020–2021. Some cities, such as Perth and Brisbane, experienced another boom in 2023–2024.

The cycle can be seen more easily if you view it in terms of the 'rate of property growth', as not all markets have downturns, or bust phases, accompanied by price declines. In some markets, the 'down' phase of the cycle manifests merely as a slowing in price rises.

The cycle can also vary from city to city and can also vary within cities ('micro-markets').

One of the main factors driving property cycles across Australia is the cycle in interest rates, with periods of rate cuts eventually driving upswings in the property cycle, and vice versa for rate hikes.

Around this, the supply of and demand for property also have an impact, as do factors such as job security and unemployment.

In a world of high inflation and wages growth that is not keeping up with inflation, cost of living problems are created and property price growth can leave a lot of people out of the market.

How to predict Australian property prices

Forecasting the movement of Australian house prices isn't as easy as it seems, because there isn't just one Australian property market. There are different markets in Sydney, Melbourne, Brisbane, Adelaide and Perth. In fact, there is a property market in every suburb of every region, of every city in Australia, and within these suburbs there are even micro-burbs. This means that certain streets in a suburb perform very differently from neighbouring streets. As an example, beachfront houses will perform differently and be more expensive than houses on the next street without the beachfront.

Australian property prices are based on the economics of supply and demand alongside inflation. Drivers can be broadly referred to as population, income, employment rates, credit availability and borrowing capacity (which depends on the interest rate).

Understanding these factors can assist you in predicting how the property market will react to any event. Also keep in mind that the property market will move organically through cycles of growth and decline. (Experts often refer to this organic movement as 'the property clock'.) This is why economists' predictions are often wrong — there are so many factors to consider.

Population growth

Australian population growth was fairly stagnant during the pandemic. When the international borders reopened we saw the population begin to grow again. What happened then was a completely unexpected level of growth in house prices, followed by a massive increase in rental prices.

What caused the increases? There were not enough properties around for the numbers of people needing somewhere to live. A lot of that had to do with people migrating from overseas. The population of Australia's capital cities grew by more than 500 000 in one year (June 2022–23), the largest annual growth recorded by the Australian Bureau of Statistics (ABS).

Melbourne (up 167 500) and Sydney (up 146 700) had the biggest increase in 2022–23, with Perth and Brisbane each also adding more than 80 000 people. With the addition of Adelaide (28 100), these five cities had their largest annual population growth since 1971.

The government has instituted a lot of funding and planned how many houses they want to be built over the next five years. But beyond the rhetoric I don't see any way they can actually make it happen. They're certainly not going to meet their current housing targets, yet immigration continues apace.

COST OF LIVING

The high cost of living impacts property affordability for buyers, especially if they are currently renting. Landlords are raising rents to recoup their interest rate expenses, and this is putting pressure on the property market. Many renters are becoming increasingly frustrated and are weighing up whether it might be more beneficial for them to buy a property rather than pay rising rentals.

BUILDING INDUSTRY

The slowdown in new building is inhibiting supply. When demand is greater than supply, prices will start to rise. This slowdown is being fuelled by the lack of materials, as well as their rising cost, which is compelling more property owners to wait before they build or renovate. Many builders just cannot get their hands on materials fast enough to support their builds, which is also slowing things down and impacting the market supply. All of this supports property price hikes.

INTERNATIONAL TRAVEL

More foreign travellers are entering the country looking to live, work or study here, which is increasing population growth. Also, more foreign investors are entering the Australian property market, which is increasing the demand for properties.

GOVERNMENT INCENTIVES

State governments have introduced new incentives to help first-time home buyers enter the property market. Buyers who were previously unable to borrow or save enough for a deposit are now entering the market. This has increased the demand for property, especially in the lower price brackets.

MEDIA

A lot of what you hear in the media about property prices are predictions fuelled by economists who are not active in the real estate industry and do not fully understand the strength and resilience of the Australian property markets.

Unfortunately, the media still has a tight grip on the supply and demand for properties. When there are reports of a looming property market crash (no matter how unfounded), we see buyers running scared and leaving the market. When there are reports of a property boom, buyers who are on the sideline will suddenly be persuaded to enter the market.

INTEREST RATES

Interest rates affect a buyer's borrowing capacity, but it's a double-edged sword as rising interest rates should be helping to grow any cash savings. For example, when retirees and others have their savings in the bank and interest rates increase, their savings grow. When interest rates go up, it can stop growth, but that's not what we're seeing at the moment. We've got really high interest rates and the market's still spinning along.

Why is this important? Just as property prices run in cycles, so do cash rates. Not all markets are equal. Each property market is likely to respond differently to rising interest rates.

When interest rates rise, many borrowers can no longer borrow as much as they might have been able to previously, so they will start to look at purchasing properties at a cheaper price point. This puts further pressure and demand on the cheaper properties in the market (which doesn't help the demand from first home buyers). The properties that will be most impacted by this are those at the higher end of the market as buyers shift to cheaper properties. Sellers hold the upper hand when there are lots of buyers going for the same properties.

For investors, interest rates will impact cashflow and yield on their investment properties.

When rates rise, we see many investors shift to properties in regional centres, smaller coastal towns or outer suburbs where they can invest mainly for cashflow benefits, sacrificing long-term capital growth to supplement the rising interest rates on their mortgages.

HOW TO CONTROL THE MARKET

We've talked a lot about what to look for in an investment location, and you will learn more about Australian locations in this chapter, as well as *when* in a property cycle to invest. But I want you to work harder than your average property investor. You truly can safeguard your property from market downturns through manufacturing your own equity rather than relying on the capital growth of the markets.

Once you learn to create equity in your investment property, you won't need to stress over speculation about market falls. You will see growth and cashflow no matter what is happening to other investors. *You will control the market.* With this kind of security, all the hype around market highs and lows will seem to you irrelevant, if not downright mythical.

Let's bust some of the myths around Australia's property cycles now.

🏠 MYTH 1: INFLATED HOUSE PRICES ARE JUST PROPERTY OWNERS BEING GREEDY

Yes, people definitely see dollar signs when their properties are valued high, but as I have explained, prices are not determined by landowners.

Property prices increase when houses aren't built quickly enough to meet demand. There's greater demand for housing when the population — and investor interest — increases, which is why such a large amount of growth occurs in Sydney and Melbourne. That's not the full picture, though.

There are several reasons that may account for an undersupply of properties, including a lack of available land, a lack of government investment and regulations preventing people from building in certain areas.

Banks come into it as well. Because most people can't afford to buy a home based on savings alone, they'll typically take out a mortgage, or loan, that they'll have to pay back over a long period of time. This means demand for housing can be controlled to an extent by how much the banks will lend.

When the Australian Prudential Regulation Authority (APRA) directed banks to make lending more difficult, it slowed increases in property prices substantially, as it became trickier for people to get loans. This was APRA's intention.

The amount Australian banks will lend depends on several factors. These include regulations from APRA; how well they think the economy is doing, and therefore how likely they think it is that people will be able to pay back their loans; and how much governmental support is in place for homeowners. Banks generally like lending in the form of mortgages because these are less risky than other types of loans. This is because if a bank lends someone money to buy a house, and a few years down the line that person fails to repay, the bank can simply take back the house and sell it through a mortgagee sale.

Politics also plays a vital role. Town planning, government investment and political choices can all affect property prices. For example, the idea of abolishing negative gearing always seems to be on the table around election time and can decrease interest in property, because whenever people are worried about negative gearing, those people who have negatively geared properties think, 'Well, I'm not going to invest any more because I can't save money on tax.' That can have negative effects on the market. I don't believe the government will ever get rid of negative gearing, as too many politicians are invested in negatively geared properties. Now I hope you understand more about why *you can't predict exactly how long a cycle or downturn will last.*

🏠 MYTH 2: ALWAYS BUY WHEN IT'S BOOMING

Figure 5.1, the 'property clock', shows each phase in a typical property market cycle. The upswing starts at around seven on the clock face and keeps going up until the peak of the market, at 12. Then it's on the downswing. The bottom of the market is at six.

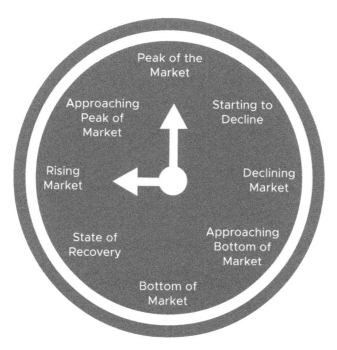

Figure 5.1: the property clock

Never buy at the peak of the market or at the start of a downturn, as you will lose equity almost immediately. There are advisers out there who encourage people to buy in booming markets, but you need to avoid this and to buy in a rising market, before it booms. *You should buy at around seven or eight on the clock face so you can capitalise on the growth that is about to occur.*

It is difficult to know exactly when a market cycle has 'bottomed out' until prices in that market start increasing again.

How else can we determine that an upswing is coming? There are several signs that suggest an upswing is likely on the way:

- Auction clearance rates start increasing.

- Days on the market (DOM) decrease — that is, properties start selling more quickly.

- FOMO ('fear of missing out') pushes prices up as people start offering more.

- More people are viewing open homes and real-estate listings.

In terms of location, should you buy in any area in which the property market clock is somewhere between seven and eight o'clock? Well, that depends on your investment strategy, of course.

Bear in mind that, unlike those of a real clock, the hands of the property market clock don't move in a regular, completely predictable way. *Even within the same geographical area or suburb, the length of a property cycle will change.* How long a full cycle takes is more about what's happening in individual markets, so let's take a look at some of those.

SYDNEY

Sydney is Australia's largest city. Almost six million people live here today. It is a highly desirable and livable city. The growth drivers are immigration from overseas, strong economic growth and jobs creation, and government infrastructure and spending.

When investing in Sydney it is important to understand the importance of the harbour and the beaches as focal points. There's nothing like that harbour anywhere else in Australia. It's a unique, spectacular hub of activity, including the New Year's Eve fireworks, the Sydney to Hobart yacht race, and cruise ships arriving and departing through the Heads every week over the summer. Then of course there's the iconic Harbour Bridge and the distinctive sails of the Sydney Opera House, one of the most outstanding buildings in the world.

You need deep pockets to buy property in Sydney, but a savvy and strategically planned investment strategy can help you get your foot on the property ladder here.

I tend not to focus as much on developments in Sydney, as acquisition costs for land here are very high and the returns are not necessarily as good or better than those you'd get from developing property in less expensive markets.

One in three people in Sydney lives in an apartment for the affordability. They embrace medium to high density. This also means that apartments in Sydney can make good investments, although I recommend staying clear of them in other cities. Either way, if you purchase an apartment in Sydney, a property near the city or near the water, such as on the lower North Shore or Northern Beaches, could do very well.

There is a scarcity of affordable townhouses and larger apartments in the city, which is one thing that's driving house prices up, particularly in the first home buyer segment. A lot of the clients I deal with are people who come to me wanting to buy a home, often with a healthy budget such as $2 million. But when we look at where they want to live, they just can't afford it. And we end up pivoting to an investment strategy where they can buy outside of Sydney, and buy three or four investment properties, and get up the ladder by rent-vesting.

For example, at a recent auction we managed to scrape in just under $2 million, which was my clients' budget, but the property was a two-bedroom townhouse. There were 80 people at the auction and about 10 registered bidders. It was crazy. It was so lucky that we won that auction for our client. The townhouse was in St Peter's, which is in the west of Sydney, traditionally a lower socioeconomic area. It was directly under a flight path too, which is somewhere I would never recommend buying. But I discussed that with the clients, and they were happy to live under a flight path. Because that's what their budget dictated and because they wanted to live in that area.

Then there's the bank of mum and dad — parents who are willing to chip in for their kids to get that property. So a property that was eight or nine hundred thousand suddenly goes over a million because the bank of mum and dad is also pushing up house prices. This is very unfair for those who don't have that help and are on a tight budget, because they are quickly outbid at the auction.

 **MELBOURNE**

Melbourne's property cycle varies each time around. This 'constant change' occurs because of the city's continual growth. With more than five million people, the job market is great in Melbourne. As in Sydney, improving infrastructure is driving the growth and causing property prices to move very strongly there.

Victoria has a diverse property market, from vibrant Melbourne, which has a median property value of $1 150 000 (April 2024), to beautiful regional areas like the Mornington Peninsula, with a median house price of almost $2 million. However, property investors are now wary of investing in the state due to recent government policy changes impacting profitability and cashflow.

One notable change was the introduction of a 7.5 per cent levy on revenue from short-stay accommodations, effective as of 2025, aimed at promoting affordable housing options. Many complain that these levies may negatively impact the Victorian tourism industry and prompt other states to follow suit. The levy also impacts investors' bottom line.

Furthermore, as of 2024, the land tax thresholds changed in Victoria so land tax is now payable on land values of $50 000, down from the previous threshold of $300 000. This adjustment aimed to catch out more property investors and secondary property (holiday home) owners, but it backfired, leading investors to sell to avoid the increased tax burden. These changes also slowed down the market, chasing away buyers.

In fact, many Melburnians are migrating to regional Victoria's affordable open spaces, scenic landscapes and vibrant communities. Government initiatives focused on decentralisation and regional development have further enhanced the investment appeal of regional Victoria, making it a compelling option.

 BRISBANE

You have already read my case study for Brisbane, home to almost three million people, as an ideal investment market. The markets in Brisbane used to move more slowly than those in Melbourne, but lately Brisbane has been through a couple of cycles much more quickly and the market is moving faster than Melbourne.

The main drivers of growth here are interstate migration, major exports and government infrastructure.

I own an apartment in the inner-city Brisbane suburb of Newstead, which is something I wouldn't necessarily recommend. I bought it a few years ago and it has rented solidly, but it doesn't fit with my current strategy of creating equity and cashflow. It has increased in value significantly since the pandemic but growth was sluggish prior to that. I am holding it as a long-term investment.

I've also got a house with a granny flat attached in a growth area in Brisbane's western corridor that is generating really good cashflow and has seen good growth.

The interesting thing about Brisbane is that often when you buy a little bit further out, especially on the north side, such as in the Moreton Bay Regional Council area, the growth can be a little better than when you buy an apartment near the city, which challenges some people's beliefs!

 # HOBART

Hobart has a population of a quarter of a million. The city's main growth drivers are agriculture and forestry. In addition, the state has a major health care sector. In 2016 through 2018 Hobart had among the highest growth rates in the country, even as most other capital cities were starting to decline.

Hobart was on the move because people were going down there chasing cheaper prices and better yields. Because properties can be purchased at quite low price points and the rental yields are quite high, you're buying cashflow-positive properties in Hobart, which is good news.

The problem I have with Hobart is that population growth there is too slow and there are not enough growth drivers in place to sustain long-term growth. So those people who got excited about getting into the Hobart market a few years back may not be seeing the long-term gains they'd have got if they'd invested in property in one of Australia's other capital cities, particularly Sydney or Melbourne.

Hobart experienced a sharp upswing over just a few short years. So you might have a cycle that lasts for a number of years, but it was only in the last couple of years of that cycle that it started to really take off, because property markets in other places were declining, which meant people were going down to Hobart to invest, mainly for the cheaper prices and higher rental yields.

It is normal for a property market to flatline for a number of years before it starts to take off; again, the exceptions are Sydney and Melbourne, both of which tend to move pretty quickly.

 # CANBERRA

Canberra is less than 300 kilometres south-west of Sydney and, like Sydney, has enjoyed solid capital growth over the past five years. Home to almost half a million people, Canberra has one of the strongest economies in Australia, surpassed only by those of NSW and Victoria. This strong economy has a lot to do with the affordability of property.

Despite being a small city, Canberra's largest industry is retail trade, but tradespeople aren't doing badly in Canberra either, thanks to the number of apartments and townhouses that are being built in the region. And since the nation's capital has such a high concentration of public servants, we've seen that public-sector wages have outperformed those of the private sector on the jobs-growth front.

I would not be tempted to buy an apartment in Canberra. Apartments are an increasing focus of government revenue as the boom in apartment building continues and the number of new standalone homes stagnates. Units and apartments faced a big rates hike in 2017 as the ACT Government moved to bring apartment rates into line with those of freestanding houses.

On top of that, rates for all ACT homeowners, including owners of apartments, have been rising each year, as part of the ACT Government's shift to higher rates and lower stamp duty.

Also, if an ACT-based apartment is rented out, its owners — property investors — will face a substantial increase in land tax. This may result in many investors selling their properties in Canberra.

 ADELAIDE

Adelaide has a population of almost 1.5 million. This is a place that doesn't grow much but doesn't bust, either, so you don't have the upswings and downswings that you get in Sydney and Melbourne. You'll get a little bit of growth then it will slow down, but you won't lose much money. It experienced an unusual amount of growth in the post-pandemic boom.

There are billions of dollars of government projects underway in South Australia at the moment. Large investments in the Lot Fourteen and the BioMed City innovation districts are underpinning new jobs in space, machine learning, big data, health and medical sciences, as well as other emerging sectors.

Adelaide's commitment to its technology infrastructure, most notably Australia's first 10 GBps fibre optic network connected to thousands of local organisations and businesses, makes it a safe place to invest.

PERTH

Perth has a population approaching 2.5 million and a good deal of new and emerging infrastructure to support apartment developments. However, it is very reliant on the resources sector. The city's property market is known for its cyclical nature, so investors should be mindful of past boom-and-bust cycles and approach investments with careful consideration to navigate market fluctuations effectively.

With a high concentration of residential units and rising median house prices, the city offers strong rental yields compared with other Australian capitals. Perth has had good growth in recent years, and I have bought here for a few clients.

The Perth market is going to be slightly less stable than most capital cities. You'll get some growth, then it will fall back, because it's overly reliant on the fortunes of the mining sector. Investors need to be cautious of overpaying in the upswings, as bidding wars are common and can lead to potential negative equity when the market corrects.

 DARWIN

Darwin, home to around 150 000 people, is small, with many locals living outside the city. It is, however, a major export centre, particularly to South-East Asia. It is a big service centre for mining, offshore oil and gas production, pastoralism and tropical horticulture. It is also a major tourism hub for businesspeople en route to Asia.

The problem with Darwin is the city is too reliant on the mining and tourism sectors. For this reason, it has never been part of my property portfolio.

Darwin experienced a big downturn during COVID, with the town's GDP decreasing by 8.6 per cent. However, visitors soon returned and the city is focused on promoting Darwin as a place to live, invest, travel and study.

🏠 MYTH 3: YOU CAN MAKE MONEY DURING A MINING BOOM

It's not great for investing when whole cities, such as Perth and Darwin, and even whole states (Western Australia and the Northern Territory), are reliant on what's happening in the various mining sectors. That's because when mining jobs disappear, so do the bulk of the people in that area.

As you see in table 5.1 (page 87), Perth and Darwin were the only cities in Australia to experience an overall decline in house prices in the decade to January 2020, even as the other cities were reaching record highs.

Perth went through four or five years of downturn after the last mining boom, which was a longer period of downturn than has been experienced by any other Australian capital city. Darwin was similarly afflicted.

If you had a crystal ball, you might be able to take advantage of a boom and buy property then get out before the bust. I don't have one.

I wouldn't recommend doing anything in a regional 'one-horse' mining town either, because it too is a 'boom and bust' risk. Yes, early in my investing career I bought a property in the central Queensland mining town of Blackwater, but it's not something I would do again.

Smaller mining towns such as Port Hedland and South Hedland in Western Australia and Moranbah and Emerald in central Queensland saw a lot of growth during the mining boom and after the Sydney 2000 Olympics, and it lasted right through until 2013. People were making a lot of money just buying property here, then not really doing anything with it — but when it bust, people lost big-time.

In Port Hedland, for example, a house would be renting to a fly in, fly out (FIFO) worker for $2000 a week because the mining company was paying that worker's rent. When the mining industry collapsed, that miner flew out and did not fly back in again. Of course, your average mum and dad can't afford $2000 a week in rent, so when the mining company leaves town, there's no-one to rent the house.

It was the same with property prices. You'd have a four-bedroom house that would be worth over $1 million but when the market bust, it *really* bust, and that house wouldn't even sell for $250 000. In fact, the average house price in South Hedland plunged from $800 000 in 2012 to just $216 000 in 2018!

My property in Blackwater is also worth less than what I bought it for. I'm still holding it, but it certainly hasn't been an ideal investment. Many of the people who bought several of those properties in the boom times went bankrupt.

Again, the best course is to *buy in areas that have good infrastructure and more than one — preferably several — growth drivers.*

MYTH 4: YOU MUST BUY CLOSE TO THE CITY

I do like to challenge people's thinking about buying investment properties close to the city, which are obviously going to be more expensive, but many people are convinced that properties in 'desirable' inner-city areas are going to see the most growth.

It really comes back to strategy: are you looking to buy for the long term, or for cashflow, or to add value to a property?

For example, a client might tell me, 'I want to buy an apartment in Brisbane.' That's fine if they want to live in it, but if they want an apartment to invest in, I'd generally try to talk them out of it. Having explained about the recent oversupply of apartments in that city, I'd propose a strategy around what they *should* be doing as an investment. The same applies to Melbourne: given the oversupply issues, don't buy a unit near the city.

You're going to get sick of me harping on about apartment oversupply, but it always comes down to this: *You need to buy in areas where there's scarcity.* And while the inner suburbs will always do well over the long term, they are definitely not the only areas in which we should buy.

Campbelltown, a suburb 50 kilometres south-west of Sydney's city centre, experienced enormous growth during the last boom in Sydney. People were moving there; there was infrastructure happening there; and when growth in Sydney property prices started to decline, the wealthier suburbs in the city's east and inner west lost more in value than cheaper Campbelltown, which makes the latter a good investment, given the lower entry prices.

It's interesting to note, if we're looking at the Sydney market specifically, the more affordable markets are in the south-west and western suburbs, places like Campbelltown, and places out further from the CBD, like Penrith, and Mount Druitt. Those areas are more affordable to buy and more affordable to live in because there's land out there, and that's where there are new housing developments going on. The rest of these infill areas — just about everywhere else in Sydney — there's just not a lot of housing being built, and people are competing for limited properties.

That's just pushing the prices higher and higher. And we're seeing that in lots of different markets around the country. It really does come down to the low supply of properties with a lack of dwellings being built.

The other thing is that in some areas where there is land and it is possible to build new homes, there's just not enough infrastructure going in there. I get people coming to me who want to live close to the city or where they're on a main train line or near the beach, and those are the areas that are seeing continuously increasing rental and house prices.

The idea of buying in lower socioeconomic areas does scare people a little, and they have a point: you need to be careful. I'd never buy a property that's close to a public housing development, for instance, because those properties are difficult to sell and can be even harder to rent. If you have evidence that the government will be selling off the public housing, that's different.

If there's some gentrification going on in an area or really good growth happening in the suburb next door, then rather than buying in a suburb that's already boomed, buy in the suburb that's a little bit cheaper but is set to see some growth in the near future because it adjoins a nice suburb. That way, thanks to the ripple effect, you'll find yourself with a good long-term investment.

MYTH 5: DON'T INVEST IN REGIONAL AREAS

Australia has a lot of emerging regions that can provide great opportunities to enter the market. But even established regional towns don't really have growth cycles as such. They don't boom like the capital cities do, but they don't decline as much in a downturn either.

Regional towns that have a lot happening can tick all the boxes when you're choosing a good location in which to invest.

WHAT TO LOOK OUT FOR WHEN BUYING IN A REGIONAL AREA

Here are some key pointers:

- A rapidly rising population is a must; large-scale infrastructure in the pipeline is another indicator of capital growth.

- A strong local economy is also key. If growth in median household income is higher than inflation, it indicates that the area is becoming affluent and people are spending money here. Evidence of lots of new businesses establishing in the area — and not too many closing down — is a good sign.

- Economic diversity is important. It's very risky to invest in a town that relies on only one industry. Look for a town close to a prominent regional centre with a large established population, as these towns are more likely to have several strong industries in the vicinity. They also tend to have a good mix of employers, which helps keep property vacancies low and demand for them high.

- A big development such as an airport or hospital, while not essential, will attract people for employment and the property market will tend to follow.

- Some investors fall into the trap of buying in an area where they'd like to take a holiday or retire. Steer clear of tourist 'hotspots' that have nothing else going for them. They can be unstable and seasonal, and can easily fall out of favour (as the Gold Coast has, for example). It's far better to choose your property based on solid fundamentals; then you'll be able to afford to holiday or retire wherever you like.

WHEN TO JUMP ON A SMALL-TOWN PROPERTY INVESTMENT

Timing your entry is more important in smaller markets, as 'time in the market' doesn't always serve you well. Look for areas with low supply and high demand from purchasers. This is more easily said than done; however, here are a few barometers you can use to compare one area with the next:

- Low discount rates and high clearance rates typically mean demand is strong.

- Low vacancy rates indicate that an area is popular with renters, which usually puts upward pressure on rents and yields.

- At the same time, high rents can push renters towards buying, putting more upward pressure on prices.

- A low number of days on the market points to demand exceeding supply.

- A low amount of stock on the market means supply is low compared with demand, and properties tend to get snapped up by eager buyers.

Now you know where and when to buy, and what not to do — namely, *avoid investing or building in a location that's at the start of a downturn*, because there will almost certainly be better opportunities elsewhere.

While all this information is good for investor education, you can make money at any point in the property market cycle if you go about it properly.

That's what this book is about, because with my strategy, it doesn't matter so much what the markets are doing or where they are in their respective cycles, as you are controlling your properties and your portfolio growth. I am all about creating equity.

LLOYD'S STRATEGY

My pick of regional towns? Go to my website, auspropertyprofessionals.com.au/cherrypick. I keep an up-to-date list of my favourite towns, suburbs and micro-burbs there for my PG readers to peruse.

CASE STUDY
Location — Newcastle, NSW

Newcastle has all the growth drivers of a capital city without the high price tag. This area definitely hits the investment property trifecta: equity, high rental yields (positive cashflow) and good long-term growth.

THE PROPERTY TRIFECTA

EQUITY   +   CASHFLOW   +   GROWTH

With its modern infrastructure, vibrant city and coastal culture, diverse industry base, and opportunities for education and training—not to mention its proximity to the Hunter Valley and Sydney's metropolitan area—the Newcastle region appeals to a broad range of people. If you know where to look, and what to look for, it also offers affordable, positive-cash flow properties and should bring solid returns on your investment over time.

Around 2014 I began to realise that Newcastle, NSW, was what many would term a 'hotspot', potentially ripe for enormous growth. I identified it as an area in which demand for blocks of land and duplex developments was starting to outweigh supply. I could see there would be high demand in the future and limited stock available, which always pushes up property prices. What's more, no more land releases in the area were planned, which pointed to land scarcity in the near future as well.

Already there was a scarcity of land suitable for developing duplexes, but fortunately I found some vacant blocks off market and managed to negotiate significant discounts, buying them under market value, and achieving *instant equity* from the start.

In one case, we had to sleep out overnight to ensure we were the first to put an expression of interest (EOI) on a block once the developer made it available that morning.

On another occasion, I was negotiating on a block at 10 pm on a Friday night, with my client on one line and the real estate agent on the other! At the same time, another buyer was also negotiating on the block but still checking the finance with their broker and doing some last-minute due diligence. We had pre-approval but if we'd waited even until the next day to get our offer in, we would have missed out.

(continued)

CASE STUDY
Location — Newcastle, NSW
(*cont'd*)

All of this pointed to the popularity of the area.

Sure enough, Newcastle really started to boom around 2016–17. At one point house prices were rising by $1000 a week. Sales agents couldn't believe what was happening in front of their eyes in this formerly blue-collar port.

The trick was to get in at the right time, and thankfully I had predicted it well and got into the Newcastle market before it boomed, so I could take advantage of the increases in prices when they occurred.

Here's what I spotted in the pipeline (which I hope will help you to identify growth potential in other places around Australia over the coming decades).

WHY INVEST IN NEWCASTLE?

There are numerous reasons why Newcastle is a great place in which to invest. It has all the fundamentals I look for in areas where I consider investing:

- The city is on the V8 Touring Car circuit, and there are dozens of year-round attractions within an hour's drive of the Newcastle CBD, from top wineries and horse studs to glorious lakes, beaches and wilderness areas.

- Right now, massive amounts of infrastructure spending (half a billion) are going on in the CBD and its port, transforming it from its industrial city background into a cultural and entertainment hotspot.

- The NSW Government has also contributed to revitalising Newcastle's CBD with new architecture, beautiful walkways, galleries, reserves and family-friendly facilities.

- $9 billion is being invested in developing Newcastle's port to allow for international cruises and larger capacities for exports and imports.

- It also benefits from the presence of a major regional hospital, a large university and a new light rail system.

That covered, I try to 'get ahead of the market', predicting what areas within the chosen region are most likely to be in high demand—because properties in these valued pockets will almost certainly experience enormous growth.

A growing population

According to the ABS, Newcastle's resident population in 2023 was 185 000 and it continues to expand, thanks to the diverse opportunities the region provides. Experts predict that by 2036, the region's population will have grown by 14.97 per cent.

A great geographical location

Newcastle, in the heart of the Hunter Region just 160 kilometres north of Sydney, is Australia's seventh-largest city. It's a thriving metropolis flanking a coastline dotted with great surf and swimming beaches.

Ideally positioned, the city is less than an hour's drive from numerous world-class attractions: glorious beaches; the Hunter Valley's wineries and the Upper Hunter's horse studs; the UNESCO World Heritage–listed rainforest at Barrington Tops; and Australia's largest saltwater lake, Lake Macquarie.

A sector with big potential for international growth, the region's visitor economy attracts more than eight million tourists annually, contributing to strong employment growth in the accommodation and food services sectors, and in retail trade.

Fantastic access via car, bus, boat, bike, train and plane

The Port of Newcastle, which lays claim to being Australia's first port, is central to the economic life of the city and the adjacent, highly populated Hunter Valley region. Each year millions of tonnes of coal are shipped through the facility, making it the largest coal exporting port in the world.

Newcastle is well connected to other towns and cities by the Pacific Motorway (south); Hunter Expressway and New England Highway

(continued)

CASE STUDY
Location—Newcastle, NSW
(*cont'd*)

(west); and Pacific Highway (north and south). It's approximately two hours and 15 minutes from Sydney via the Pacific Highway.

Easily accessible by plane, with daily flights to and from Newcastle Airport and several capital cities, the region is also well serviced by local and long-distance bus, rail and boat services; Newcastle city public transport, including buses and the new light rail; and picturesque walking tracks and cycleways.

A diverse, growing employment base

In the Newcastle region, the manufacturing sector, including metals processing; transport, machinery and equipment manufacture; chemical processing; and defence, are all major employers and key economic drivers. Manufactured products are the region's top exports, followed by utilities, construction, healthcare and social assistance.

Potential improvements to the Port of Newcastle's operations should have a positive impact on the productivity of the region and improve its export potential.

Australia's trade agreements with Japan, the Republic of Korea, China and Indonesia have helped the region's wine and agriculture industries become more competitive in these markets.

Key defence companies, including Boeing, BAE Systems, Thales, Lockheed Martin, Northrop Grumman and Raytheon, are all well established in the Newcastle region. Another driver of growth is the RAAF Base at Williamtown, one of two main bases for the 72 new F-35A Joint Strike Fighter (JSF) aircraft. The presence of the Federal Government's JSF-35 fleet will ensure that the region's large aviation companies continue to flourish.

More opportunities are expected from regional expansion in the knowledge-based service sectors, including tertiary education, spearheaded by the University of Newcastle—which, in 2015, was ranked number 2 in Australia and number 30 in the world for universities under 50 years of age by *Times Higher Education*. The University has spent $95 million on its NewSpace campus in the Newcastle CBD, with another campus to come, driving substantial job creation. Dedicated research and innovation centres such as the Hunter Medical Research Institute (HMRI) and the Newcastle Institute for Energy and Resources (NIER) also drive innovation in the region.

The services sectors, including healthcare, social assistance and retail, are also a growth driver and the largest source of employment in the region, followed by manufacturing, retail, then education and training.

Prime investment region

It's no longer just a port for shipping coal. These days the Newcastle region of New South Wales is thriving, with some outstanding opportunities for savvy property investment.

Of course, with all this infrastructure and growth occurring in Newcastle, the trick is to locate the best suburbs to invest in and determine the best strategy. I have been very successful in this in both my own investments and those of many clients. Since I predicted the boom times in Newcastle I have had clients do extremely well both from duplex developments (instant equity and cashflow) and from holding property and simply seeing the prices rise.

SUCCESS STORY
Duplex profits north of a quarter of a million

George, a Melbourne-based businessman, engaged us to manage the development of a duplex in Newcastle, New South Wales. George and his wife Lynn wanted to create equity as part of a broader strategy to fast-track their portfolio and pay off existing

(continued)

SUCCESS STORY
Duplex profits north of a quarter of a million (*cont'd*)

debts. The duplex project was a huge success, netting them more than $300 000 in profit and putting their business back in the black.

It's a very common story that people who have made bad property decisions in the past accrue a heavy debt load. George and Lynn were in this position when they came to us seeking help in 2016.

CHALLENGES

George was in his late fifties, about seven years away from retirement. He and his wife owned a couple of apartments in his hometown, plus a property in the US they'd bought during the GFC. They also had a business that was severely in debt and on the verge of going under.

Because they had substantial debt and owned all these properties that weren't performing very well, George and Lynn weren't in a great position to borrow or fund better-performing properties, so we needed a good broker and some excellent lending strategies.

They'd bought their Melbourne properties within the previous 10 years, a period during which the city was oversupplied with poorly constructed apartments. Another flaw in their property-investment strategy was that, lacking knowledge of the market, they'd bought in suburbs that subsequently decreased in value. These properties weren't renting very well either.

THE GOAL

George came to us because he'd heard about my duplex projects from when I was featured on Sydney radio regarding one of my own successful projects. His aim was to get out of debt and get some reliable cashflow happening before retirement.

They needed to achieve a large amount of equity to advance their investment portfolio and pay off existing debt. They didn't have the time to invest, then sit and wait for the market to increase over the long term; their portfolio had to have positive cashflow from day one.

As I saw it, to achieve their dream, they'd have to start getting rid of their 'dead-weight' properties and create real growth.

Given their current financial position, we calculated that it would probably take three or, at most, four duplex projects for them to become totally debt-free, with some cashflow as well.

THE STRATEGY

We decided that their best course of action would be to buy land in an affordable up-and-coming area, construct a duplex, subdivide it, then sell both units, taking the profits to pay off the debt on George's business and, if possible, on the couple's other properties. Meanwhile, they'd work to get rid of their other, underperforming properties.

To start to see growth they'd need to sell the first duplex, and possibly the second, to pay off their existing debts and fund the next deal, but by the third or fourth duplex projects, we figured, they should be in the position to hold those duplexes and use them to produce a good income with positive cashflow.

(continued)

SUCCESS STORY
Duplex profits north of a quarter of a million (*cont'd*)

With the help of a great mortgage broker, George and Lynn had a maximum available budget for their first project of $750 000, including land, construction and council costs. We advised them to invest in Newcastle and to start their new investment property portfolio with a duplex project.

THE LOCATION

At the time they were looking to invest, rental yields in Newcastle were strong, and comparative sales showed excellent value. We knew the Newcastle market was starting to rise but it was not yet the 'hot market' it is today. This meant we should be able to achieve excellent results, hitting *the property 'trifecta': growth, instant equity and cashflow.*

THE PROPERTY TRIFECTA

EQUITY   CASHFLOW   GROWTH

For this particular project, we pinpointed West Wallsend, 19 kilometres from Newcastle's CBD and not far from the Pacific Motorway and Hunter Expressway. West Wallsend had a number of larger-sized blocks suitable for development. Neighbouring Cameron Park, a desirable family suburb, had recently enjoyed a major hike in land prices, and West Wallsend had the potential to undergo a 'ripple effect' from this upswing.

THE BUILD

We helped them secure a fantastic 1050m² corner block in West Wallsend for just $270 000. Our team managed the development application (DA) process. After a couple of floor-plan revisions, we were given the go-ahead to build, and arranged a Construction Certificate in under three weeks.

We were able to contract a builder we knew who specialised in high-quality investment properties. He prioritised George's job, completing construction in under six months, even throwing in some upgraded inclusions: ducted air conditioning and 2.7m ceilings (standard height is 2.4m).

The total cost of the project was $720 000, well under their budget of $750 000.

SUBDIVISION AND SALE

Given the generous size of the block, we were able to obtain Torrens titles for the duplex, which meant each unit was a separate property and could be sold separately. With Torrens titles, the equity potential (if holding) and development profits (if selling), the duplex was now 'supercharged'.

Since our clients' strategy was to sell at the end of the project in order to reinvest funds in another project and pay off more debt, the units were put on the market for $519 950 and $509 950, respectively. Unit 1 sold for the asking price of $519 950 in under two weeks; unit 2 soon had an offer accepted for $509 950. The sales price for both totalled $1 029 900.

Duplex project costs

 Land price (1050m²): $270 000

 Construction price (including council costs): $430 000

 Stamp duty (payable on the land): $7940

 NSW stamp duty rebate (abolished 1 July 2017): $5000

 Holding costs during construction: $17 060

(continued)

SUCCESS STORY
Duplex profits north of a quarter of a million (*cont'd*)

 Total project costs: $720 000

Independent valuation (after strata titling):

 Unit 1: $519 950

 Unit 2: $509 950

Total development cost: $730 000

Instant equity: $299 900

THE RESULTS

George and Lynn made almost $300 000 on the deal. Because they sold 12 months after purchase, they also got a 50 per cent reduction in capital gains tax, which was part of our strategy.

With that profit, George got his business out of debt and paid off some of the debt with other properties. He also sold one of the Melbourne properties that he wasn't making any money from.

THE FUTURE

Before they sold the duplex, George's business was going to fold—no-one wants to buy a business that's in a lot of debt. But now it's back in the black, there's potential to sell or close it down as part of his retirement strategy.

Happy with the results of the first duplex deal, they moved on to a second, and they will sell or keep that depending on the market and their circumstances. Our flexible duplex strategy is helping George to achieve his goal of financial independence by the time he's 65.

CHAPTER 6
BUY LIKE A BUYER'S AGENT

My secrets — from valuations to negotiations through to settlement.

While a real estate agent is paid to represent the property seller, a buyer's agent is a licensed professional who represents you, the property buyer. This chapter is all about how a buyer's agent can help you from end to end in the property purchasing process.

Buying a property is easily one of the largest, most complex purchases you're likely to make. It can take months, even years for some people to find the right property, then weeks for the transaction to close after negotiations, building and pest inspections, valuations and so on.

Most Australians fortunate enough to be able to buy property will make only a few real estate transactions in their lifetime — and if you do something just a couple of times in your life, it's not unlikely you'll make a costly mistake in the process.

When you're looking to buy such a significant asset, having an expert on your side to help you negotiate the right price for the right property and under the right terms makes a lot of sense. An established buyer's agent has gone through hundreds of such transactions and knows how to avoid mistakes that could end up costing you thousands of dollars.

WHEN SHOULD I USE A BUYER'S AGENT?

A buyer's agent can be used for purchasing a home or an investment property, or for managing a development project. A good buyer's agent can also discuss strategies on how to build a multiple property portfolio so you can reach longer-term goals.

They will have a vast knowledge of the various property markets and extensive experience in searching across markets and ascertaining the best markets to buy in. They'll be excellent at evaluating properties within those markets, negotiating the purchase price and bidding at auctions on behalf of their clients. A good buyer's agent will also support the buyer through all facets of the purchasing process right through to settlement.

If you're looking at taking on a development, a buyer's agent with experience in this field will be an invaluable asset to you. With their knowledge of the process, they will do all the due diligence before you buy the land, speaking with council, town planners, builders and architects to ensure the land you are looking to purchase can be approved for the type of property you plan to build, whether a house, a duplex, townhouses or something else.

Your buyer's agent can organise everything and can project-manage the build from start to finish, ensuring a seamless process throughout the transaction.

Much of what we do as buyer's agents consists of sourcing land, finding suitable builders for our clients and managing the whole process, including taking care of council applications. The aim is to achieve substantial instant equity once the development has been valued so we are very picky about the areas in which we develop. We'll even assist a client in finding the right property manager!

We also buy completed developments for clients looking to buy at under market value who want to achieve good cashflow without having to go through the entire construction process. Again, I am very picky about which duplexes I present to a client and a lot of due diligence is done on each deal we look at.

Ten reasons to employ a buyer's agent

1. You lack the time to visit lots of open homes.
2. You feel unsure about the process.
3. You are not confident about property negotiation and bidding at auction.
4. You feel unmotivated, as you've been looking for some time.
5. You do not live near where you want to buy.
6. You feel frustrated with real estate agents, who keep presenting you with the wrong homes.
7. You are worried about paying too much for an investment property.
8. You want access to opportunities not available to the general public.
9. You keep missing out at auction.
10. You are unsure of your investment goals.

The top three reasons why people come to me are that (1) they're time-poor, (2) they lack the knowledge they need and (3) they lack the confidence to go it alone.

Generally, people come to me for advice because they don't know exactly what they're doing. Perhaps they think they want to buy a property but are unsure about how they can get ahead at the same time. I began like that. When I bought that first unit in Rockdale I thought, it's near the shops, it's near the water — it makes sense. But I had no strategy in place. Had someone been there to mentor me at the time, I might have progressed a little more quickly than I did.

A lot of people come to me because they've come to realise that negative gearing isn't going to work for them and they want clarity around the types of properties that could be positively geared. They want to know how they can buy a cashflow-positive property and still spend only $400 000. Maybe they want to do a duplex development and make good equity but they don't have the money to do that right now. They want to do a couple of other property deals with me first and build up to that duplex so they can get some really good equity and cashflow down the track.

I've noted that when I went looking for cashflow, my buyer's agent found me a house in a mining town. He could have made me aware of the risks, but he didn't. I believe a good buyer's agent should be a mentor who will educate you about how to make well-informed decisions and about the risks associated with a particular property. They will guide you around the traps that await the unwary.

That's how I run my business, why I have so many repeat and long-term clients, and why past clients as well as colleagues in the industry refer friends and family to me. Among my biggest clients are mortgage brokers, accountants, financial planners, solicitors and other industry professionals, which shows how useful the services of a good buyer's agent can be.

THE DREAM TEAM

Buying and developing property involves working with a team of experts from diverse fields. A reputable buyer's agent can tap into their network of trusted professionals to help you along the way. This network will include:

- solicitors/conveyancers
- mortgage brokers

- financial planners

- accountants

- town planners

- property valuers

- building and pest inspectors

- builders

- architects

- land surveyors and quantity surveyors

- insurance reps.

I put the whole 'dream team' together for my clients, starting with the accountant, solicitor and mortgage broker. I'm very particular about who I refer, but once I've found someone who's good at what they do, I'll make sure I give them some good clients to work with.

Even if my client already has their own team, I deal with everyone along the way and keep everyone in the loop. The first step after we have had an offer accepted is getting the buyer's details to the selling agent and advising them who the solicitor is. Then I'll make sure the solicitor is aware that the contract is coming their way and that the broker gets the contract; and if we need to talk to the accountant, I make sure that happens too. For an existing house or unit we organise the building and pest inspections. If a depreciation report is needed, we'll see to that. We do *everything* involved in the property purchasing process for our clients.

Following the purchase of your property, we can put you in touch with reputable industry experts such as insurance brokers to ensure your property is properly covered, as well as with property managers who can find you quality tenants quickly.

TIME FRAMES

How quickly everything happens really depends on your expectations and how tricky the search is, but usually we can have our clients in a property within one to three months of engaging our services. We've had people who've been looking for a couple of years and have kept missing out. They come to me and we get them focused and straight into a property.

Sometimes it can take longer than three months. Much depends on the client's strategy, how unique their property goal is and what's on the market at the time. But generally we move pretty quickly. We're not emotionally attached to any property so it's always about getting the right property at the right price.

There are many steps to the purchase process. Here's how we get it done so fast.

THE STRATEGY SESSION

As I've already outlined, we start by taking a step back from your immediate property goals to look at the bigger picture, setting some long-term financial and lifestyle goals over the next five, 10 or 15 years. I'm not a financial adviser, so this part of the process will typically involve your mortgage broker and/or financial planner.

We then kick off our complimentary tailored strategy session, in which we outline how we can help you to achieve your lifestyle goals. In this session, we'll discuss your needs and current situation, including evaluating where you are in your current property portfolio and your desired outcomes. We'll also perform your cost–benefit analysis and set up your budget.

If you want help in finding a suitable investment property, we devise a strategy around what type of property will perform best for you with regard to achieving your goals. If you are looking for help in getting that dream home for your family, we'll prepare a full brief on your requirements.

And, as I've shown, we offer a value-adding strategy whereby you can increase the value of your property without having to wait for the natural growth of the market, through cosmetic renovations, major renovations, the addition of a granny flat/auxiliary dwelling, subdivision of an existing block or development of a duplex.

Whatever the case, we first need to ascertain your goals to be able to decide what property scenario will best help you to achieve them.

Having a strategy in place saves time, as we now know exactly what we are looking for as well as what we don't want. We liaise with your mortgage broker to make sure the numbers line up with your goals. Then we prepare a brief for the purchase of your first property.

THE PROPERTY SEARCH

With many years' experience in buying all kinds of properties, we know how to find the one that fits! Once your property strategy is laid out, we save you from having to plough through hundreds of real-estate ads by researching properties for sale in your price range that fit your criteria.

We stay in tune with market trends by evaluating hundreds of properties each week that are for sale or have recently sold. That way, we always have an accurate assessment of where the markets are heading, and can choose locations that will work for your budget and your goals.

We do all the due diligence required to ensure that we've identified the best possible locations for you. This includes acquiring a sound understanding of the demographics of the area or areas we're considering for you, and investigating the long-term capital growth potential, as indicated by planned infrastructure projects (new hospitals, schools and roads), increased employment opportunities and a growing population.

We source properties with the best capital-growth prospects, and compare any properties that match your strategy with similar properties that are on the market or have sold recently.

For clients looking to do cosmetic renovations and developments, we evaluate the instant equity creation potential as well as the likely rental return before and after the planned changes. We do this by performing a thorough feasibility analysis on every property we shortlist for you.

Our real estate experience saves you from being pestered by over-eager agents. We negotiate with them on your behalf. We can interpret all the sales talk and sales tactics real estate agents typically use in language you will understand.

PROPERTY INSPECTIONS

Typically, property hunters trawl through the likely open homes every Saturday, visiting as many as six or seven properties a week, and if they don't find or miss out on what they're looking for, they go through the same dance the following Saturday. This can become extremely frustrating.

If you work with me, though, I'll take your brief and start sourcing and inspecting suitable properties for you straight away, then arrange convenient times for you to inspect only those properties that meet your specific criteria.

This saves you loads of time. Better still, I can get you into private viewings so you're not looking at properties with a crowd of other prospective buyers. As we are out there doing it every day, we have the sort of experience that gives us a significant advantage over the average punter trying to secure the property they want via cursory Saturday morning inspections.

OFF-MARKET OPPORTUNITIES

Having a buyer's agent on your side means you get 'insider info' such as access to off-market and pre-market opportunities — properties for sale that are not available to the general public.

You may not know that many properties don't ever hit the public listings. There are thousands of these properties, and they represent opportunities denied the average property hunter. Through my contacts with real estate agents I find out about many off-market properties. Pre-market opportunities are great, as my clients will often get the first look at them, being able to inspect these properties before they are listed.

Once I have a client's criteria, I'll start calling agents. At the same time, I have agents calling me most days saying they've got a certain property that hasn't been listed. They love that I can bring them pre-approved buyers. There's a lot of opportunity there that can help with negotiations and a smooth purchase for my clients.

What it means is that my clients are the first people to see that property; no-one else gets that exclusive viewing. And we can look through it on a Monday or Tuesday night after work — we don't need to wait until the following weekend.

WHEN A BUYER'S AGENT DOES DUE DILIGENCE

Building faults, pest infestations and problematic sales contracts are things you don't want to discover after you've signed on the dotted line. But they're rarely obvious to the untrained eye during a 10-minute inspection.

When you're satisfied that a property is worth buying, we bring in the heavy artillery. We arrange inspection by a qualified building and pest inspector and a legal review of the contract of sale. You'd be amazed at the elementary errors and omissions we find in some contracts!

We check the land survey plan as well as the property's zoning, its sewerage plan, the strata report (if applicable), any easements or covenants on the property, and the fittings and chattels inclusions list.

But our research doesn't stop there. We also investigate:

- the property's sales history
- how much buyer interest it has attracted
- the vendor's reason for selling
- the market's position in the property cycle
- the local property market's economic drivers
- planned development and land releases in the area
- likely future housing demand.

Does the vendor need a longer-than-normal settlement period? Do they need to sell urgently? All this information can make a big difference to the final price and settlement terms we're able to negotiate.

By getting an understanding of the vendor's position and the reasons they're selling, we ensure we're in the best possible position when it comes time to negotiate on price and terms.

The thorough homework a buyer's agent will do on your behalf can save you tens of thousands of dollars.

FEASIBILITY STUDY

Our due diligence also ensures that any work you do on the property will add real value to it.

If you plan to add a second dwelling or subdivide your block, a feasibility study is very important. It gives you an accurate picture of how much the whole process will cost and what the result will be.

This is where our experience comes into play once again, as we understand all aspects of subdivisions and developments. We will carry out all the due diligence with council, town planners, builders and the like to ensure the proposed dwelling or subdivision will be permitted on your existing block and can proceed as planned.

TRUE MARKET VALUE

Not sure what to offer? If you don't know a property's true value, it's likely you'll pay too much for it. We have access to industry-leading resources and data that is not available to the general public. This allows us to provide you with a true market appraisal of the property you're looking to purchase, ensuring you'll get good value.

Quite often, what a property is listed for is not what the vendor actually wants for it. Sometimes they want more than the asking price; other times, they have an inflated asking price and after some negotiating we can get it a lot cheaper.

It is always wise to be very familiar with prices and comparable sales in the suburb in order to get a true understanding of a property's value.

If a house is listed for sale at, say, $560 000, I'll work out its true value by working through the comparables — what has sold in that area over the past six months; what's currently for sale; where the property is located compared with other, similar properties; its street appeal; its internal and external condition; its floor plan and any micro-markets within the suburb.

It's not enough simply to find similar-looking, recently sold properties in the suburb. They may look the same from the outside, but every property is unique.

Many factors contribute to determining the true value of a property, including:

 any special features

 the condition of the property

 existing improvements

 its floor plan and functionality

 land size as well as the internal size

 location and proximity to amenities

 current market trends

 average days on market.

The detailed report we prepare addresses all these issues, drawing on real data to ensure that your market appraisal is accurate. This allows you to make a fully informed decision on how much to offer.

If the property is worth $520 000 based on comparables, I'd put in an offer under $500 000, and negotiate upwards until we settle on a decent price for it. Ultimately, though, it does depend on what price the vendors are prepared to accept. If the vendors want more than fair market value, we usually walk away and move on to the next property.

Underquoting happens a lot at auctions as a means of attracting buyer interest. A property might have an auction 'price guide' of around $900 000, for example, but when I look at comparables in the area I can see that the property is probably going to sell for around $1 million or even $1 050 000; there's no way it's going to sell for $900 000.

Prospective buyers with a budget of $900 000 who are unaware of this are frequently frustrated when they keep missing out at auction. But they're missing out because they're looking at the wrong properties. They aren't educated around the true value of the property.

When clients come to me I give them the information they need. I might tell them, 'Okay, so this property has a guide of $800 000, but I reckon it's going to sell for about $900 000.' It's sometimes a bit of a reality check for them, but I'm usually pretty accurate. I might then show them what they can *actually* buy for $800 000, which may not be the beautiful dream home they thought they could get, but they need to know what they can truly afford. In some states, such as Queensland, agents are not allowed to tell a prospective purchaser the price guide. You need to work it out yourself by studying comparables.

Having an accurate market appraisal will benefit you in three big ways:

- **It will save you money.** By knowing the property's true value, you will be in a position to negotiate a better price, rather than just paying what the seller's agent is asking.

- **It will save you time.** When you've found your ideal property, it's important to act quickly and secure the deal before someone else does. To make an informed decision on how much to offer, you will need to have all the information in front of you, and without expert help it could take you weeks to gather this information. A buyer's agent who does this daily and understands the different markets intimately can provide you with an accurate market appraisal quickly so you can submit your offer fast and not miss out.

- **It will improve the property valuation.** If the seller is asking an inflated price for the property, this may be reflected in a valuation that comes in at under the contract price. If you pay less for the property, the valuers and your bank will likely be happier with the property!

LLOYD'S STRATEGY

I managed to secure the deal for a client at 10 pm on a Friday evening on a much-sought-after property that was being shown to the public the next day, simply because we had done all our due diligence in advance, and had the confidence to move ahead while other buyers were still doing their research. This is a true benefit of using a buyer's agent.

NEGOTIATIONS AND AUCTIONS

Buyer's agents are licensed to negotiate with real estate agents and to bid at auction on your behalf, or they can guide you through the process.

You may think you know what you're doing, but a buyer's agent makes offers and purchases properties day in and day out. Having one act on your behalf during this stressful time will help you to avoid the common trap of letting emotions push the price above your budget.

In a private treaty sale I do all the negotiations with the real estate agent or the vendor on my client's behalf. The client need deal only with me while I deal with everyone else.

Experienced real estate agents are professional negotiators, trained to extract every last dollar from unsuspecting buyers. I know all the tricks of the trade and can negotiate strongly in order to get the lowest possible price and most favourable terms for my client.

At auction, employing a pro gives you an edge over other buyers while ensuring you don't get into hot water — we know when to hold 'em and when to fold 'em!

I'm with my clients the whole way. They can attend the auction but I'm the one doing the bidding. It takes the guesswork, the scariness and unpleasant surprises out of the equation.

I have a success rate at auctions of about 90 per cent because I enter the process with a highly accurate appraisal of the true market value of property—I *know* what it should go for. I educate every client on that, making sure the property they're hoping to buy aligns with their budget and I never bid on a property I think is going to sell for more than my client's budget will permit.

SUCCESS STORY
We negotiated 10 per cent off the asking price!

A lot of people worry that they will not be taken seriously if they submit an offer well below the agent's asking price. My team and I always submit lower offers with real data to back them up. This means we are taken seriously and positions us well to have our offers accepted.

THE BRIEF

Peter, in his late fifties, was from regional Victoria. He had made some investments earlier in life that hadn't gone so well, and eventually, after going through a divorce, he had had to sell them. This meant he had to start all over again.

Now remarried, Peter's goal was to try to create some equity through investments so he could look forward to a comfortable retirement. Given his past experience, he was set on growth, cashflow and instant equity. He came to us with a low borrowing capacity and a limited deposit of $40 000.

It was important for us to find Peter an investment-grade property that would help him set the foundation for building a property portfolio. So we needed to find a property that would provide excellent cashflow to help with serviceability, as well as creating some equity up front when purchasing the property through buying under market value. If we could do all of this, Peter would be able to 'recycle' his initial deposit from this purchase, using it to help buy his next property.

THE LOCATION

We discussed with Peter a few different locations that would work within his loan budget of $400000, settling for the greater Newcastle/Maitland region.

There is a lot of growth potential there, which has been recognised by the increase in values over the years as a result of improved transport links into Newcastle, planned infrastructure, the new Maitland hospital and many more developments. We knew these areas quite well already, having helped many clients successfully purchase or build property there.

So our search began.

CHALLENGES

As market conditions in the area had started shifting in a positive way, vendors had begun holding off on accepting lower offers on their properties. Stock levels were at their lowest in over a decade, reducing the availability of properties.

NEGOTIATIONS

After inspecting a number of properties, we shortlisted a fantastic freestanding three-bedroom house on a large corner block of more than 600 square metres that would provide high yield and future development potential.

As the property was vacant at the time, we knew the vendor had no cashflow coming in, which would give us some leverage with our offer. After thoroughly researching comparable properties and determining the sale property's true market value, it was time to make our offer.

ACQUISITION

We started with a much lower offer to 'test the water'. With some back-and-forth negotiating, and standing firm on our final offer, we were able to secure the property for 10 per cent less than the asking price, at $371000.

(continued)

SUCCESS STORY
We negotiated 10 per cent off the asking price! (*cont'd*)

With more than $30 000 shaved off his original budget, and with an expected rental return of $460 per week in an area ripe for some serious growth, this property was the perfect first investment for Peter, and an opportunity to start building his portfolio.

RESULTS

Peter's property was cashflow positive from day one. This meant it was not costing him a cent from his own pocket. In fact, the property is paying him some funds, after expenses. This also puts Peter in a great position with the banks moving forward, as banks love to see a good injection of cashflow into people's portfolios when assessing them for future lending.

Peter now feels that the future is looking far more secure for him and his wife, and he's thrilled with the result.

FROM SIGNING TO SETTLEMENT

As a buyer's agent, I also coordinate and supervise each stage of the settlement process, from the signing of the sales contract until settlement day. This way everything happens efficiently and without stress for the client.

This is the part where we make sure that all the *i*'s are dotted and the *t*'s are crossed. Getting the details right is important when you're buying property, because of the amount of money you're spending and the number of professionals and organisations involved in making the transaction. We talk their language, then translate it into plain English for you.

CONTRACT EXCHANGE

Once your offer has been accepted, contracts must be signed between you and the vendor. There will be two contracts — one for you and one for the vendor — that both parties must sign and exchange. In some states execution of the contract involves both parties signing the same contract.

These days the signing of contracts is usually done by DocuSign and arranged by your solicitor, conveyancer or the agent, who will explain how the process works in your state or territory.

WHAT IS INCLUDED IN A CONTRACT OF SALE?

Firstly, the Contract of Sale (CoS) needs to list all parties and their representatives, and include the full addresses of the buyer and seller, and the selling price.

Additional clauses in the CoS might include whether the purchase is subject to finance, whether it has a cooling-off period or no cooling-off period (which would therefore include a 66w certificate), as well as the reports from any building and pest inspections conducted on the property.

The following information can usually be found in a Contract of Sale (although some of these inclusions vary between different states and territories of Australia):

- the full name of the selling agent
- the full name(s) of the purchasing party or parties
- the seller's name
- the property price
- the initial deposit, payment terms and conditions
- loan details, if applicable (in some states)
- the property address
- details of any improvements to the property
- details of any exclusions from the sale
- details about anything else included within the title
- a full list of any household fixtures, furnishings and chattels
- the length of the cooling-off period, if there is one

- the intended property settlement date and period, including penalty rates (between 30 and 90 days from date of purchase, unless agreed on between the parties)

- warnings about the necessity of installing/maintaining smoke alarms on the premises

- Certificate of Title information

- details of any encumbrances on the property, such as a mortgage or lease agreement.

SPECIAL CONDITIONS AND DISCLOSURES

While most property contracts have standard terms to cover, there may also be special conditions attached to the sale of the particular property you are buying or selling. These conditions will be included in the Contract of Sale and can override the standard terms and conditions as necessary. Always ensure you understand what these terms relate to before signing. Seek advice from your solicitor or conveyancer if you are unsure.

The seller is responsible for attaching any relevant disclosure documents, conditions of sale, warranties and notification of any defects.

These disclosures may include:

- plans for sewer lines

- zoning certificates

- property certificates

- plans for the land, including subdivision or strata plans

- covenants, restrictions and/or easement documentation

- home warranty insurance certification — necessary only if the property is less than seven years old.

Unless otherwise noted, a Contract of Sale usually also states that:

1. the land contains no sewers owned by other authorities

2. the information in the zoning or planning certificates is true and accurate

3. there are no adverse affectations, such as public authority plans to purchase the land.

INSURANCE

In some states, the property is at the risk of the purchaser from the date of signing the contract. If this is the case in your state, you should arrange insurance on that property immediately. Banks won't settle on a property until it has insurance. With all our clients, an insurance rep is part of your dream team, so we can arrange this at the time the contract is signed.

WHAT CAN BE NEGOTIATED IN A CONTRACT OF SALE?

From a buyer's perspective, it is imperative that any legal advice, finance approval and building inspections are carried out before the exchange of contracts.

 ### THE COOLING-OFF PERIOD

While the cooling-off period is waived when you purchase a property through an auction, cooling-off terms relating to private treaty sales can be negotiated. They can be longer or shorter or can be removed from the terms of sale altogether. In a 'hot market', vendors like to have the cooling-off periods waived.

If the cooling-off period is waived, a written certificate from the buyer's solicitor indicating the nature and effect of the terms is necessary. Some states allow a finance clause that enables the buyer to get formal approval even after the contracts are signed. In states where a cooling-off period applies, this period can be used to finalise the formal approval, because in a hot market you might be at risk of losing the property by delaying the signing of the contract.

 ## THE SETTLEMENT PERIOD

The sale is considered final when the balance of the purchase price and other adjustments have been paid and the title and transfer documents have been exchanged. Settlement usually occurs two to six weeks after contracts have been signed by both parties. At settlement, you become the legal owner.

The property settlement period — the time between the exchange of contracts and the date when the new owner takes possession of the property and title — can also be negotiated.

 ## DEPOSIT AMOUNT

A vendor generally asks for 10 per cent of the property's purchase price as the deposit, but often this can be negotiated down to 5 per cent. The deposit is transferred into the vendor's solicitor's trust account.

The vendor won't receive the deposit until settlement day when all the necessary funds have been paid, unless there is a 'release of deposit' clause in the contract. I warn strongly against allowing that clause, as it can cause major issues for the buyer if the sale falls through.

 ## FITTINGS AND FIXTURES

It is important for a purchaser to identify what the vendor means by 'fittings', as usually these don't include appliances such as fridges, televisions and sound systems. Typically, ovens, cooktops and dishwashers are included in the fittings. Ensure that all included fittings and fixtures are detailed clearly in the contract; then you can negotiate on items you might like to have included with the property that are not already included with the sale.

When Renee and I bought our house in Lilli Pilli, we also took ownership of three fridges — two of them bar fridges. The family we bought the property from threw in their pool table free of charge. We wanted something to fill that space and they couldn't be bothered moving it as it was so heavy. I guess they were happy with the price we paid them for the house. I'm still no better at pool, though!

STATE TAX/STAMP DUTY

Stamp duty is a government tax that must be paid on settlement. It is calculated as a percentage of the sale price or the property's market value. Stamp duty exemptions may apply for first home owners or concession card holders. This may vary between states and territories. Your solicitor or conveyancer can explain the stamp duty payable in your state or territory.

WHAT HAPPENS ON SETTLEMENT DAY?

On settlement day, all representatives of the parties, including any financiers, communicate with each other to exchange legal documents. Your buyer's agent will assist. This is the day when:

- final checks are performed

- payment of the purchase price is made to the seller

- the bank pays the balance (minus the deposit and any funds you've already paid) if you are financing the property

- all relevant legal documents are exchanged.

The property transfer needs to be completed at the Land Titles Office — or Land Registry Service, as it is called in some states.

Note that any funds the buyer owes must be transferred to the solicitor's trust account before settlement day. Direct deposit is the way to go.

I recently had a client who decided to deposit a cheque into their solicitor's trust account just two days before settlement. As cheques take five days to clear, the funds weren't available by settlement day and therefore settlement was delayed. I didn't even know anyone used cheques any more!

OVERSEAS AND INTERSTATE CLIENTS

My clients who live interstate and overseas generally don't come and inspect properties in person. We communicate over email and hold meetings, using the technologies of the day, but it's the same process; I just carry out all the steps myself.

Most contracts can be signed and sent by email. You email things to the bank; you email things to the solicitor. If required, they'll be posted. So it's the same service wherever you are in the world, but you'll do a final inspection with me through Facetime before you buy.

CHAPTER 7
WINNING AUCTIONS

Arm yourself with a bulletproof strategy for your big auction day.

Auctions are about tactics, strategy and knowledge — *not* luck! I have a success record of around 90 per cent at auctions because I know exactly what advice to give to my clients to prepare them and what to do on the day.

There will always be some things out of your control at an auction, but in this chapter I will share with you all the factors that impact the fall of the hammer, so you can do everything in your power to be that last bidder.

Buying property at auction is very different from other property purchases. At an auction potential buyers gather together publicly to bid for a property. It is conducted by an accredited auctioneer. Not just any real estate agent can be an auctioneer; a licenced auctioneer requires additional training and qualifications.

Most bidders at auctions are inexperienced and emotional. This can be dangerous, because auctions are a high-pressure battlefield where you face a very real risk of spending more than you need to or, worse, more than you can afford to.

The bidding process is public, and if the hammer falls and you are the highest bidder, you must sign the Contract of Sale and pay your deposit then and there. If you forfeit the purchase, you will lose your deposit and may be liable for any damages suffered by the vendor.

You must be sure about the property and well prepared to buy on the day! This means you must:

 have conducted inspections of the property prior to the auction

 have your finances pre-approved (and know your limit)

 have the relevant legal documents checked by your solicitor/ conveyancer

 have had the building and pest inspections done

 have carried out any relevant strata reports

 be ready to hand over your deposit on the spot by bank transfer into the agent's trust account

 ensure you have increased your daily limit in advance, so you can make the deposit if and when required.

Here's how we make it all happen...

WHAT IS AN AUCTION CAMPAIGN?

An auction campaign means you don't normally buy the property by putting in an offer. A property being sold by auction does not have a list price. Auction rules are different in every state: in some states the property will have an auction guide price; in others, such as Queensland, it is illegal to quote a price guide. In this case the interested parties must rely totally on their own due diligence to ascertain the true market value of the property.

Where there is a price guide, instead of 'For Sale for $850 000', for example, the marketing materials will state, 'Auction guide $850 000'.

The goal of any auction campaign is for the hammer to be brought down at a price that meets or exceeds the vendor's expectations. The benefit of an auction, for the seller's real estate agent, is that the owner will quickly understand what their property is actually worth.

Auction campaigns usually run over a four-week period that culminates in the auction itself. Typically, there are viewings or 'open inspections' on Saturdays, and on at least one weekday over those four weeks. And you may have a chance of a private inspection if your buyer's agent can arrange it.

Some vendors will consider offers prior to auction. Whether they'll countenance this usually comes down to what the market is doing and the vendor's motivation to sell. If the vendor agrees to consider pre-auction offers, you can make a pre-auction bid through the selling agent. If you are going to do this, you need to put your best foot forward and put in your highest and best offer, as the vendor and agent won't entertain a significant amount of negotiating. At the same time, the agent will also ask any other interested parties to put in their best offers.

If the vendors are keen and you have the strongest offer, you can buy the property before auction day. But sometimes the vendors will say, 'No, we're definitely going to auction.' That's completely up to the vendor.

AUCTION CLEARANCE RATES

When you find your ideal property and it's going to auction, don't be swayed by the auction clearance rates (ACR) for that location. ACRs are often spruiked in the media to indicate a *sellers' market*, where demand is high, or a *buyers' market* (when the ACR is below 60 per cent).

One of the main issues with using ACRs is that often these figures are general, relating to a major capital city as a whole rather than to individual micro-markets within that city. Another risk of using ACRs to determine market strength is that the data is impacted by multiple factors and is not comparable month on month.

Also, auctions are not suited to all markets. The tactic is best suited to properties that are unique, and therefore difficult to put a clear value on, such as premium homes or homes in popular locations, or when the market is heating up. In less expensive markets, properties are usually sold by private treaty; therefore the ACR is not a true indication of the overall market strength.

There are many other more reliable indicators of potential growth in the market in which you're about to buy, such as the rise or decline of property values, days on market (DOM) to sell properties, average rates of vendor discounting to sell and vacancy rates of rentals in that location.

EXPECTED SALE PRICE OF THE PROPERTY

I win a lot of auctions precisely because I do a lot of due diligence and know, as closely as I possibly can, the true market value of each property that is being sold at auction and what it should go for, whether or not there is a price guide.

Often the auction will begin under the price guide figure, so it's important you don't assume, 'Oh well, my budget's $1 million and that property's got a price guide of $1 million, so let's go to the auction and see what happens.'

When people talk about properties selling for $100 000 more than their budget it's because they're looking at the wrong properties. As I've mentioned, real estate agents often underquote the sale price as they have no way of knowing what a property will really sell for at auction. But when the sale price is underquoted, it can draw more attention and interest. There are two possible outcomes if you become emotionally attached to a property, believing it is within your price guide: you can win at auction and may end up paying more than you can afford; or, if you don't win, you've wasted time and effort looking at a property beyond your budget.

When I bought our house in Lilli Pilli, the real estate agent said, 'It should probably go for this much,' but at the end of the day we paid $1 million more than that, and about $600 000 more than the reserve price. In this instance, it did not necessarily mean the property was underquoted by a million dollars, as it is a unique property that generated a lot of interest, and fierce competition from other buyers.

The agent was probably surprised by what it sold for, but I knew that he knew it would sell for more than the 'guide price' he was quoting. So on the day I came prepared and completely ignored his guide. I started my bidding at just under the guide price, and that is where Renee thought I was going to finish, which is why she was so anxious!

If you don't want to waste time, you need to really research the market, look at the comparables and how much these properties are going for, and work out for yourself how much the property's worth. Inspect as many similar properties in your chosen areas as you can. Go to auctions for similar properties and learn the auction process.

Another reason to get to know a property's true market value before going to auction is that there are many upfront, additional costs when you're seriously preparing to buy at auction (such as obtaining a building report, a strata report and a pest inspection report for the property). That is, unless you are going to a 'friendly auction', where there are no costs attached to those items (more on that in a moment). You don't want to spend extra money up front on a property you've undervalued, and then end up missing out on it at auction.

No COOLING-OFF PERIOD

There are a few scary rules around auction campaigns. Normally, when you buy a property, you either have the finance clause in place or you have a two-, five- or 10-day cooling-off period. The cooling-off period means you can sign the contract and if you get 'cold feet' a few days later, or find issues with the property, you can pull out of the contract, as long as you do so within the designated period.

With an auction campaign, if you're the highest bidder when the hammer falls you *must* take the property, which basically means there's no cooling-off period, and you have to pay your previously negotiated deposit of 5 or 10 per cent of your winning bid on the spot.

This means you need to have your finance in order before the auction date. Check with your mortgage broker or lender the maximum amount you can borrow and have a conditional approval letter from your lender before auction day confirming this. The bank will need to see the signed Contract of Sale, which you will have straight after winning the auction!

This is why, before auction day, you need to organise a professional building inspection and pest inspection and to review any strata reports if the property is in a strata scheme.

Get your solicitor to look at the contract, which will be available to all prospective buyers throughout the marketing campaign. If you want to make changes to the contract, such as paying a 5 per cent deposit instead of the usual 10 per cent, or setting a longer settlement term, these conditions need to be negotiated well before auction day.

What is a 'friendly auction'?

The 'friendly auction' system is a more transparent form of auction designed for the modern marketplace, and is often used for properties that might be purchased by first home buyers.

In the friendly auction system, interested buyers receive price guides. They receive building, pest and strata reports at no charge, along with assistance in finance preparations—though I recommend you always use your own broker, even with a friendly auction.

You also get access to solicitors, and there is usually more flexibility when it comes to deposit and settlement conditions.

This allows potential buyers to prepare and to offer their best price in a transparent and comfortable environment before and during the auction.

HOW MOTIVATED IS THE SELLER?

Another secret to my auction success is to find out as much as I can about the vendor's situation, either by asking the selling agent or through my inspections, as this can affect the urgency of the sale and the vendor's price expectations.

At open houses, I ask why the vendor is selling the property. Maybe they got a job transfer and are moving interstate. If the agent doesn't come out and tell me, or it takes them a while to reach the seller for questions, it might be a clue that the vendor lives interstate or even overseas. Maybe they are getting married or getting divorced. Either scenario could necessitate a sale.

Maybe the house has been fitted with disabled-accessible facilities. This could be a sign that the vendor is on the way to a nursing home. The family may need to sell the house as quickly as possible to enable them to afford the steep cost of such facilities. Or we might learn that the owner has died and the family needs to wrap up a quick sale.

A house that's sitting empty means the owner has already moved and is probably now paying mortgage and utilities on two separate properties. If they have been in this situation for a few months, they may be desperate to sell. And they probably have less of an emotional attachment to their home than a seller who is still living there.

If the vendor or agent admits that the basement floods, or the roof leaks and that they have no intention of fixing it before the sale, they probably don't have cash to put into the house. They don't want to waste time waiting for you to find these things out during an inspection. They might simply want all of this off their hands.

This sort of intelligence can assist you in determining whether the vendor is likely to consider offers prior to auction, and also if they might have set a 'realistic' reserve price.

AUCTION DAY

On the day of the auction, the property will be open for inspection — if the auction is being held at the property. Sometimes auctions are held at an auction house or a local club, as agents might want to run a few auctions on the same night.

Whether the auction is held on the property or at an auction house could affect your bid. You'll potentially be more influenced by emotion if you're at the property itself. So be aware of that, and set your limit *before* the auction.

To participate in an auction, you must first present your ID and register with the vendor's agent. You'll be given a bidder's number and a copy of the auction rules or bidder's guide. It is a legal requirement that the auction rules are on public display at the auction. You can also take another look at the contract at this time.

You won't find out how many bidders there are until the start of the auction, once all bidders are registered. There will also be a number of casual observers. These may be neighbours, or other prospective buyers or sellers doing 'market research', or even just people walking in off the street. So be mentally prepared for a crowd.

The auctioneer oversees the bidding process. He or she takes bids from potential buyers and keeps track of the current bid price.

Auction laws and requirements differ between states and territories, but some laws apply Australia-wide:

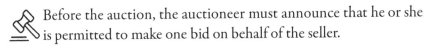 Before the auction, the auctioneer must announce that he or she is permitted to make one bid on behalf of the seller.

The auctioneer must announce immediately before or when making the bid that he/she is making a vendor bid.

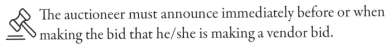 As soon as the bidding level passes the vendor's reserve price, the property is *on the market* and will be sold when the hammer falls.

The highest bidder is the buyer, subject to any reserve price.

If bidding doesn't reach the vendor's reserve price, the highest bidder has the first right to negotiate with the vendor.

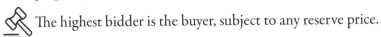 Contracts are signed and a deposit is paid immediately after the auction is completed.

Auction sales are unconditional; in other words, you have no right to make the contract subject to any further conditions once a sale is made.

There is no cooling-off period. This means that if you're the highest bidder when the hammer goes down, you will be required to go through with the purchase.

LOCATION

Bidding at auction is tactical. Location in the context of an auction refers to your physical position, because where you stand during an auction can make or break your bidding strategy. It's all about perception and the impression you create on the day.

I like to be very visible. I don't like to hide at the back as I don't want to risk the auctioneer not seeing my bid. I stand up at the front, near the auctioneer, and look like I mean business. I face the auctioneer, keep calm but also wear my poker face. I don't watch the other bidders; I'm not interested in what they are doing.

CONTROL THE SCENE

One of the biggest mistakes an inexperienced buyer can make is bidding at the wrong time, or at the wrong price increment. There are a few things that I like to do at an auction around timing, bid amounts and exit strategy, to control the scene.

I always like to put in the first bid. Some people like to wait around and see what's happening. I don't. As soon as the auctioneer asks for bids, I put in the opening bid, which is usually quite low. And from there, when someone else puts in a bid, I usually come back with a counterbid straight away — though this may depend on other people's strategies, as sometimes I also like to slow down the bidding process.

I also vary the amount of my bid. The auctioneer tries to set the bidding increments, depending on the price bracket of the property, at $10 000, say. So sometimes I might raise it by $10 000, sometimes by only $5000. Sometimes I might really try to scare the other bidders by upping it by $50 000 in a single increment. But as we go higher in price, the increments usually decrease, and often I find myself upping the bid by just $500, or even $250, or by something random like $380 to really make the auctioneer think as he adds up the bids. More than once, I have caused an auctioneer to get lost using these tactics!

I also like to control the process so the opposition — everyone else trying to buy the property — knows I'm serious about buying and thinks we've got limitless funds. I've even had auctioneers tell the crowd, 'Oh, this guy's got a limit. You just need to find out where it is!'

THE RESERVE PRICE

Before auctioning a property, the seller will nominate a reserve price, which is essentially the minimum price they will accept for the property. If no bidder at that auction meets the reserve, then the property will be *passed in*.

Before the auction only the seller's agent and the seller know the reserve price. You might have an auction price guide of $1 million but a vendor with a reserve of $1.1 million. Once the bidding meets that reserve, the auctioneer will call out, 'The property is now on the market.' That's how you know it's met the reserve, and the property is going to be sold to the highest bidder.

The auctioneer can place a *vendor's bid* on behalf of the seller, often to kick off proceedings if no-one else has bid yet. Or, if things haven't quite met the reserve, the auctioneer can put in a vendor's bid then, which might be at around the reserve price.

WHAT IS A 'DUMMY BID'?

'Dummy bidding' is done by the vendor but is not the same as vendor bidding. By law, vendor bids are announced and made by the auctioneer, and they must not continue once bidding for the property has reached its reserve price. Dummy bidding, on the other hand, occurs when the vendor has someone pretending to be a buyer standing in the crowd at the auction, making fake bids to keep other prospective buyers upping the price even after the reserve price has been reached.

If it's not right, use your rights

If you suspect something illegal happened at an auction, contact your local state or territory's consumer protection agency (sometimes called 'Consumer Affairs') for advice about your rights and options. This body may also be able to help negotiate a resolution between you and the seller.

Australia's consumer affairs and protection agencies include:

 ACT Government — Access Canberra: *accesscanberra.act.gov.au*

 NSW Government — Office of Fair Trading: *fairtrading.nsw.gov.au*

 Northern Territory — Consumer Affairs: *consumeraffairs.nt.gov.au*

 Queensland Government — Office of Fair Trading: *qld.gov.au/law/fair-trading*

 Government of South Australia — Consumer and Business Services (CBS), Attorney-General's Department: *cbs.sa.gov.au*

 Tasmanian Government — Consumer, Building and Occupational Services (CBOS): *cbos.tas.gov.au*

 Victorian Government — Consumer Affairs Victoria (CAV): *consumer.vic.gov.au*

 Government of Western Australia — Consumer Protection — Department of Mines, Industry Regulation and Safety: *commerce.wa.gov.au/consumer-protection*

HOW DO YOU NOT LOSE AT AUCTION?

You won't win them all. You can't avoid losing at auction if someone else has deeper pockets than you and is prepared to pay more for the property.

I once lost an auction for a client in the rising Sydney market, when I was very confident that I understood the true market value of the property.

But most importantly, we'd set a budget for the client and we knew what strategy we would employ. We were simply outbid by someone who was more emotionally attached to the property, had deeper pockets and was also probably suffering from FOMO, fear of missing out, on the day. But that was fine. I will never let my clients pay too much for a property and we will never bid above their agreed maximum. So we shook hands, congratulated the winning bidder and moved on with our search.

However, unless the market's very hot and people with FOMO are jumping in to make all sorts of high offers, it's unusual for properties to sell for a lot more than what they're actually worth.

STICK TO YOUR LIMIT

It's most important that before you go to auction you know exactly what your budget limit is and accept your maximum purchase price as set in stone. This is because it's easy to get carried away in the heat of the moment. The price can escalate and keep getting higher...and higher. You might have an approved budget of, say, $1 million, and in no time the bidding has reached that limit and continued to climb — to $1.1 million. *You need to stop* if you can't afford that, because if you're the highest bidder you will be forking out to buy that property.

If you go over your maximum approved limit and need to borrow more, you may have to pay for lender's mortgage insurance on top, which will blow your budget even further. Or, worse still, you may not get approved at all for that higher amount.

It's not worth the risk.

TAKE THE EMOTION OUT OF IT

To eliminate the risk of a FOMO bid on the day, you must be disciplined, or use someone independent who is *not* emotionally involved to bid for you and who will not exceed the agreed limit.

Clients who use me for auctions are often either uncomfortable speaking out publicly, or are time-poor, or simply recognise they don't have the knowledge or experience to bring to the task. They know I can do a good job because I do it most Saturdays and I know all the tricks of the trade. It's my favourite part of the job.

When I'm the one bidding, there's no emotion there. I've educated my client and we've found a property within budget. I've told them my strategy for the auction. If we get to our limit, I simply seek confirmation from my client: 'This is your maximum purchase price; you can't go any higher, right?' And they need to agree with me that they don't want to go higher.

On one occasion clients got cold feet and decided against bidding to their maximum purchase price. They actually missed out on a property because they panicked about the numbers and stopped me. By doing so they likely did themselves a disservice, because they could have bought the property if they'd bid up to their budget.

GIVING PERMISSION TO PURCHASE

If my clients are not bidding at auction — perhaps they're overseas, or maybe they are attending but have asked me to bid on their behalf — they need to sign an 'authority to bid on behalf of another person', which gives me permission to do the bidding for them. The letter must include their name, address and proof of identity, such as a driver's licence or passport.

I pass this written authority, along with my own ID, to the selling agent before the auction starts. If the purchaser is not going to be at auction, they also need to give permission in writing to the auctioneer for me to sign the Contract of Sale on their behalf. This is usually done via a Power of Attorney.

SUCCESS STORY
An exciting auction day in Eastwood

Let me tell you about one particular auction I remember winning under fierce competition.

My clients, Sam and Mary, had a growing family. They had been renting for a few years and with the oldest of their children about to start high school, they really wanted to settle down in a home of their own.

THE BRIEF

Sam and Mary had been searching for their dream home around the Ryde, Macquarie Park and Eastwood areas of Sydney for almost two years. You might think that having a budget of $1.6 million is a healthy position to be in—and it would be almost anywhere else in Australia—but for my clients their dream home seemed out of reach as they negotiated and attended auctions on homes they liked that continued to sell for prices that were closer to $2 million than to their budgeted limit.

Sam and Mary were referred to me by friends of theirs—people I'd already helped to purchase two investment properties. I told Mary I would be more than happy to help and visited the couple at their rental property. This gave me an understanding of the kind of property they liked to live in, and also gave me the opportunity to get a very detailed brief from them.

THE LOCATION

We discussed suburbs, street appeal and where they were planning to send their kids to high school, as well as school catchment zones for the youngest, who was still in day care. Then there was the number of rooms, whether they wanted an office, the types of appliances they wanted in the kitchen, and so on. And of course, most importantly, their budget maximum of $1.6 million, which for those of you familiar with the Sydney market will know does not get you a lot.

CHALLENGES

Knowing their preferred suburbs well, I could immediately manage my clients' expectations. I let them know that to stay within their budget, we should start looking for good townhouse or duplex properties rather than those larger standalone houses, which were way over their budget. I showed them comparable sales.

At first this seemed a bit of a letdown for them, but they understood the strategy; it's all about education and getting to know the market. Within two weeks I had presented them with three properties that met their revised brief.

I inspected the properties with Mary, Sam and the kids and they chose a fantastic three-bedroom, two-bathroom duplex in Eastwood with a nice backyard for the kids. We inspected it at the start of a four-week auction campaign. Based on comparable sales and where the market was headed, along with a scarcity of such properties, I advised Sam and Mary that the likely sales price would be close to their budget of $1.6 million and told them I believed that other buyers in the market would likely underestimate this price. I said we needed to be prepared to bid to our maximum and give it our best crack.

THE AUCTION

There was a large crowd on auction day. Sam and Mary were spectators but there were also 12 registered bidders. I stood with my clients right up the front so the auctioneer had a good view of me and could see and hear my bids. Once he called for opening bids, I jumped right in with a bid of $990 000, starting low, as I always do. There was quite a bit of action, with other bids coming in at $50 000 increments, then $25 000, then $20 000, and so on. As soon as anyone else put in a bid I came back with a counterbid, as I wanted it to look like we didn't have a limit and could and would outbid anyone.

As the price was starting to edge towards $1.4 million, I decided to take control of the auction and decrease the bid increments, so I put in a $5000 bid, then my next bid raised the price by just $1000. Once we got to around $1.5 million the bidding started to slow down, but there were still two other bidders in the race with us.

(continued)

SUCCESS STORY
An exciting auction day in Eastwood (*cont'd*)

What had started with 12 bidders was now down to just three. I continued to control the process until there was just one other bidder left. The other remaining party put in a bid for $1570000. I upped that by $1000. There was no further bid from our competitor. They had finished and could go no higher.

RESULTS

Finally, the hammer fell. We secured a fantastic duplex for them for $1571000, which was $29000 under their budget, leaving them some money for the kitchen upgrade and painting they wanted to do.

I have kept in touch with Mary and Sam ever since, and they are extremely happy with the purchase and love living in that part of Sydney.

SUCCESS STORY
My first duplex in Armidale

Of all the property strategies I have executed to create instant equity and cashflow and add to my portfolio, I have the most experience with developing duplexes. In the next two chapters I will explain how to develop your own duplex. But before I do, let me tell you about my very first experience and what I learned through the biggest 'aha' moment of my life.

When I did my first subdivision, I was still teaching. I owned five properties but growth was slow, and it seemed to be going nowhere. I knew I didn't want to teach forever, and I wanted to set up my finances better for retirement. I was thinking there must be better ways to invest in property than I was currently using.

What I needed was advice from the right people.

MY INFLUENCERS

I read *Rich Dad Poor Dad* by Robert Kiyosaki and *Think and Grow Rich* by Napoleon Hill. For me, this was all about learning how I could do things better. I was inspired by books on success in business, like *What it Takes* by Mark Burris and *The Accidental Entrepreneur* by Janine Allis. I attended seminars and started speaking to people who were successful in property, as well as reading a lot about how equity can be created.

The idea of subdivision and manufacturing equity came up and I thought, that's more interesting than waiting for growth.

I had enough equity to do my first development, but I didn't want any nasty surprises and I didn't want to invest in something I didn't know anything about ever again. One of my golden rules of investing now was 'only invest in something you understand', so I made sure I understood how this would work.

Like everything I did, I put a lot of research into my first project, but I was also very nervous. There were a lot of unknowns. How could I know what was a good area to build a duplex in? How would I choose a good builder? Where could I get that advice?

THE RIGHT LOCATION

I knew what to look for in a location, both from my previous investing experience and from the wide research I was currently doing and my involvement with other investors, and I'm sharing this knowledge with you throughout this book.

I knew I couldn't afford to buy and develop land in Sydney, so I started to look in established regional centres around New South Wales, like my home town of Orange, and Albury and Armidale. I did a lot of due diligence and a feasibility study and found the vacancy rates on rentals were very low in Armidale, particularly for new properties. While older properties could take a while to rent out, newer properties were in demand, driven by the university.

I thought, there's some money to be made here—maybe $50000 or $60000, but that's better than nothing.

(continued)

SUCCESS STORY
My first duplex in Armidale (*cont'd*)

Armidale location snapshot

 Armidale is an inland city in the Northern Tablelands region of New South Wales, 105 kilometres north-east of Tamworth, Australia's 'country music capital', and 467 kilometres south-west of Brisbane. Armidale is located on the New England Highway, which links Brisbane with Newcastle in NSW then joins the Pacific Highway and Pacific Motorway, which take you through to Sydney.

 Armidale is on the main north–south railway line, served by daily passenger trains to and from Sydney. There are multiple daily flights between Armidale and Sydney.

 Armidale differs from most inland rural centres because the long-established University of New England has transformed it into a small but sophisticated and cosmopolitan city. Through its university, TAFE, and private and public schools, the city has become a significant education hub, creating a wider range of jobs and business opportunities than are usually found in the country. It has a well-educated and diverse population who stimulate change and demand a high standard of living.

 Armidale's best-kept secret is the four national parks, each with extraordinary natural attractions, within an hour's drive of the city centre.

Clearly, Armidale ticked all the boxes of a good growth location, but I was unsure whether it was the right market because at that time, in 2011, nobody was recommending it.

Around then, every man and his dog was telling people they should invest in Gladstone or Toowoomba in Queensland, the number-one 'hot spots' in the country. I could see some potential issues with these areas becoming oversupplied with developments.

I am really glad I decided not to follow the crowd. I have a favourite quote from the world's greatest investor, Warren Buffett, which I've reflected on many times throughout my investing career. Buffett said it is wise 'to be fearful when others are greedy and to be greedy only when others are fearful'.

And he was right.

The Gladstone market collapsed and many investors went bankrupt. The Toowoomba market hasn't done much either, having been saturated with investors until recent years when we have seen some growth there.

Guided by Buffett's wisdom, a feasibility study and my own gut feeling, I decided to take the gamble and go with Armidale.

BUYING THE BLOCK

Buying my first block of land in Armidale was an interesting process.

After a bit of searching I saw a corner block listed for sale on realestate.com.au for $185 000. It was in Grandview Crescent, in a nice family-oriented estate (and in my opinion, the best subdivision in Armidale), in which most of the blocks had owner-occupied properties with lovely views of the town and the surrounding mountains and countryside.

My research showed that similar blocks of land in Grandview Crescent had been selling for between $180 000 and $200 000.

Nevertheless, this block had been sitting on the market for a while, because it had in fact sold but had then come back onto the market after the previous sale had fallen through.

I learned through the selling agent that the vendor wanted to sell urgently and, while the previous contract had come in at close to the asking price, I now had the chance to put in quite a low offer of around $150 000. It was all about the numbers for me and how

(*continued*)

SUCCESS STORY
My first duplex in Armidale (*cont'd*)

much I could make—I needed to make sure I didn't pay too much for the property.

So we went backward and forward a few times and I finally got that block for $159 000. This was significantly under the asking price, and under true market value. I was thrilled because it meant I had already made a profit there.

MY FIRST CONSTRUCTION CONTRACT

Buying the land was only half the deal. The other half was getting a builder and the build price right so I was building for less than I could sell the completed property for.

I'd heard a lot of 'construction disaster' stories, so I researched possible reasons why people developing properties were having such disastrous results. And I thought, but they're not protected in their build contracts, which were all about protecting the builder. I wanted to make sure I too was protected in the contract. I put together a build contract that included clauses around fixed price, fixed time frame and liquidated damages.

For that first project I had to negotiate with two or three builders and try to convince them to take on my job under my terms before I found the right one. I ended up using that builder on future developments and, later, recommended them for clients of mine as well.

Because I sought out good advice from the start, that first build went quite smoothly.

It can be a little bit scary at first when you try to talk to people about stuff you don't know much about. But the builders knew I was a novice investor and they shared the information I needed fairly openly, so it wasn't as intimidating as it could have been because, again, I surrounded myself with experienced people and mentors with different areas of expertise who could assist and provide advice.

At the end of the day, when you're employing a builder, you don't have to deal with every individual tradie. If you have it set up the right way, the builder employs and deals with the tradies and you only deal with the actual building company and the site supervisor.

When you have a lot going on with your developments or your property portfolio, you don't have time to micro-manage people. That's why it's so valuable to build a team you can trust.

Having a watertight contract was something I insisted on from my very first project, and each project I have added to my portfolio has got better and easier to manage. My clients also benefit from my ability to negotiate watertight construction contracts with the best builders and in that way mitigate the risks.

Of course, on my first development I also had a lot to learn about the council development application (DA) process.

The frustrating thing was that the council didn't submit all their requests for amendments in one go, which is not unusual. They would, for example, give a determination and say that the builder had to change the way the lounge room was facing because they wanted the sun to come in from the north instead of the south. After we'd satisfied them with that particular amendment, they'd come back and say, 'We're not happy with the landscaping plan and we want some extra trees planted in the front yards for street appeal'. They even specified the type of tree that we needed to use because council were trying to make it aesthetically pleasing to align with the rest of the owner-occupied properties in Grandview Crescent. And there was something about the fence, or there was something about the garage...and so on and so on, until my DA was finally approved.

It was a steep learning curve, but I loved it.

I put a duplex on the land, with entrances from two different streets so it looks like a house on one street and a house on the other street, adding more value than I'd have got from building a regular, side-by-side duplex.

(continued)

SUCCESS STORY
My first duplex in Armidale (*cont'd*)

MY FIRST DUPLEX REMAINS POSITIVELY GEARED

When I went out to Armidale and saw the completed project, I was very relieved and satisfied. For me it had been all about the numbers—until I walked in and saw the new paintwork, the nice stone benchtops and the lovely landscaping that council had insisted on. And I realised, oh, this is a nice property, and people are actually living in it and paying me lots of rent!

It was exciting. I had bought quite a few properties previously but this was the first time I had facilitated and overseen the build from the ground up. I wasn't sure how it would turn out, being my first development, but I've still got that property and both units have been rented every single day since.

From day one, those duplex units were renting for $410 a week each, so I was getting $820 a week in rent, which equates to a 6.7 per cent gross yield on the initial project cost. Not bad for my first duplex!

They were cashflow-positive, because the income more than covered what I was paying to keep the property. So this property wasn't costing me anything to hold, and I had enough money left over after paying the mortgage to buy a whole McDonald's Happy Meal® plus a Soft Serve Cone® every night if I wanted to!

Not only was I getting this great cashflow but, to my surprise, I also made $141 000 in virtually instant equity—more than twice what I expected, and twice what I was earning in a whole year as a teacher. This was the real kicker for me.

I paid $159 000 for the land and $440 000 to build the property, which included council and subdivision costs, then an additional $30 000 or so in legals, stamp duty and holding costs, which are things like bank interest and council land rates. So we're looking at $629 000 for the whole project.

My first valuation on that duplex development came back at only about $80 000 higher than what I paid for it, so I thought, let's go for another one...and then another one. The best of the valuations was the third, which came back at $380 000 for one unit and $390 000 for the other, for a total of $770 000, and when I deducted the combined project costs and holding costs of $629 000 I was left with a neat $141 000 in additional equity.

When I got that higher number, I was very excited. A light bulb went off in my head and I thought, I need to try to repeat this process. Now, when I need another 10 per cent deposit for another property, I can take it out of the property I've built. I don't need to try to find $60 000 from somewhere else; it's equity in the property! That is exactly what I did to start building my portfolio faster. And the rest is history, as they say.

I ended up buying a further five properties in 2013 alone, including doing another duplex development, using the equity I'd created in Armidale along with equity I had created in other properties, without the need to use any of my own money. This is also called using OPM — other people's money. Money that the bank can lend you, based on your successful properties.

The Armidale duplex turned out to be a great investment and, thanks to that project, my portfolio was really starting to go places. It wasn't only about Armidale, as there are many other great markets to invest in, as I have pointed out, where the same strategy can work. It's about duplex projects and how they can really help you achieve your goals. As you've seen through our success stories, and as I hope the next two chapters will show even more clearly, there's no reason why the same thing can't happen for you.

Chapter 8

Duplex Developer — Pre-Build Plan

Get the land, the loan and the plans, and get the DA approved.

 Do you want to build a duplex, and potentially make hundreds of thousands of dollars for your efforts? This chapter will educate you on the elements of building a duplex and provide useful information and tips — from how to source a suitable block to how to secure finance for the build and get your development application (DA) through council — so you know how to go about it *before* you start your project.

There are many elements to building a duplex and, as you'd expect, the process is quite complex. Stick with this strategy, though, and you will certainly make serious returns for your money.

Remember, this is how I created enough equity to leave my full-time teaching job. A client of mine recently made over $800 000 in instant equity in under 12 months (I'll present that inspiring success story at the end of the chapter). This was just one of many great results I and my clients have enjoyed using the duplex strategy.

If you follow the process I'm going to outline for you, you can build a duplex in 15 to 18 months. If you make $250 000 or even $200 000 on your duplex, that's two to three times the average Australian's annual income. By building a duplex, you can make that type of equity straight away — and that's when you're doing the development on the side while holding down your day job.

A profit of that size can help you to buy another property almost immediately, accelerating the growth of your portfolio. Then of course there's the positive cashflow from your two rents, which the banks will love when they're assessing you for your next loan. Plus, the dual incomes from renting a duplex can bring the next item on your wish list that much closer! That could be paying for your kids' education, paying down your home mortgage or even buying a boat.

WHAT IS A DUPLEX?

A duplex is two separate homes built on the same block of land (that is, on a single title) that can be subdivided into two separate titles after construction.

Typically, the duplex is a single building with the two homes separated by a party wall — which isn't as much fun as it sounds. A party wall must have a 60-60-60 fire rating, which means that if one unit is on fire, that fire can't spread to the next unit. This requires a very strong brick wall with extra cladding. With that wall, and with each unit having separate amenities, such as water meters and electricity meters, they can be subdivided into two separate properties. Essentially it's a big house on the outside with two units on the inside.

But duplexes don't have to be joined. You can build two separate units on one block if the council allows it. This is known as a 'detached duplex' and is more expensive to build because of the extra brickwork. In some cases, however, a detached duplex can be worth more in the long run.

THE NEW 'GREAT AUSTRALIAN DREAM'

I've talked about apartment oversupply in Melbourne and Brisbane, but that doesn't mean there isn't a burgeoning market for duplexes and triplexes, from which you can even graduate to quadplexes and small townhouse developments for some serious profits!

There is definitely a market for smaller housing. The 'great Australian dream' of owning the quarter-acre block and the big home has started to change in recent years, mostly because it has become so expensive that for most of us this lifestyle is way out of reach.

When you're creating these smaller units on smaller blocks, you're selling them to people who can afford to buy something smaller but can't afford the traditional big dream home — at least not in their chosen location. Often they are young professional couples or young families who are time-poor and don't want a high-maintenance property. Duplexes are perfect for that.

The best news is that there's a high demand for duplex properties, not just from buyers but from tenants. Tenants also want low-maintenance homes. They don't necessarily want to rent a big house if they can rent a duplex unit. A three-bedroom duplex means less rent and lower maintenance than a four- or five-bedroom house. But as the owner and landlord of a six-bedroom duplex that's subdivided into two units, you get two lots of rent, so the lower rents don't affect you.

Then you've got downsizers, often people who are retiring for lifestyle benefits. Maybe they are empty-nesters whose kids have left home, or they are moving away from the city for a clean break. We build popular properties for downsizers near the water — say, on the NSW South Coast or up on the NSW Central Coast or the Sunshine Coast in Queensland. Typically, these rent out even before they are finished.

There are all sorts of reasons that Australians are moving into these types of properties. When you choose a high-growth location, building duplexes near universities, hospitals and schools and lots of amenities, you'll find that there's always a demographic that wants to live in this sort of housing, and an opportunity to provide it.

Not surprisingly, building a duplex is an attractive option for many property investors because of this high demand.

A duplex development also maximises the potential of the land and usually doesn't require land subdivision before having the two properties built. This means you can also build a duplex, keep it on one title (without subdividing) and still rent it out as two properties. For cashflow, this is great, and you may even save a bit on council rates. But if your strategy is equity gain, I always recommend you build in a high-demand area and subdivide on completion.

The instant equity will come from the properties having their own valuations as two separate properties.

Here are some advantages of building a duplex:

 It's a high-growth, high-yield investment.

 It's positively geared.

 It reduces your build costs: a duplex is much more cost-effective to build than a single dwelling, and you get double of everything.

 You have the flexibility to rent or sell at the end of the project — you can rent out both, sell one and keep one, or sell both.

But the greatest advantage of a duplex is that it gives you the chance to create equity quickly with a high rate of return on your investment. Manufacturing this instant equity means you don't have to wait for organic capital growth in the market.

You'll also have enough equity that you won't need to save for your next deposit.

THE FEASIBILITY STUDY

It's vital to do a feasibility study before you get started so you know your budget for your block and your build, as well as the expected outcomes.

When you build a duplex, the idea is to be able to build it for less than you can sell it for. Using some round numbers, let's say it's going to cost you $400000 for the land and $900,000 in construction and council costs; that gives you $1.3 million for duplex project costs.

When you build a duplex consisting of two three-bedroom units, for example, you're building it as one six-bedroom property, so costs are aligned with those of constructing one property. The kicker here is that you're building something for which you'll manufacture equity through subdivision on completion. Then you'll have two properties, each of which has its own identity, title and valuation.

This is where doing a feasibility study is so important, as you need to look at comparable sales in the area *before* you decide to take on any project. For example, if you're planning on building two three-bedroom units, you need to look at what three-bedroom units are selling for in your chosen location in the current market.

If we determine that you can sell a three-bedroom unit for $900000 and you're building two of them, this means that on completion, the duplex you've paid only $1.3 million for is going to be worth $1.8 million.

Now, if you do everything the right way, you'll make $500000 profit on your duplex, and that gets you off to a good start with your long-term strategy.

As I've mentioned, you will need to consider *holding costs* — your bank loan while the property is being constructed — and *stamp duty* in your total costs. The great news is that when you build a new dwelling on vacant land, you're paying stamp duty only on the land, not on the dwelling. This is a considerable saving and will help your bottom-line profit.

For example, when I built my Armidale duplex, stamp duty was a small cost — around $4500 — as I only had to pay it on the land. Had I purchased a block with a house on it, or a completed duplex that someone else had built for $600 000, stamp duty would have been in excess of $22 000. So you can see the savings benefits of buying vacant land and building yourself.

With that $500 000 or so gain in equity, you can refinance up to 90 per cent of that increased equity, if your lender agrees you have the financial capacity to do so. The other option is to keep one unit and sell the other to pay off some debt in order to move forward if you have to.

I have a large portfolio, but I have sold some properties from time to time, simply because I needed to free up some borrowing power to be able to take the next step or pay down mortgages on other properties. A good broker is worth their weight in gold when it comes to financial strategy.

Either way, you've got that profit there.

And you can take that profit and reinvest it in another property. The next one may not necessarily be a duplex; it could be a cheaper property. We might go to an area where we can get a nice $500 000 house that just needs a little bit of TLC. Then we'd organise some contractors to go in there, do some painting, replace the old carpets with some floating floorboards or hardwood floors, update the kitchen and the bathroom, and actually create equity on that property.

You'll be able to use that equity to buy another property — maybe another duplex. And we'll revisit your longer-term strategy as we go, checking on your borrowing capacity and what the various property markets are doing.

BASIC UPDATES

We've touched on renovation as a strategy. Let's talk some more about that here. I'm about micro- to mid-sized developments and holding property, not flipping houses. So when I suggest a renovation, we need to ensure you don't overcapitalise.

We aim to increase your property's value by up to three dollars for every dollar spent, so it is important to know what work will get you the best results. In some cases, doing basic cosmetic work such as a fresh coat of paint and updating floor coverings and window furnishings can provide you with a better return on your investment than putting in a new kitchen or bathroom would. So it's important to understand what upgrades your property will benefit from most.

It is commonly said that the kitchen and bathroom add the most value to a property; they are also usually the most expensive areas to replace, however. You might find yourself overcapitalising simply by putting in a new kitchen or bathroom. Try to upgrade them instead. Be sure to develop a clear picture of your budget and expected returns, and the demographic in the area you are looking to serve.

For renos, we start with a feasibility study. We look carefully at comparable properties in the area that have sold recently. If similar properties that have been renovated are selling for around what your property is already worth, we won't bother updating your property or pursuing a renovation strategy, as doing so won't add value. Instead, we need to look for areas where there is a considerable difference in value between renovated and unrenovated properties.

We also consider the demographics of the area, making sure that any changes are likely to suit the people living there and their lifestyles. There's no point adding a second bathroom to your property when most people who live in the area are either singles or couples with no children. You can better utilise these funds on upgrades that will appeal to the demographic, such as new floorboards, painting and window coverings, resulting in an increase in the value of your property and a higher rental return, which will increase your cashflow.

SOURCING DUPLEX LOCATIONS

The thing about building duplex properties is that we're looking for *the trifecta*, which you'll remember is *instant equity*, *good cashflow* and *capital growth*. So even though you're getting that instant equity, if you're going to be keeping the property long-term you want to make sure you're getting that capital growth as well as great rental returns for cashflow.

THE PROPERTY TRIFECTA

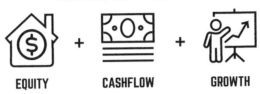

EQUITY   CASHFLOW   GROWTH

By now you know all about how to find a good location with everything required for capital growth. I always maintain it's important to get into an area before everyone else follows, as this will allow you to maximise on the area's growth very early on, and this has proven to be a successful strategy for my clients time and time again.

It's good to get in early — but not too early. This goes for any type of property but obviously if you're looking to do a duplex development, you want to buy land where there's some scarcity. You don't want to buy where heaps of new land is being released, because if there's heaps of vacant land around for sale, then there's no pressure to get a piece of it, and pressure is what causes prices to increase in an area.

If there's too much available land, you're buying property that may sell at the same price or may even go down in value, which means the land prices in that area are likely to stay low and that property won't sell very well.

My advice is to *check for suitable vacant blocks in established areas.* We're always trying to build among owner-occupied properties, because most homeowners are house-proud and look after their properties, and that's what drives the market value up. If you build in those kinds of areas, this can really drive the growth of your property.

Remember, you'll want to sell in the future to an owner-occupier who will pay more for your property because they are emotional. Investors will always try to pay less, so it pays to get into the right area in the first place.

Most of the land I find is off-market. Often the developer is actually keeping it off-market and selling it without even advertising. That's one of the tricks of the trade when it comes to getting your hands on a good piece of land.

In established areas with low supply, such as areas near the water, I can often find blocks for clients where there is literally nothing publicly available. For example, when a block comes back on the market because someone else's finance fell through, we are often the first to hear of it through local developers and real estate agents, and we'll snap it up straight away.

DUPLEX BLOCKS

Once you know your finance, budget and location, you can start looking at the blocks available.

Duplex blocks can be quite difficult to find, because a lot of blocks out there are not big enough or are not approved for duplex development. There are a few specific things that are important when it comes to finding a development block.

Each local council will specify a minimum block size for this kind of build but, essentially, the bigger the better when it comes to a good block.

Most of the time we *try to build on a vacant block*. Sometimes we find a block in a good area but it has a house on it, so we'd need to knock the house down to build the duplex. You should do that only if the numbers stack up, because you're probably adding at least $20 000 in demolition and removal costs before you can build. And don't forget the stamp-duty factor. Finding a vacant block with nothing on it to remove is going to be cheaper.

The other option is to find a large block of land with a house on it that you want to keep. In this case I have a three-pronged strategy: renovate the house and rent it out, subdivide the block through a Torrens title subdivision, and build a duplex at the back.

The problem is the duplex is likely to be what's called a 'battle-axe' property, which means it sits behind the house, so it may not be worth quite as much as properties with street frontage. And it does cost a bit more to build because you've got to pay for service connections and a long access driveway.

Nonetheless, with that strategy you've turned one property into three — a house and two duplex units — and you've got options, such as keeping and renting the house then selling the duplex. We occasionally do that for clients with a slightly bigger budget.

These triple-residence properties don't always have to involve battle-axes; it depends on the shape and size of the block. For example, you can build a duplex next to a house on a corner block so when you subdivide the block next to the house has street frontage as well — in which case, the build could actually increase the property value further.

Corner blocks are hard to come by so they're often more expensive, but they're very good for duplexes because they allow you to have entrances from two different streets. In this way your duplex is more like two houses than one duplex, which adds value and appeal.

LOCAL COUNCIL REQUIREMENTS — ZONING AND MINIMUM SIZE

A lot of people make the mistake of buying a block first and finding out later whether the land's going to be approved for a duplex. Once you've shortlisted a suitable site, *check that council zoning allows duplex development* on the land being considered before you put in your offer.

The two sets of building guidelines local councils have in place are the Development Control Plan (DCP) and the Local Environmental Plan (LEP). Your duplex development must meet all the requirements set out in these plans.

Your property must be in the right zoning for a duplex. For example, council will allow dual-occupancy properties to be built in areas of NSW with R3 zoning. It can be frustrating to find a fantastic block of land then find out that the local council will allow only single-dwelling houses on it.

When Renee and I were living in our inner-west house in Lewisham, we had a block of land next to us and we enjoyed it being vacant. It sold to a guy who tried to get DA approval to build a duplex. He fought for about four years and still couldn't get approval.

Next he tried to get it approved for a childcare centre, then for a house. He couldn't get it approved for anything. Now he's stuck with a block of land he paid half a million dollars for, and while the land is going up in value he's probably got a mortgage on it and he still can't do anything with it. It's no good to sell either, because most people do their own research and they'll see that he bought it a long while back and hasn't been able to build on it.

Meanwhile, Renee and I still enjoyed the open space. Nothing was built there while we were living next door, and as far as we know it's still vacant.

It's also very important to *find a block of land that fits into the DCP's minimum size*. This will vary according to the council area it's in. Some require you to have at least a 600m² block before they'll let you build a duplex on it; others require at least 700m². In some suburbs they'll allow a double-storey duplex to be built on only 500m² — we've done that on occasion.

In one instance I had difficulty with Lake Macquarie City Council in the Greater Newcastle area. The DCP said you could build a duplex on anything over 600m², so I bought a block of land that was 660m².

Then, while my development application (DA) was with council, it changed its DCP requirement to 700m². They said they weren't going to approve my DA, and I ended getting into a massive argument with council because the town planner had already told us it would be approved.

In the end, we did get approval, but since then no-one has been allowed to build a duplex on a block of under 700m² in that council area. These days you can only build a house on a block of that size, which makes mine an extremely valuable duplex block.

If you're buying from a developer, you also need to *check for covenants*. Your block might be in the right zoning with council, and be the right size to build a duplex on, but then the developer says, 'We're not allowing any duplexes in this estate.' So you need to ask the developer up front, 'Are you happy to have a duplex on this block?' And if they say no, then you either don't buy the block or you convince them to change their mind (they need to give you that approval in writing). I've done that a few times too.

It's all about knowing the DCP and talking to the authorities up front. Having conversations with the town planner and with council, then also speaking with architects and builders, is vital. You crosscheck everything to make sure that you won't have any problem constructing a duplex on this block of land.

It's all part of your due diligence.

MORE DUE DILIGENCE

Once you have made certain that you'll get approval for a development, you need to do further due diligence on the land, inspecting the terrain and surroundings to ensure there are no costly obstacles to your development plans. As I always say, it's about the numbers: if you spend too much, you're not going to make the profit you hope for.

Firstly, you don't want trees on the spot where you're going to build because it will cost money to remove them. Secondly, you want a flat block. Sloping blocks cost more money to build on and you end up having a sloped backyard.

If your block does slope, it needs to slope towards the road so stormwater can run off. If it slopes to the back or to the side, you may find you need to create an easement to drain that stormwater. And that drainage easement will need to be on the neighbour's property, which means you'll need to get approval from the neighbour, who'll usually come back with a big fat no. Even if they agree to it, you could end up having to pay them compensation for building a stormwater drainage easement on their land. This could add $15 000 or more to your costs.

Easements allow a right of way across a piece of someone else's land, commonly used either for drainage or underground electrical cables so electricians can enter the property without trespassing, for example. In most circumstances you can't build over an easement, so the easement must not affect the 'building envelope'.

An easement across the middle of a block is no good to you. You can (potentially) still get approval from council subject to the easement, but we try to avoid that so we don't strike any roadblocks with council.

We had an issue with one particular, notoriously difficult council (which will remain nameless). One block of land had a very gentle slope to the back. The council in question approved the DA on the condition that we create a stormwater easement. Fortunately, one of those neighbouring blocks at the back was council land, so we managed to convince council to approve the easement on their land and approve the DA as well.

This was a lesson learned. The point is, I got all this checked out up front by a town planner, and he assured us there would be no need for a stormwater easement and no issues getting the DA approved. It demonstrated that speaking with town planners is just one part of the due diligence you need to do on any property you're planning to purchase, particularly for a duplex development. This particular council balked at the slightest slope, which another council might well have allowed.

Before you buy land to build a duplex on, you also need to *test the soil* to make sure there are no issues, such as radioactive or other poisonous residues, that might affect your property later on. At this stage of due diligence, you'll also be talking with a builder, and soil tests can be arranged through the builder.

FINANCING, OFFERS AND NEGOTIATIONS

Once you have a shortlist of suitable blocks, have chosen a block and have settled on a builder (along with the construction costs and inclusions), you can look at negotiating the lowest possible purchase price on the land.

Whether there's wriggle room on the price will depend on how popular the area is and how many interested parties there are. But it's not uncommon for me to negotiate $40 000 or $50 000 off the price of the land, with terms that suit my client.

Then a conveyancer or property solicitor comes in and does the checks on the land. Once we are satisfied, we can sign the land contract and exchange contracts. This process varies in different states; in Queensland, for example, both purchaser and seller sign the same contract, which is called 'execution'.

So you exchange or execute on the land, and meanwhile you're also working on your finance with your broker. Then you lodge both the land contract and the construction contract with your lender, and apply for a construction loan.

Here's a tricky one for you: you need to prove you've got finance to get a builder on board, but you need the builder's signed construction contract to get your finance. Yes, this is complicated, and that's why it's vital to get the help of a good mortgage broker.

Some brokers do things the wrong way and try to get a land loan first and then a construction loan, but I prefer to get financing for the land and the build at the same time, and put them both through as one loan.

It's all about timing, so having your broker arrange pre-approval of your finance is key. This is also important so you know the maximum you can spend on a project before you begin the search.

Then, after the exchange of land contracts you have a brief time in which you must gather everything you need for the final approval of your construction loan. Some states have mandatory finance clauses, which may allow up to 21 days to get your finance approved, while other states may allow only a five-day cooling-off period or none at all, depending on how popular the land is, the vendor's intentions and also whether it has been bought at auction, in which case different rules apply, as I outlined in chapter 7.

Your construction loan application will need to include the plans and elevations for the block of land you've got the contract on, and your construction contract, including the builder specifications and inclusions. As we've touched on, all construction contracts are subject to finance. That means the builder needs to see a letter from the bank saying you've got unconditional financing, before they start work.

As banks never lend you 100 per cent of the costs, the builder usually requires proof, via a bank statement, that you have sufficient funds to make up the shortfall, which is the difference between what the bank is lending you and the total project costs. These usually equate to the deposits required for both land and build.

In other words, if you have a project that is costing a total of $1 million and the bank is lending you $800 000, the builder will want to see that you have the $200 000 in your bank. The bank will also want to see that same bank statement as part of their approvals process.

If you are financing the construction entirely with your own cash, then you will need to produce a bank statement for the builder showing that you have sufficient funds available to pay for the entire build.

A construction loan is unique in that you finance the loan in stages as the builder builds, but it also requires several points of negotiation, which I'll cover in more detail in the next chapter.

Once you have all of this documentation, your broker will be able to finalise your loan with the bank, and you can close on your block of land.

PREPARING YOUR DEVELOPMENT APPLICATION (DA)

We always have our DAs approved — even the tricky ones — because we've always done our research up front, before we buy the land.

You need to lodge your application with the full set of *architectural plans*, so the council assessment officer can see what's being built on the property. They also need to see what the inclusions are, so if you're going to have ducted air-con or a solar heating unit on your roof, they need to see all of that in the plans.

This means you need to liaise with the architect or draftsperson to produce working drawings of the proposed duplex. The architect typically takes seven to 10 days to complete the plans. Once they're finalised, we submit them to council along with the DA.

The DA goes through six different stages in council.

1. Pre-lodgement

The pre-lodgement stage is the front end of the development assessment process. Giving council an assessment-ready application, with all required information, will not 'guarantee' approval. However, if you get this right, you are likely to have a simpler DA process, saving time and money for all involved.

Planning controls

There are a couple of ways you can determine the controls that apply to your site:

a. A planning certificate lists the planning instruments that apply to your land. They usually form part of the Contract of Sale, or you can purchase one from council.

b. Council's website is a great source of planning information and deals specifically with the controls that apply to your local area.

Site analysis

When you are planning and designing your development project, you should analyse how your site fits into the neighbourhood, and how your development will relate to neighbouring developments and to the streetscape. This will help you understand its development capacity.

Your street will have its own character, which is created by the sizes and shapes of lots along that street, the form of buildings (such as setbacks, heights) and the nature of the landscape. There may also be heritage overlays, depending on the age and style of the buildings in the street. A site analysis will help ensure that any development you undertake fits in with the character of the street.

A site analysis can be carried out by an architect, draftsperson or designer, and shows the key characteristics of your site and its relationship to adjoining land, such as the path of the sun and the location of buildings, trees and other key features on your site and on adjoining sites in your street. The plan considers how your proposed development will affect your neighbours, such as its impacts on their privacy, and overshadowing. The slope of your land, creeks and drainage are also key issues that can impact how and where you can build on your land.

2. LODGING YOUR DA WITH COUNCIL

When you have filled out all the required forms, you can lodge your DA with council. It is your responsibility to provide all the required information, and to make sure your DA provides enough detail to enable council to make a decision. If not, you'll receive a request from council for further information.

An assessment-ready DA will generally include:

a.   any necessary specialist reports

b.   council's DA form and checklist

c.   all matters required for a DA as listed in the Environmental Planning and Assessment (EP&A) Regulation (Schedule 1, Part 1)

d.   the required DA fee.

Lodgement is the formal start of the DA process. Council will check that all the information has been provided. If the information you provide is adequate, the 'clock' that measures the time council has to assess your application will start. If the information is inadequate, the clock stops until the required information is provided.

The amount of time council takes to issue approvals varies between states and also depends on the type of development you are proposing.

WHO MAKES THE DECISION ON YOUR DA?

For small housing developments such as duplexes, most decisions will be made by your assessment officer or the council's general manager. The assessment officer prepares a report and a recommendation on the DA, then submits his or her report to the council's delegates for determination.

NEIGHBOUR NOTIFICATION

Once your DA has been lodged and checked, the council may engage in formal neighbour notification and advertising. Neighbour notification is a key element in the process.

It may sound like you're opening your development up to being shut down, but raising issues can be a positive, value-adding exercise, as all stakeholders work together for a mutually beneficial outcome.

Public notification can take a number of forms, such as:

a. individual letters to local residents

b. an onsite notice

c. an ad in the local newspaper.

The onsite notice and newspaper ad mean your DA is on public exhibition, and any person can make a submission with regard to it.

Your development plans and application are also made available at the local council offices, and sometimes at other locations (such as the local library) for public inspection. They're usually listed on council's website as well.

The public notification is usually out there for about a month, giving people time to lodge any objections. This very rarely happens if it's a house or duplex, unless your proposed development is some kind of monstrosity. People usually object formally only to large developments.

REFERRALS (INTERNAL AND EXTERNAL)

Council has internal experts who will comment on different environmental issues. Many councils have a meeting of experts to check DAs after they are lodged to ensure the information provided is adequate to enable them to make a decision.

Some government agencies have special roles to provide comment or agreement/approval within their areas of expertise by way of a consultation or 'concurrence'. Examples in NSW might include a consultation with the NSW Rural Fire Service if your property adjoins bushfire-prone land; or with the Department of Planning, Industry and Environment (DPIE) if your proposal is near a state heritage site.

ALLOCATION TO YOUR ASSESSMENT OFFICER

When your DA is considered ready for assessment, an officer will be allocated to you. That person will be your key point of contact during the process. It is good practice for council to set a future 'call-back' date when the assessment officer will ring you to introduce themselves, discuss progress and address any issues, if necessary.

Key points of contact will be:

a. the initial setting of a future call-back date

b. the site inspection

c. the call-back date

d. council seeking additional information

e. council advising you of its decision regarding your DA.

In some instances, council may request to speak to a member of your specialist team, such as your engineer.

Remember, if you have engaged someone else to be the applicant on your behalf, such as a buyer's agent, project manager or builder, then council will contact them, not you.

3. ASSESSMENT

All DAs must be formally assessed by the local council. This means the site must be inspected, applicants and neighbours engaged, reports drafted and recommendations made.

The matters that council must consider are:

a. all plans and policies that apply, such as LEPs and DCPs

b. impacts of your proposed development on the environment as well as economic impacts in the area

c. the suitability of your site for the proposed development (such as physical characteristics, access and services)

d. any submissions or objections (such as from neighbours)

e. the broader public interest.

COUNCIL'S DA TRACKING SYSTEM

You can consult your council's online DA tracking system, if available in your area, to monitor the progress of your DA. The system may give you access to the assessment officer's report and recommendation.

LIAISON WITH COUNCIL – ADDITIONAL INFORMATION REQUESTS

If you get the 'front end' right, then the assessment officer will most likely have all the information required to make a decision. However, it may be necessary for the assessment officer to contact you or your representative and request clarification and additional information if you haven't provided something, or maybe they want something more.

Recently we did a project down at Sussex Inlet on the NSW South Coast, where we submitted everything we normally do in that area. A couple of months later the council came back and said they wanted a bushfire report on the property. They'd never asked for that with other developments we had done in that same council municipality. It delayed council approval for another couple of months, which was a little frustrating, but we got there in the end, with our DA approved.

It's helpful if you can respond quickly to any additional council requests, and it's best to get your experts to talk directly with council if further clarification is needed.

COMPLYING DEVELOPMENT CERTIFICATE (CDC)

Instead of a DA, you can also do a CDC, which is where your application doesn't have to go to council, it can be ticked off by a certifier. A CDC is a combined planning and construction approval for straightforward developments. A CDC can be approved when a proposed development complies with predetermined development standards set under State Environmental Planning Policies (SEPP).

This process allows a fast-track assessment by a certifying authority, which may be either Council or an Accredited Certifier. The purpose of this certificate is to receive assurance that the building works will comply with all relevant legislation and building standards. A CDC can often take less than three months. A DA process can certainly take longer to get through the approval stream.

Not every council jurisdiction allows it. If you're doing a more complicated or difficult design, like a unique custom duplex, it has to go through a DA. But for a straightforward design, a CDC will work.

4. THE CONDITIONS OF YOUR CONSENT

When council does come back with its decision on a DA, there are usually conditions attached to the approval by the Local Environmental Planning authority that are designed to reduce the impacts of the development on the environment. Some conditions relate to the provision of infrastructure to adequately service the property and protect the environment post-development. And there's usually a time frame for each condition to be met — for example, within 24 months.

The DA consent lasts for five years unless another period is specified by council or construction has occurred, in which case it does not lapse. This means that you need to commence your build within five years of getting your approvals, or they will lapse, and you will need to start all over again.

Conditions of consent (such as requirements that you reduce height, delete elements, add a privacy screen, build a retaining wall, or create an easement) can require you to modify your plans. These changes may increase the cost of your construction. Getting it right at the start of the application process will help minimise unexpected and unplanned costs as a consequence of having conditions imposed. That's why enlisting the help of a buyer's agent who is very experienced in this field will really help you, and can safeguard you against some of the costly issues that could arise.

Conditions also require you and your team to take steps prior to or at key stages of the development — before the issue of a Construction Certificate, before or during construction, and before the issue of an Occupation Certificate.

These conditions include:

a. the erection of signs onsite with details about your Principal Certifying Authority (PCA) and principal contractor

b. ensuring that operations on the site (such as hours of work, waste management, and controlling water run-off and erosion) do not adversely affect the neighbourhood

c. organising any bonds to be paid (such as to protect the footpath)

d. payment of development contributions, which go towards local infrastructure; otherwise known as section 94 contributions, these are required conditions in most cases (I always have them included as part of the build contract so the builder will forward the funds to council on your behalf).

WHY CONDITIONS ARE IMPORTANT

Your development consent is a legal document and is extremely important. You must build according to the conditions specified to avoid possible penalties or the need for costly rectification measures. As the owner, you should read carefully and discuss these conditions with your builder or representative (such as your buyer's agent).

Some conditions are mandatory and must be applied on all development consents. For example, your development must meet the Building Code of Australia (BCA).

DA REFUSAL

If your DA is refused, or granted but with unacceptable conditions, you have three options, all of which will require some time and cost:

- **Option 1:** Request a Review of Determination by your council (with amended plans, if you wish). A fee applies and you have six months from the date of the decision for this request to be lodged and determined. You need to allow sufficient time for this.

- **Option 2:** Lodge an appeal to the Land and Environment Court (in NSW) or its equivalent in other states or territories. In NSW, you have six months to lodge an appeal. The court hears from you or your representative, council, relevant experts and (potentially) the community, and determines whether the DA should be approved and what conditions should apply to it. The appeal process can be time-consuming and costly, particularly if a matter is not resolved through mediation before going to a hearing.

- **Option 3:** Modify and relodge your DA.

DA MODIFICATIONS AND REVIEWS

If you change your mind and wish to make changes to your approved plans (or the conditions), you can submit an application for a modification of your development consent. Again, this is called different things in different states and territories.

The development you seek to modify must remain substantially the same as the development the original consent was granted for. If the application varies too much from the original consent, a new DA must be lodged. For example, adding ducted air-con instead of a split system is fine, but you can't change the number of bedrooms or the total footprint of your development without lodging a new DA.

5. CONSTRUCTION CERTIFICATE OR BUILDING CERTIFICATE

After the DA comes through, the builder can start — but first they will need either a Building Certificate or Construction Certificate (depending on the state or territory in which you're building).

There are three steps to finalising the Building or Construction Certificate:

a. Get a Construction Certificate (CC) — building approval. The CC must be obtained from your council or an accredited certifier and includes your detailed building plans/engineering details and specifications. The plans will most likely contain a lot more information than your approved DA plans, to allow your builder to work directly from them, as the building must be consistent with these plans and the development consent.

b. Appoint a Principal Certifying Authority (PCA) to monitor construction. This can be your council or an accredited certifier. I set things up so my builder does this on my behalf. It's all part of having that great team around you.

c. Your builder needs to complete any works listed in the 'Prior to commencing work' part of the consent.

6. OCCUPATION CERTIFICATE

Note that this certificate goes by different names in different states and territories. The Occupation Certificate (OC) authorises the occupation and use of a new building or building section.

This is the final certifier check by council and occurs once the building is complete; it indicates that everything has been built according to BCA standards.

Once the OC is issued, the property can be leased. Banks won't settle on the property without it and you can't legally have people living in there without it.

Now, time to start developing!

CHAPTER 9

DUPLEX DEVELOPER – CONSTRUCTION AND PROFITS

Build that duplex and dig deep into my equity goldmine.

At last, we're ready to build your bricks-and-mortar investment. Let's go through what you need to do to get your builders on site and constructing your duplex, and what to do once they're there. Then it's time to get your hands on that usable equity.

Before we get started with the nuts and bolts, let's backtrack a bit to securing your financing for the build.

Once your builder is on board, you can apply for your construction loan, which covers your build and your land purchase (unless you are paying cash).

Without a builder on board, you're just buying a block of land, and it's much harder to get finance that way as there's no cashflow on a vacant block. You can, of course, buy a block with an existing house on it and get finance; however, that is a different strategy again and can be more complicated to finance.

Another mistake people sometimes make is they buy a block of land and only then go find a builder. When the builder comes in too expensive they find they can't afford it. So it's important to get the builder on board as soon as you find the land.

HOW DO YOU FIND A GOOD BUILDER?

Sometimes the media run stories reporting that a lot of builders are going broke because of supply chain delays and increases in tradie and other costs. That's mostly media hype and you don't need to pay too much attention to it. Do your own proper research on the builders and talk to them. Ask to see what they're up to. And ask to see financial records such as their P & Ls. Speak to their past clients and get testimonials so you can be confident you're making the right decision.

Most of the builders I use for my clients are ones I've used myself to build my own duplexes. So I've got some skin in the game there, which is road-tested builders. My advice is do not go with the cheapest builder. The cheap ones undercut the market then can't pay their tradies.

When we're building in a new location, I do a lot of research on builders in the local area. It counts if they've won awards. I also find out their track record to make sure they finish jobs on time and that there have never been any bad delays on their builds or price increases. And I make sure they've got good reviews online. Apart from Google reviews, I have found online forums and the ACCC to be good sources of information.

Then obviously I meet with the director or owner of the company and discuss what we're looking for. I always look at their work too. I visit their showroom. They usually have a display home. Where possible, I find builders who have a display duplex. I inspect it all — not just the display homes but some of their other completed properties, then some of their partially completed properties, the ones under construction. This way I get a good feel for how they're going.

I also go down to the building sites for a chinwag with a few of their tradies, who can offer objective insights given that most of them will be subcontractors who don't actually work for the builder. So I have a bit of a chat to see how the contractors are going, if they're happy doing what they're doing and if things are bubbling along well.

When it comes to signing the contract, finding someone I feel will do a good job and negotiate well is very important so I know they're looking after our client. If I find a builder who's going to look after us and offer good inclusions and good pricing, because he knows he's going to get a fair bit of work from us, then we're on the right track.

I was on site recently inspecting some of our properties and the construction manager told me he's giving all our projects priority over the rest of their builds. That's the way it's been set up, and it's good to have that reinforced — they will try to finish our projects before other people's. That might sound unfair if you are one of those 'other people', but if you are one of my clients then you will have that advantage.

People sometimes wonder, should I just go directly to a builder or should I use a buyer's agent? As you can see, it's good value to go through a professional who can facilitate the whole process rather than just trying to do it yourself.

THE KEYS TO A SMOOTH BUILD

One important consideration when looking to ensure a successful project is to negotiate a great price with your builder. I have a fair bit of success with that, as the volume of work we give them enables us to negotiate construction contracts well below what they would offer on the open market.

Being smart about the fine print in your contract will go a long way to ensuring that the builder doesn't spring any nasty surprises on you later on by increasing costs, or changing time frames or inclusions through variations to the contract that you weren't aware of. Many people come unstuck that way and get themselves into trouble as a result, losing potential profits and the good cashflow they calculated initially.

When managing your own project, having a *full turnkey construction contract* will mitigate your risk as much as possible.

Every build contract I sign is a fixed-price contract and has a *fixed time frame* clause, so I know up front exactly what we're paying for the build and how much time it will take.

You also need to look carefully at the *inclusions* on the builder's specification sheet so you know that all the features being installed are right for your demographic and, more importantly, are what you want in your duplex. Will your duplex include stone benchtops? Is it ducted air-con or split system? Are 2.4-metre ceilings okay or do you want higher ones? I tend to put in 2.7-metre ceilings in our duplexes, with 2.4-metre-high doors. It gives the feeling of a larger, higher-end property.

If you don't understand any part of the construction contract, get a solicitor to look it over before you sign.

All this sounds complicated, but again, enlisting the help of a professional in this field can really pay dividends. Best-case scenario, whoever you engage to help you has duplexes in their own portfolio and they're not just trying to sell you someone else's product without having been through the process themselves.

FIXED PRICE

There are two kinds of basic construction contracts: *cost plus* and *fixed price*.

A cost-plus contract is one in which the builder is paid for all their allowed expenses and expects additional payments to allow for profit. This presents a lot of risk to the client.

Fixed price is self-explanatory: there are no variations to the contract price unless you request them, so the builder has to stick to that contract price, with everything included.

There are only a couple of minor exceptions that will result in a price variation on a fixed-price contract, and one of those is finding rock. The builder isn't to know that there will be rock under the ground so they will charge extra to break it up and dispose of it.

The way I mitigate that risk is to ensure that we're not building near volcanoes or where large amounts of rock have been found before. In all the hundreds of duplexes I have been involved in developing, we have hit rock on only *one* occasion. That's a pretty good track record! The client had to pay $4000 to have it excavated, which was not actually a big deal in the context of the large profit on the project.

Everything plus the kitchen sink

When the build contract is a *full turnkey contract*, on completion of the project you simply pick up the keys to your property and it's ready to live in.

There are many stories of people who didn't read their contract carefully and discovered that the builder didn't do the driveway or the landscaping (which weren't included), so the client had to organise their own landscaper after the fact.

Lots of builders don't do those things. *I make sure my builders do absolutely everything.* The construction contract is going to include driveways, fencing, landscaping, soil tests, working drawings and all the architect's costs, all the engineering, the subdivision, and all the council costs including the DA, the section 94 contributions and Construction Certificate costs. Everything's in there.

Inclusions

Your builder's job specification sheets contain hundreds of standard items, from skirting boards to flooring to roofing materials, needed for the build and included in their pricing.

When negotiating with my builders on behalf of clients, I ask them to throw in a lot of extra inclusions over and above the standard specifications, either at greatly reduced pricing or for free. I've gained these privileges through many years of good work and negotiations with these builders, and I share them freely with my clients.

Job spec extras might include:

- higher ceilings
- stone benchtops in the kitchens and bathrooms
- downlights
- ducted air-conditioning systems
- freestanding bathtubs
- floor-to-ceiling bathroom tiles
- a solar power system
- goose-neck kitchen mixers
- larger-than-standard kitchen sinks
- 900-millimetre appliances
- dishwashers
- roller blinds (as these present better than vertical blinds).

These upgrades create a higher-quality duplex than most, which benefits both its rentability and the equity — and, in the end, the sale price. Of course, it is also important to build for the demographics of the area.

Your duplex will feel more like a home than an investment property if you build with quality inclusions. The goal should always be to sell to someone who wants to purchase it as a home, as this sort of buyer will pay more, typically bringing more emotion to the purchase, whereas investors will pay less, thinking only about the numbers.

A BUILD THAT FINISHES ON TIME?

Yes, you read that right. You'll have heard a lot of nightmare stories in which it takes three years for people to get a house built because the builder keeps stuffing them around. You may even have experienced something like this yourself. Another thing I put into the contract to mitigate risk is a *fixed time frame*.

With a fixed time frame the builder must finish by a certain date — say, 180 days or six months from the contract sign-off date (the time will vary depending on the type of development we're doing). If they go overtime, then the *late-completion clause* specifies that the builder must actually pay *you*, the client, liquidated damages. I usually try to have that payment set high, at about $100 a day, to cover any potential loss of rent you might face because of the delays.

So if your builder doesn't finish on time, they end up paying you $500 per working week, which gives them a strong incentive to keep to the schedule!

No, most builders don't like to include liquidated damages in a contract. But if I can't get a builder to agree to liquidated damages, I'll walk away, because if they're not prepared to provide some mitigation for myself or my client, there's something dodgy there, and without a late-completion clause in the construction contract, it's not going to cost them anything to drag the chain.

That said, I have never actually needed to enforce the late-completion clause with any of my builders, which is great. But if you are putting together a deal for yourself, make sure you include such a clause.

THE PLANS FOR YOUR DUPLEX

Once you have a signed builder's contract, we can proceed to the next stage, in which the architect or draftsperson prepares the full set of floor-plan drawings and elevations (side profiles) for the property.

This is often done before or at the same time as getting finance approved, as banks usually require these drawings. If the property is in New South Wales, the builder will also need to order a BASIX certificate. BASIX is the building sustainability index, which regulates the energy efficiency of residential buildings. Once we have all the drawings and the BASIX, we then submit these to council.

Most builders have their own draftsperson, which saves a bit of money because the fixed-price contract includes the cost of the engineer and the draftsperson.

These days I make sure thorough due diligence is done before we submit, so the council approvals don't drag out for up to a year. I've already made phone calls to make sure the local council will allow a duplex development on the block. And (for NSW) I've checked the Development Control Plans and the Local Environmental Plan. All states have their own planning guidelines and use different names.

I've also checked the *setbacks* of the property — that is, the requirement that buildings on that land have to be a certain distance from the boundary fence and the footpath. And, of course, where the land is sloping, potential stormwater issues. These are all things you need to ask the local council about.

Once we have our answers we have the architect design the property accordingly, then submit those plans to council as soon as we have our finance approved.

When you lodge an architecturally designed plan with council, it must show exactly what the property will look like, and all the inclusions. So, for example, you can't just say, 'It's going to have ducted air-con but we might change to split system later on.' You've got to show exactly what you're going to have there. If you're going to include a skylight or solar, you've got to show it in the plans.

You've also got to give the council an estimate of what the duplex will cost to build. You don't have to show them the construction contract, but you must give them an approximation of how much you're planning to spend on the construction of the property.

And if council comes back with an amendment request for anything, these days I actually ask them, 'Is there anything else that needs to be done?' so we're not still waiting six months down the track for approvals to come through because they're being slack. As I keep saying, my clients these days benefit a lot from my past experiences!

This all sounds like a heap of work but I get all this stuff done in a couple of days.

Once we find the block of land, I know the builders; I know the town planners. I get right onto the case and put everything together, including a feasibility study to show my clients the exact cost of the proposed development, and the projected profit at the end.

MANAGING THE BUILD

During the construction phase we're in constant communication with the building company's director or owner. This is crucial when it comes to facilitating progress claims with the bank. The progress claims come at deposit, slab, frame, enclosed (brickwork, roof and roller doors completed), fixing and completion. There are several points of contact with the builders I manage as well.

If you're halfway through a project and it's not going anywhere, you need to visit the site and speak to the construction supervisor. Make sure you know who your construction supervisor is and develop that relationship up front. 'Oh yeah, who should I be talking to?' is not something you want to be asking mid-build.

I speak to the construction site supervisor every week, which means I speak to supervisors every day because I'm doing lots of different projects at the same time. But for every individual project I expect a weekly progress update, along with photos.

In addition, to ensure everything is on track and going to plan, we (I myself or a member of my team) will actually go to the site to get updates from the builder and take onsite photos and videos ourselves, which we can then send through to clients.

The construction supervisor also takes photos at various stages and sends them to me. So there are lots of updates, keeping my clients very well informed about how their duplex is coming along.

Some clients drive over to visit their property themselves, but a lot of them don't. And if they're in Sydney and they're building a property in Brisbane, they might go up to see it only once, when it's finished. They rely on having us manage the project and check that everything is progressing on schedule. My expat clients in Dubai, Singapore, Hong Kong, the USA and the UK usually don't see their properties at all, but they engage us to facilitate the projects and manage their property portfolio growth.

LEGAL ASSISTANCE

You don't get a lawyer involved unless things go very wrong. I had friends (not clients) who were halfway through a build and came to me when things were going badly with the builder. I sat them down for an hour and gave them some advice, but finally I said, 'You might need to speak to a litigation lawyer about the situation, because what's happening to you doesn't sound right.'

In this instance the builder kept giving them more and more variations, and increasing the price, but didn't seem to be doing any work. Nothing seemed to be happening on site, and there were no photos to show otherwise. And they just kept demanding more money from the client. That suggested the builder either had bad financials or was just doing the wrong thing.

AFTER THE BUILD

When the builder is finished we organise a handover. This is when you make your final payment to the builder, and they give you the keys to your property — and it's all yours.

Before handover, I highly recommend getting an independent building inspection done by someone who is not associated with the builder. This offers extra peace of mind: you can be sure that everything is in order and has been built to the highest standards.

Building inspectors examine and crosscheck everything, and zero in on any defects they find. The builder is responsible for fixing any defects, usually within 14 days, before you make the final payment and get those keys, completing your turnkey build.

It's standard for there to be a mandatory 13-week 'defect period' after the build during which the builder is obliged to fix any small issues immediately. I have been able to convince some of my builders to make this period 12 months, on top of the structural warranty.

Your structural warranty covers you for 'structural defects' and issues arising as a result of the original build for at least six years, which is the Australian minimum standard. Some builders offer warranty periods of longer than six years. All of this is spelt out in your construction contract.

REALISING THE PROFITS ON YOUR DUPLEX

The best way to get results is to do something differently from other people — because if you do the same thing as everyone else, you get the same results as everyone else.

There are multiple ways to access profits from your duplex projects, and this flexibility is also very attractive.

When the subdivision process is completed, the property can be refinanced. Banks will usually allow you to refinance up to 90 per cent of the improved equity in your property on revaluation (depending on your serviceability and financial circumstances).

Or, depending on your strategy and what you're trying to achieve, on completion you have the option to sell both units or one unit (renting the other), or you can choose to keep and rent both.

I generally recommend that people don't sell. If you sell property within the first five years, you've usually got to pay GST and you've also got capital gains tax, which can impact your profits considerably. I always recommend my clients seek advice from a property-savvy accountant prior to selling a property.

LLOYD'S STRATEGY

Quite often, it's better to hold and refinance the property, only selling when you have to sell.

Again, this depends on your borrowing capacity moving forward, so regular discussions around strategy and finance with a mortgage broker are crucial here.

SUBDIVISION

Developing a duplex block often involves a Torrens title subdivision. Strata titling essentially facilitates individual ownership of a lot or unit while sharing ownership of the common grounds it is built on, such as the driveway and hallway.

If you're building a duplex on a smaller block of land, then it's usually going to be strata titled, whereas on a large block of land, you can get your duplex Torrens titled.

The subdivision needs a lot of approvals and can only be completed after the build. However, the surveyor can go in and take measurements and start the process once all the walls are up, so the process can commence while construction is still in progress.

Before the build, when you submit the DA, you apply to build one dual-occupancy property, and throughout the whole process the property has just one address — 1 Equity Street, or Lot 1, for example. It's only when it's completed that you'll have two mailboxes, because then you'll have two units.

You don't need to have the property subdivided to rent it out; the two units can be the same property on one title; in that case they'll be Unit 1/1 Equity Street and Unit 2/1 Equity Street, for example. But you must have them subdivided through strata or Torrens titling if you want to sell them as separate properties or realise your increased equity.

It's unlikely you will get much equity uplift if you just refinance the duplex before subdivision as it will still be the one property, on one title. This is great news for cashflow as you can rent the properties immediately, before subdivision. Once they've been subdivided, however, you're getting two separate valuations and realising some good profits from the project because you've refinanced them individually.

The following are the main steps to getting a subdivision through (remember, though, that all this can happen on the side, as it did for me on my first duplex, while you are working at your regular job):

- Your application for subdivision goes through the surveyor.

- The council signs off on it.

- You, the owner, sign off.

- If the property is financed, the next step is for the bank to sign off on it.

- It then goes in to the Land Registry Services (LRS) in NSW, or each state or territory's equivalent, who sign off and release the separate titles.

ONE INTO THREE SUBDIVISIONS

If you have built a triplex, you can get each unit strata titled and you will have three lots of valuations and be able to sell them off individually for increased profits.

If your block is large enough and meets the council's DCP minimum size, you may want to do a one-into-three-lot subdivision. In this scenario, you would submit a development application to council to subdivide the property into two further blocks, so you have three blocks in total.

For example, we had a 2000m² block in Newcastle with a house on the front of it and we did a one-into-three subdivision, creating two extra blocks of 650m² each and one block of 700m² with the house on it.

By adopting this strategy, you have the option to sell the two new blocks as individual vacant blocks of land, or to keep them and 'land bank' them for future capital growth. Or you can build houses on them, council permitting. Then you have the option of keeping the new houses for cashflow and further growth.

Remember: always do a feasibility study to check that the numbers will work in your favour, and be sure to seek advice from your accountant before selling any properties to realise profit.

Either way, when you chop blocks up, you are creating extra value. Subdivisions are fantastic for this reason, as long as you are doing them in the right locations. As the old saying goes, land values increase because they are not making any more land. In this case, you are creating additional blocks from existing land, so you are forcing value and equity into land.

Property management

We'll cover the basics of property management in chapter 10, but there are a few things you should do when your duplex is close to completion so it's not just sitting there afterwards.

As part of my process, I arrange for our clients to get tenants in place so they've got cashflow coming in and paying the mortgage straight away post-construction. Ideally, you should start advertising for tenants while the properties are being built. We usually have tenants lining up before the properties are even finished.

I strongly recommend having a property manager for each of your properties. Don't try doing it yourself; you need to run it like a business. I work with a number of reputable property managers, who make being 'a good landlord' very easy for me. Be sure to thoroughly research any property manager you are considering taking on board.

I also arrange for our clients to get insurance, because the bank won't pay the final instalment to the builder unless the property is insured.

Finally, I arrange for the quantity surveyor to do the depreciation report you'll need for your tax return.

VALUATIONS

When your property has been subdivided, you can go ahead and get a revaluation done.

If you find valuations baffling, you're not alone — everyone does. It's a minefield, as the value of a property can be more than a little subjective. That's something I still battle with every day, whether dealing with my clients' properties or my own.

The broker orders a valuation through the bank. You can't choose your valuation company; you can only choose your bank, and that bank orders the valuation. They don't usually get to choose which valuation company to go with either, as valuation companies are supposed to be independent of banks.

The bank registers for a valuation on your behalf through RP data. All the banks use this system, which automatically picks a valuer for them by rotation, so you have no way of knowing who you're going to get most of the time.

The valuer gives your property a value based on their opinion of what you could sell each unit for in the current market, so they look at 'comparables' in the market.

If your feasibility study was right in the first place and you've built, say, a six-bedroom property for $1.3 million including the land purchase, estimating that each three-bedroom unit could be worth $900 000, then at the end of the process the valuations should be something similar to that.

As you are getting each unit valued, you will get two valuations of $900 000 each. Or perhaps 1/1 Equity Street is valued at $880 000 and 2/1 Equity Street at $920 000. This can happen even if the units are identical. Either way, you have a project valued at $1.8 million that cost you only $1.3 million.

As another example, if you get valuations back for a lower price of, say, $750 000, giving you a total of $1.5 million, you may feel disappointed that it didn't meet your feasibility estimate. But given the whole project cost you just $1.3 million, you've still gained $200 000 in equity. Your feasibility should have a contingency to allow for a slight variation in the results as the markets can and do change from when you enter a project to when it is completed and refinanced or sold.

Because the valuation is being done on behalf of the bank, they tend to give a value that is a bit more conservative than the actual sales price could be, because they want to be able to sell the property quickly if the owner forecloses on them, so a lower value benefits them.

LLOYD'S STRATEGY

I recommend you get two or three property valuations done with different lenders.

DON'T STOP AT ONE

I've known two different people to give valuations on the same property that differ by as much as $100 000. To you, that could mean the difference between going into another property and not, or the difference between buying only one more property and buying two. So be persistent with your valuations, and remember your goals and why you are doing this.

Different valuers *do* value things differently, particularly if they're from outside the area and don't know the suburb or town very well. They may not look at the right comparables — or if the valuer has had a bad day stuck in traffic, they may not be in the best mood. You never know, it does happen!

I had three valuations done on my Armidale property. One suggested $141 000 in additional equity; another $120 000; and the third valuation came in at $80 000. Three very different valuations, with $61 000 difference between the lowest and the highest valuation for the same property. That could be a year's salary.

Of course I went with the bank that gave me the highest valuation!

BANKING ON IT

The whole property game depends on finance, so you need to be prepared for that.

I work closely with mortgage brokers on getting these valuations through. I also organise valuations with different banks from the one with which I currently have the loan, because my current bank already has the security, so they're often not that interested in giving you more equity on something they've already got. If you go to another bank, they may be more interested in taking that security and giving you some equity.

Once you have your highest valuation you can refinance your property with the bank that gave you that high valuation. The bank will need to hold the whole property as security so you will need to shift the original loan to the new bank, and they will lend 80 per cent or 90 per cent of the new value they have placed on that property.

If you do get a satisfactory valuation from the lender who had your original loan, you can keep your loan with that bank and they will give you what is called an equity loan for a percentage of that increased value. The percentage they give you is based on a few factors, including the bank's criteria, your serviceability and whether you want to refinance the whole amount or just take, say, 50 per cent of the improved value, leaving substantial equity in the property.

CALCULATING YOUR EQUITY

Equity is the difference between the loan you have on a property and how much the property is worth. So, in lay terms, if you buy a property and put down a 20 per cent deposit, and you have an 80 per cent loan, you've got 20 per cent of the property's value in equity and you're borrowing 80 per cent.

To work out how much equity you have in your property, you'll need to subtract any debt remaining on your mortgage from the property's overall value. For example, if your combined duplex property is worth $1.3 million and you have $900 000 left on your mortgage, your equity is $400 000.

You won't be able to access all this equity, but the portion lenders will allow you to borrow, called *usable equity*, is usually up to 80 per cent or 90 per cent of the total equity, depending on individual circumstances.

To access the usable equity, you can refinance your mortgage, as I have described.

That new loan comes to you in the form of cash that you can use for whatever you like. But if you're being savvy about it, you have a strategy to pay down a debt, pay down your home or use it as a deposit to get into another property to keep working towards your dreams.

Banks will ask what the money is going to be used for. They are happy for it to be used for investment purposes, or even to do a renovation. Just don't tell the bank you intend to buy the latest model jet ski with your equity!

That's what you can do differently to get ahead as a property investor and get into another project without waiting for years for your property to increase in value, because you've already increased it in value. So simple it should be obvious, right? If you're ready to go, table 9.1 outlines what we do for clients and will help you keep track of your first development. Good luck!

Table 9.1: equity creation checklist (developments)

Item	Notes
Location	
Shortlist suitable locations based on region's growth drivers	
Approved development plans in surrounding area	
Increased government spending has been approved	
Excellent transport links	
Increasing jobs growth	
Desirable for both families and workers	
Low vacancy rates	
Education and childcare facilities	
Land acquisition	
Seek new land releases	
In established areas, seek vacant blocks among quality owner-occupied homes	

Item	Notes
Check council zoning will allow development	
Check easements and covenants	
Check contour plans, including terrain surroundings	
Check flood and bushfire zoning, as well as mine subsidence	
Organise soil testing	
Negotiate lowest price on suitable block	
Receive working drawings from surveyor and architect of proposed development	
Arrange lodgement of the DA	
Construction contract	
Negotiate lowest price on construction cost with your builders	
Negotiate contract for inclusions such as landscaping, soil tests, working drawings, section 94 contributions and DA	
Negotiate contract for build inclusions such as ceiling heights and air conditioning	
Contract review for maximum completion date, turnkey handover, structural warranty, warranty check-up after six months	
Construction timeline	
Project management throughout build including weekly meeting with site manager	
Ask for regular updates and progress photos throughout construction	
Ensure your project is on track through regular site manager calls and, if possible, site visits	
Arrange handover, including final inspection, independent building inspection and approval	
Completion	
Arrange strata or Torrens titling of your new duplex	
Interview suitable property managers, and get your property listed for rent as quickly as possible	
Find appropriate insurance cover	
Arrange your tax depreciation report	
Refinance your loan if you want to purchase another property or pay down other debt	
Exit strategy	
Get advice on the most appropriate exit strategy for your individual circumstances (hold, sell one, sell both, and so on).	

CASE STUDY
Duplex location — South Coast — Illawarra, NSW

An easy two- to three-hour drive or train ride south of the Sydney metropolitan area, the South Coast region of New South Wales is powering ahead and ripe for further growth. A multitude of market drivers in this breathtakingly scenic and economically valuable region make it a great place to spend property-investment dollars.

This area definitely ticks the investment property trifecta: equity, high rental yields and good long-term growth.

SOUTH COAST NSW

In New South Wales, the Illawarra, with the city of Wollongong at its centre, is one of Australia's top regional areas for investment, with continued growth since 2017.

There are several solid market drivers energising the region, with the education hub around Wollongong University, massive industry, increased government spending, booming tourism and more, and this has been reflected in consistent house prices in recent years. And being just 90 kilometres from Sydney, it is an easy commute by car or train.

We have done a lot of developments in the area, with some massive results achieved. We look for the ripple effect and invest in areas close to the 'Gong' that we think will do well.

Banks love the area for valuations because there's a scarcity of land, which means it's a good prospect for growth, and the land sells quickly so it's very popular with buyers as well. We've done some good developments in Vincentia, which is a beautiful spot near some of Australia's finest beaches that's really popular: house prices are strong, meaning growth is almost assured. Rental returns are high, bringing positive cashflow from day one. We've also done some cool developments in Ulladulla.

I like the region so much that we go down there every weekend to spend time at the beach in our holiday home. So, even apart from investing in the region, it's stunning.

WHY INVEST IN ILLAWARRA?

With its modern infrastructure, beautiful coastal environment, diverse industry base, and expanding education and healthcare facilities — not to mention its proximity to Sydney — the Illawarra region appeals to a broad range of people, which is why new residents move there every day.

Major infrastructure spending

More than a quarter of a billion dollars was allocated under the Restart NSW fund to improve infrastructure and foster economic growth in the South Coast – Illawarra region, drawing on proceeds from the long-term lease of Port Kembla, allowing for more accessibility and beautification, and hundreds of new jobs.

The 'Gong', an economic and cultural hub

Wollongong is a nationally significant city, poised for future prosperity through job generation in education, healthcare, business and tourism. As the third-largest city in New South Wales, Wollongong's population is projected to reach 241 700 by 2036, making it a key urban centre. This growth is supported by significant infrastructure investments, including a $2 billion redevelopment of the city centre and major upgrades to the University of Wollongong, which ranks among the top 2 per cent of universities worldwide.

(continued)

CASE STUDY
Duplex location — South Coast — Illawarra, NSW (*cont'd*)

Shellharbour Centre Expansion

The recent $573 million redevelopment of Shellharbour City Centre is set to enhance the thriving retail, commercial and residential spaces, attracting more businesses and residents to the area. The expansion of Shellharbour Hospital into a major metropolitan hospital is a significant development, as it will not only improve healthcare services in the region but also create numerous job opportunities.

Port Kembla

One of NSW's major ports, crucial for regional and international trade, Port Kembla is a key asset for the community and regional economy, playing a vital role in the logistics and transportation sectors and supporting the manufacturing, agriculture and mining industries. The port's operations handle over 34 million tonnes of cargo annually, including vehicle imports and grain exports. The port's planned expansion aims to increase capacity and support new industries, further boosting economic growth.

Growing population

Demographic projections show the entire Illawarra region's population swelling to 463 150 by 2036, representing an increase of 60 400 people in the two decades since 2016. This expansion is expected to create demand for construction of at least 35 400 new homes.

This population growth is driven by the region's attractive lifestyle, economic opportunities and strategic location. The region's three local government areas (Wollongong, Shellharbour, and Kiama) are expected to see steady growth, with Wollongong anticipating an additional 33 000 residents by 2036.

In the Shoalhaven area alone, the current population is estimated at 99 650.

New land releases

All these people need housing, and new land is being released for housing across the region. West Lake Illawarra and Nowra–Bomaderry have a combined capacity of 37 600 lots, a forecast 30- to 40-year supply of housing, of which more than half have been zoned for development. The Wollongong, Shellharbour and Shoalhaven councils have capacity to meet their projected housing needs for greenfield land supply until well beyond 2036.

The Illawarra Shoalhaven Regional Plan outlines strategies to deliver housing to meet demand, including the development of new residential areas and increased housing density in existing urban centres. The plan also highlights the importance of affordable housing initiatives to cater to a diverse population.

Tourism opportunities

With its wealth of natural assets, the Illawarra–Shoalhaven area brings in 6.7 million plus tourists a year, contributing nearly $1.3 billion to the local economy. Key attractions include the Illawarra Escarpment, Lake Illawarra and Jervis Bay.

Sustainable and adventure tourism abounds, with trails and activities in national parks, and marine-based tourism at The Waterfront Shell Cove and along the coastline. The region's commitment to sustainable tourism is evident in projects like the Grand Pacific Walk, a 60-kilometre coastal walking track that connects the Royal National Park to Lake Illawarra. Adventure tourism, including activities like skydiving, hang gliding and scuba diving, attracts thrill-seekers and nature enthusiasts to the region.

The tourism sector employs over 10 000 locals and is a significant driver of economic growth, providing support for local businesses. Visitor numbers will grow as new attractions and infrastructure projects come online, such as the $100 million investment in the upgrade of Wollongong's Blue Mile and the Shell Cove Marina.

Transport infrastructure: strategic location and transport links

The South Coast – Illawarra region is well connected by road to Sydney in the north via the Princes Motorway (M1) and Princes

(continued)

CASE STUDY
Duplex location — South Coast — Illawarra, NSW (*cont'd*)

Highway (A1), to Port Kembla in the south via the Unanderra–Moss Vale rail line and to towns and cities across the region. It has a well-established public transport network, including local and longer-distance train and bus services.

This makes it possible to live anywhere on the South Coast and commute to the Big Smoke of Sydney. Indeed, around 15 per cent of the Illawarra – South Coast region's residents have Sydney-based jobs.

The $4.3 billion South Coast Rail Corridor project will further improve connectivity to Sydney, reducing travel times and increasing the appeal of the region for both residents and businesses.

The $15.6 million upgrade of Wollongong's public transport interchange, the Albion Park Rail bypass and ongoing upgrades to the Princes Motorway, further enhance the region's convenience for local and regional travel.

Diverse and growing employment base

Traditionally, the South Coast – Illawarra has been bolstered by its strong industrial–manufacturing base, including steel and coal mining, aided by freight connections to Port Kembla, one of NSW's key international grain ports and Australia's largest vehicle importing hub. But tens of thousands of South Coast residents are employed in the retail trade and, increasingly, in local tourism and hospitality:

- **Manufacturing.** A traditional strength, contributing $1.9 billion to the economy and around 10 per cent of local jobs. The manufacturing sector in Illawarra is diverse, encompassing industries such as steel production, machinery manufacturing and food processing. The $600 million upgrade of the Port

Kembla steelworks is a testament to the sector's resilience and potential for growth. The region's manufacturing sector is also supported by advanced manufacturing initiatives and partnerships with local research institutions.

- **ICT.** With a high concentration of information and communications technology (ICT) graduates from the University of Wollongong and Shellharbour TAFE, in recent years the South Coast – Illawarra has become an ICT hub. The Innovation Campus at the University of Wollongong is a prime example, hosting over 50 businesses and research organisations, and creating a dynamic environment for tech startups and established companies alike.

- **Education and healthcare.** Significant institutions like Shellharbour TAFE and the expanded Shellharbour Hospital are central to regional employment. These institutions not only provide essential services but also offer employment opportunities in education, healthcare and related fields. The $350 million redevelopment of Wollongong Hospital and the establishment of the new University of Wollongong Health and Wellbeing Precinct are improving healthcare services and creating additional jobs in the sector.

Prime investment region

Illawarra is no longer just an industrial hub; it's evolving into a vibrant, diverse economy with promising opportunities for property investors. The region's strategic infrastructure, combined with its natural beauty and robust economic growth, makes it an attractive prospect for those looking to invest in real estate.

In my view, the savvy investor should take a second, third and fourth look at this scenic and dynamic region. I am even more excited, however, about the potential immediate returns on equity. The feasibility study on my client's duplex showed a minimum of over $800 000 in instant equity.

Let's look at this more closely.

SUCCESS STORY
Client purchases and builds successfully interstate with a 72 per cent ROI

A client from Adelaide, Stuart, a doctor, and Emma, in their late forties, had one negatively geared property that wasn't growing fast enough to provide for their retirement. They came to Aus Property Professionals looking for a new way to build wealth, because they didn't like the idea of needing to ride out the market fluctuations before they could make some solid returns, as with their existing portfolio.

THE STRATEGY

In our discovery session I learned that they were ambitious and really keen to start building their property portfolio, and they wanted to start right now.

Once we received the numbers from their broker—their borrowing capacity was $1.5 million—I was able create a strategy to best utilise their serviceability. After discussing all the finer details, we advised that they were suitable candidates for a duplex construction project.

Although they live and Stuart works in Adelaide, to get the best return they would need to invest in another state, so they would have to trust the professionals with this project.

I explained to them that we have a rigorous process of research and development. When choosing an unfamiliar area for a duplex investment, it is important to research the following questions:

- What is the demographic of the area? Is it ageing, or are more young families moving in?

- Is there government spending in the area on new roads, parks, facilities and infrastructure?

- Will there be a demand for a duplex type of property in the area?

- Will the cost to buy and develop be viable? We look at comparative sales in the area for new units compared with development costs.

We avoid areas:

- with high housing commission properties, as this may limit your growth

- with decreasing population statistics

- that have a high proportion of renters compared to owner-occupiers

- that are predominantly tourism locations without other diverse industries.

THE LOCATION

We decided on the Sapphire Coast of NSW. The main demographics in this area, with many young families and professional working couples moving in, made it the perfect place to develop a duplex.

THE LAND

When looking for suitable land, it was important to take into consideration the easements, sewer diagrams, stormwater drainage, land zoning (bushfire, flood) as well as the size of the land and whether it would be approved for a duplex. Each council has different rules, which can be found on the council websites, and when we find a site I also confirm with a local town planner that the particular site is suitable.

Despite land shortages, we were lucky enough to find a vacant block that would be cheaper to buy and more straightforward to develop on than if we had to knock a house down, and it might have been harder to get the council approvals. The land we purchased cost \$285000, and was just under 900m^2, which was permissible for a duplex construction with this council. Best of all, the block had great uninterrupted water views.

THE BUILD

The construction cost was negotiated to \$842746, full turnkey, including council and subdivision costs.

(continued)

SUCCESS STORY
Client purchases and builds successfully interstate with a 72 per cent ROI (*cont'd*)

We sourced and received quotes from a number of different builders, made our choice and performed a background check to ensure that he would provide the best quality for the price. We also checked that he had adequate insurance and had a reputation for completing projects within the schedule.

I like to work with builders with excellent communication skills so we're always clear on where the build is at and we can get right on top of any decisions that need to be made, or we are able to quickly fix any issues that sometimes come up.

Both duplex units had three bedrooms, two bathrooms and two-car parking to suit professional couples and young families.

THE RESULTS

The land and construction costs totalled $1135 946. The project took approximately 18 months and upon completion each duplex unit was valued at $980 000, for a total of $1960 000.

The resulting instant equity in the deal was $824 054, for 72 per cent return! The units were tenanted at $750, or a total of $1500 per week for both units, providing excellent cashflow and a 6.86 per cent yield.

Duplex development costs

 Land price: $285 000

 Stamp duty on land: $8200

 Construction price (inc. council and strata titling costs): $842 746

 Total project costs: $1135 946

Independent valuation (after strata titling)

 Unit 1: $980 000

 Unit 2: $980 000

 Total value: $1 960 000

Instant equity: $824 054

Current rental yield: 6.86 per cent

WHAT'S NEXT?

Stuart was now free to leverage his equity gains to move on to his next investment project and grow his portfolio. He used equity from his duplex as a deposit on his next purchase, a property in Melbourne that we renovated for him as it too was in another state. Stuart will use the equity from this to take on another duplex project. It's all about buying in growth areas of big demand and manufacturing equity.

CHAPTER 10

A LANDLORD'S TOOLKIT

Find property managers and tenants and let the cashflow roll.

 When you become a property investor, you also become a landlord. It is important to understand your responsibilities as a landlord, as this knowledge will help you avoid costly mistakes, maximise your returns and protect your investment. Never fear, though; this isn't like having a whole new side career. I want you to understand that having a property portfolio can be really easy and fun.

In this toolkit you'll find all the information and resources you need to become a successful landlord, so you can grow your property portfolio and achieve your financial and lifestyle goals. I'll be covering all matters related to owning one or more investment properties and to being a landlord. This includes relevant legislation, how to find the right property manager, rules around tenant selection, repairs and maintenance, what happens if your tenants fall behind on the rent and much more.

WHAT IS A LANDLORD?

For the benefit of those who have managed to get by without ever renting, a landlord is the owner of real property, whether a house, apartment, townhouse, villa or land, that is leased or rented to an individual or business, known as the 'tenant'.

The following are among the many benefits to becoming a landlord:

 A source of income. This is undoubtedly the main reason people become landlords. With the right strategy in place, your property portfolio should provide you with a net income cashflow. At the same time the property also gains value over the years, providing long-term benefits.

 Financial independence. With a good net income cashflow, you can achieve financial independence. Ultimately you don't want to have to rely on your job as your only source of income.

 Lifestyle freedom. We all know that with more money comes more freedom. Now you have a higher income and your assets are growing in value, you could perhaps take that holiday you've always dreamed about or reduce your work hours so you can spend more time doing the things you enjoy.

 Retirement security. Investing in property is a successful retirement strategy, providing a much higher return than superannuation or keeping your money in a bank savings account.

 Securing your children's future. Everyone wants to set their kids up for the future, whether this is by saving enough money to provide them with a better education or by giving them a head start in life with assets. This can be achieved most effectively using property.

Let's review the six steps to becoming a landlord.

Step 1: Buy a property

We've already covered buying and developing your own property in a great location set for capital growth, with low vacancy rates and high-quality tenants.

As I've mentioned, I choose investment locations so carefully that in many cases the properties we build for clients have would-be renters lining up before the build is even completed. I've had people drive by a construction site and call the builder, or me: 'I really like that duplex that's being built on [a particular street]. When will it be ready? Because I'd like to move in!'

No property should sit on the market for weeks unrented if it's in a good area. When you're building in an area where vacancies are tight, and where there's high demand for properties like yours, then it's easy to get them rented out. You can expect to earn rent and cashflow from day one.

Step 2: Understand the legislation

In this toolkit we'll cover some of the general responsibilities you take on as a landlord, as set out at the state or territory level of government. It's important to familiarise yourself with the specific rental legislation and regulations in the state or territory you're buying and/or developing property in.

State and territory government landlord info

New South Wales — Office of Fair Trading:
fairtrading.nsw.gov.au/housing-and-property

Queensland — Residential Tenancies Authority: *rta.qld.gov.au*

ACT Government — Access Canberra:
justice.act.gov.au/renting-and-occupancy-laws

(continued)

State and territory government landlord info (*cont'd*)

Victoria—Consumer Affairs Victoria (CAV):
consumer.vic.gov.au/housing/renting

South Australia—South Australian Government:
sa.gov.au/topics/housing/renting-and-letting

Western Australia—Department of Mines, Industry Regulation and Safety: *commerce.wa.gov.au/consumer-protection/renting-home*

Northern Territory—Northern Territory Government:
nt.gov.au/property

Tasmania—Consumer, Building and Occupational Services:
cbos.tas.gov.au/topics/housing/renting

STEP 3: APPOINT A PROPERTY MANAGER

People sometimes ask me, 'How can you maintain so many properties? It must be really stressful!' And my clients often ask, when they first become landlords themselves, what do they do if they get bad tenants? What if a tap leaks or the air conditioning breaks down?

I tell them, 'You're not going to be managing the properties yourself. That's what you hire a property manager for.' I have never spent any time managing or maintaining a property, because I've had management in place from the minute I rented out my first property. It's up to you whether you choose to go it alone or use a buyer's agent when buying a property, but I firmly believe that everyone should use property managers to manage their properties if they want to build a portfolio.

When I was still teaching and building a portfolio on the side, I devoted my time to due diligence research, buying properties, and talking with town planners, councillors and builders. Once I had the property, I wanted to keep moving forward. That meant that I didn't want to devote my time to collecting rent from my tenants — or, worse, chasing them up for arrears. So I had a property manager perform those roles. Now the rent just turns up in my bank account each fortnight or each month, the manager sends me statements that I can pass on to my accountant — and Bob's your uncle!

Managing your own property can easily become a full-time job. If you do it yourself, you've got to be on call all the time. If there's a plumbing problem, you've got to organise a plumber or go there and fix it yourself. If you're in Sydney and a major problem crops up in your property in Tasmania, you'll have to fly down there and sort it out.

I currently have around 18 properties — the number is fluid depending on how many I am buying/developing versus what I decide to sell. If I've got a couple of properties in a similar location, they'll be managed by the same property manager. I have 12 property managers across those 18 properties, though I don't often deal with them. In fact, I hardly ever hear from them unless something needs repairing, which doesn't happen very often.

As long as you appoint the right property managers and you buy properties in the right locations, then you can be a truly passive landlord. That said, I don't recommend being a passive property *investor*. This book is all about equity creation, which is not passive — you should be refinancing equity whenever the bank allows you to. You need to run your property portfolio like a business.

As for managing your tenants, just set and forget. Take my Rockdale property. I've had that property for many years and it's been tenanted every day of it. I honestly don't think about it. The same applies to Alexandria, Newstead, Newcastle and most of my other properties.

WHAT DO PROPERTY MANAGERS DO?

Their main responsibilities are as follows:

- They source your tenants.

- They open your property for inspections.

- They check whether your prospective tenants are blacklisted from rental.

- They check tenant references to make sure they have always paid their rent in the past.

- They collect rent.

- They pay your bills, including council, water and strata rates, from your rental monies.

- They pay you the balance of the rental income each month.

- They conduct routine inspections on your behalf and send you reports.

- They organise any repairs and maintenance that is required.

- They deal with tenant concerns.

- They chase overdue rent.

- They can represent you at the tribunal if you have any issues with your tenants.

As landlord, I receive 18 rate notices for my properties; well, in fact I don't get any. Except for our home in Lilli Pilli, they go to the property manager to pay on my behalf. When set up properly, it's entirely stress-free. It's like setting up a business then leaving the day-to-day operations to a competent manager.

If I weren't running my Aus Property Professionals buyer's agency and instead chose to be a full-time property investor, I'd be pretty much a free agent. The way I've got things set up now, I can take days off, whether to write this book or to spend time with Renee, Riley and Caelen or play in my band or go out on the water — or do whatever I feel like doing. The reason I'm running my business is that I really like helping people and I believe in contributing to society. I love being busy and property has been very kind to me, so I want to pass on at least some of what I've learned.

How much do you need to pay a property manager?

A property manager's fee is based on a percentage of the amount of rent that's coming in. The amount varies, and may be anywhere between about 8 per cent and 12 per cent. In a place like Sydney, you can get a property manager for as low as 5 per cent + GST. But even in regional areas you might need to pay 8 or 9 per cent. In Brisbane the going rate is 8 per cent to 10 per cent, but I've negotiated most of the property managers I work with, and who work for my clients, down by at least a percentage point or two to around 7 per cent, which is where it should be.

Some people think they can save money by not having a property manager. But time *is* money, and if you need to conduct open inspections on a weekday, or if you've got a tenant who is constantly firing off emails or calling you with complaints, or if repairs are needed that require letting tradespeople in and out — a property manager will take care of all of that. It's money well spent, and it's tax deductible. Just be sure you have the right property manager in place.

How do you find the right property manager?

Your property manager is a vital member of your 'dream team', yet they are often seen as the poor cousins of real estate agents. This is why it's good to deal with an agency that specialises in property management — because, to state the obvious, while real estate agents know about *selling* property, property managers know about *managing* it.

Big-name real estate agencies that offer both services typically delegate the job to staff members who are working their way up to jobs in sales. So you might have someone for six or 12 months, then someone else steps in for a while, until they too get promoted to sales. *You want someone who is a dedicated property manager.*

Finding the right property manager is as important as finding the right tenants. Every property manager works in a slightly different way, so it's important that you interview a few different operators in the local area so you can compare their approaches and identify which will be the best fit for you and your investment property.

If you're not located in the same town as your investment property, simply call them or jump on a video chat to go through the screening process. This will also help you to determine how they communicate with people. An important part of their job, after all, is to create and maintain constructive relationships with your tenants.

WHAT DO YOU NEED TO ASK A PROSPECTIVE PROPERTY MANAGER?

Many landlords jump straight to the question, 'How much do you charge?' and just go with the cheapest option, but there's so much more to consider. You need to understand what level of service you're getting and what is included in the property manager's fee structure.

Some managers charge extra on top of their management fees for providing monthly statements, for example. Some are more thorough and conscientious than others, and their tenant screening process can be much more comprehensive. So it's crucial that you ask prospective property managers the right questions.

Here are some of the questions we ask prospective property managers:

- How many properties does your office manage? And how many property managers do you have?

- How many routine inspections do you carry out per year?

- Do you charge extra fees to organise repairs or pay rates on my behalf?

- How often do you disburse payments to your landlords?

- What is your tenant screening process?

- What action do you take if a tenant doesn't pay their rent on time?

- How often do you review the rent, and will you discuss this with me?

- What is the average 'days on market' for rental properties your office manages?

Jump online and check out property managers' reviews on Google and social media to gain some insight into what their current clients — landlords and tenants — are experiencing.

STEP 4: FIND QUALITY TENANTS

Having the right tenants in your property can make all the difference when it comes to how successful (or unsuccessful) your investment is, and the tenant screening process plays an important role in this.

My Rockdale property, for example, has never been vacant and has had only two tenants. When the first tenant moved out, the second tenant moved in the very next day. With one of my properties in Brisbane, when a tenant moved out they asked if a friend of theirs could move in. Once my property manager had screened the friend they moved in right away. These are examples of how smoothly things can run if you've bought in a good area and have engaged a good property manager.

HOW DO YOU SCREEN A TENANT?

It's important for your property manager to collect as much information as possible from the applicants. How many people will move in? Do they have a stable source of income (check their employment history)? Are they likely to be short-term or long-term tenants (check their past tenancies)? Why are they looking to relocate? Do they have any pets? And so on.

Documentation that should be requested includes:

- proof of identity (driver's licence, passport or birth certificate, for example)

- proof of income (recent payslips, Centrelink statements, bank statements)

- other supporting documentation (such as a current rental ledger, written references, rates notices or current utility bills).

RUN A CREDIT CHECK

Ask for information from prospective tenants with respect to their bank accounts and credit cards to get a sense of their capacity to pay the rent. Any suggestion of high levels of debt and lots of maxed-out credit cards is not a good sign.

CHECK THEIR EMPLOYMENT HISTORY

The rental application should include details of the applicant's current and previous employers. You want to see evidence of a stable work history, because ultimately their capacity to pay the rent comes down to how solvent they are. A good salary or wage means you can usually assume they'll be able to cover the rent plus living expenses comfortably. It's wise, though, to contact their employer for a reference to make sure that applicants are who they say they are.

CONTACT THEIR REFERENCES

As mentioned, you should contact the applicant's employer, but other types of references, such as character references, are useful too.

GET FULL DETAILS OF THEIR RENTAL HISTORY

Contact applicants' previous landlords or property managers. You need to be confident that your tenants haven't defaulted in the past. Evidence of a history of late payment or, worse, if they've been taken to the rental tribunal for, say, property damage can raise an alarming 'red flag'.

It's been smooth sailing for most of my properties. An exception was my Blackwater rental, with a tenant who was getting behind on his rent. My property manager kept following it up, but the tenant got so far behind we had to give him an eviction notice. Eventually he did pay, but then he'd get behind again. This became a pattern, until one day he simply cleared out, still owing money, and my property manager was unable to contact him.

This was in Blackwater, a mining town and not the best location. I don't think my property manager did all she could have to hunt my rent down, but there were only two property managers in town.

To avoid this kind of problem it is important that, before approving any prospective tenant, you contact that applicant's former property manager: 'Does the tenant still owe you money? Do they have a history of late payment? Did they cause any damage to the unit or house? Were they disruptive to the neighbours? Would you rent to them again?'

There are lots of questions you might ask. But of course, the other way to avoid these kinds of issues is *not* to buy in a mining town!

If a tenant is behind on the rent, ask your property manager to:

1. Double-check your lease documents and payment records to make sure the tenant truly is late with their rent.

2. Send a late rent notice.

3. Call them.

4. Send a 'pay or quit' notice.

5. Take legal action!

DO A BACKGROUND CHECK

If you're unsure of someone or they don't have any references, running background checks is doubly important, because if they have ever been evicted from a property in the past, they'll be on a blacklist. Every Australian state and territory has its own tenancy database, but the largest one (tica.com.au) is Australia-wide. It isn't difficult to find out if your prospective tenant has been blacklisted.

INTERVIEW THE TENANT

Other questions to ask a prospective tenant include the following:

- Do you plan on getting any roommates in the future?

- Do you work night shifts or odd hours?

- Do you smoke? Indoors or outside?

- Do you have lots of friends who often come over at night?

- Do you have any pets?

All these steps are your property manager's responsibility, so you can see the advantage of having a good property manager on board.

STEP 5: SIGN A LEASE

Laws around lease agreements vary slightly in each state and territory. Your property manager will talk you through the ins and outs of these.

The lease agreement is a legally binding contract between the tenant and the landlord (the owner of the property). It includes the weekly rent your tenant will pay and when it is due, the deposit required and whether pets are permitted.

The deposit, which is compulsory for all tenants, is usually a bond of four weeks' rent plus two weeks' rent in advance. The bond is held by the Rental Tenancy Authority (RTA) or its equivalent, and is used to cover any damage to the property or unpaid rent. I was still out of pocket for a few weeks of rent in Blackwater, even after claiming the bond.

Why you need a buffer

We all need a financial buffer for a rainy day, and this is especially true when it comes to rental properties, as the bond may not always cover unexpected costs or losses:

- Apartments and townhouses incur annual or quarterly strata levies billed by the body corporate.

- Occasionally special levies are put on strata buildings for building repairs, in which case you'll need to come up with some additional funds, sometimes in the tens of thousands.

- Unexpected repairs may crop up on your freestanding property as well. You don't want to be in a position where you can't afford these repairs.

- If your tenants move out, there may be a couple of weeks' downtime before the property is leased again. If you have a mortgage on the property, you'll still need to make loan repayments even if it is vacant. You need a buffer to cover any weeks in which no rent is coming in.

HOW DO YOU DECIDE ON A RENTAL PRICE?

You need to make sure your property is priced correctly, so unless you are yourself a property expert, take advice from your property manager on this, because they are the experts in the field. Basically, they'll be looking at comparables.

I always recommend renting at fair market value. Don't try to rent your property cheaply, thinking it's going to get you a tenant faster, because if you're in a good area, 'market rent' will get you a good tenant.

Don't list your property for *more* than market rent, either, because then it might stay vacant for a while. A vacant property's no good; you're better off getting $10 less per week than having your property lie vacant, earning $400 less a week because you've got no tenant in it.

I also recommend that you review the rent every six months and see what the market's doing. Look at increasing your rent by about $10 a week every 12 months, depending on the market. If you're in a market that's a bit soft and hasn't moved, you might want to leave it unchanged.

There are plenty of examples of people letting their properties sit there for years at the same rent, until they find out the rents in the area are $100 higher than they were when they set it. Again, property managers should alert you to that and let you know when it's time to review your rent.

I don't put my rent up unnecessarily or simply because I need more money, but I don't like to have it 'under-rented' either, because essentially it's a business. So if the markets indicate your property is worth more due to inflation or tightening rentals, then you should increase the rent. The tenants aren't going to move out just because you increase the rent; they'd only have to find another place in the same inflated price range anyway.

I recommend a 12-month lease unless there's a good reason for doing a shorter one — say, because you're planning to live in the property or to sell it. Some landlords think offering a six-month lease gives them the opportunity to raise the rent after that period. This strategy could work if you are renting in winter and the markets seem a bit down but you are confident you will get more for your property in the warmer months. If they sign for 12 months, it gives you a bit of comfort knowing you're guaranteed tenants for the next year. Some states have introduced legislation where the landlord can increase rent only once every 12 months.

SHOULD I ALLOW PETS IN MY RENTAL PROPERTY?

Most states have rental laws to allow pets. Landlords must have a valid reason why a pet wouldn't be suitable for a property. These conditions vary from state to state. I generally allow pets in my rental properties anyway. It means I can often get higher rents and the tenants with pets generally want to make the property a home and they go out of their way to look after it.

Allowing pets in your rental property can give you:

- *a point of difference.* It can open the market a little more to good tenants who feel locked out of most properties.

- *reduced turnover.* Pet owners can be less transient than most tenants, because it can be difficult to find pet-friendly properties.

- *increased rental returns.* Advertising your property as 'pet-friendly' can increase demand, allowing you to ask for more rent. Or, if a tenant requests permission to have a pet, you can make a slight rental increase as a 'condition'.

HOW TO SAFEGUARD YOUR PROPERTY AROUND PETS

The type of property you own will often dictate whether you should allow pets. If it's a small unit with no balcony or without easy access to outdoor areas, it may be unwise to allow certain pets or breeds. If you're in a strata-managed building, the choice may be out of your hands.

The most common concerns for landlords if they allow pets are:

- *damage to your property*. Animals can scratch the floors, and chew, claw or soil the floor coverings.

- *disturbing the neighbours*. Dogs barking, birds squawking and four-legged creatures running around on floorboards can be disruptive.

- *pet odours*. 'Accidents' inside the unit or in the building's common areas will cause unwelcome smells.

- *liability*. There may be a potential risk of the animal biting another tenant or a neighbour.

To stay on top of all this, include specific clauses in your lease agreement pertaining to pet ownership, stipulating that the tenant will be liable for any damage caused by the animals and that they must fumigate the property when they vacate. You can also specify in your rental agreement the types of animals you'll allow; for example, you could stipulate that cats are permitted but that dogs are not, or enforce an age and weight limit, or say that only cats or small dogs are allowed.

Discuss additional safeguards around pets with your property manager and ensure the rental agreement includes the details of any pets to be kept at the property, including every animal's microchip number, in case you have to file an insurance claim for damage.

Your property manager should also conduct regular inspections to ensure the tenants are abiding by the terms set out in the rental agreement, and to identify any damage before it gets worse.

The tenant's personal circumstances are also an important factor, such as whether they live alone and go to work, leaving their pet(s) at home all day. When in doubt, I suggest asking your property manager to request written references from past tenancies about their pets.

If you suspect your tenant is keeping unauthorised pets, ask your property manager to inspect the property and discuss the situation with the tenants. It is important, as the landlord, to hear the tenant's case out and fully understand the circumstances around the pet(s). In most cases, the tenant probably didn't realise they had to seek permission to home additional animals.

YOUR LANDLORD INSURANCE

Never try to save on costs by cutting back on landlord insurance. Your insurance covers you, should something major happen to the property; it can be used to recoup costs from damage caused by domestic pets or by the tenants; and it can compensate you for loss of rental income if your property is severely damaged. Check with your insurer that you are covered for all items pertaining to investment property.

When setting a value on your property for insurance purposes, always include an amount (approximately $30 000–$50 000) above the rebuild value. This is an allowance for land clearing, should you experience a total loss of your property.

Review the level of your property insurance annually to determine that you're not underinsured as build costs increase.

If you own an apartment or townhouse in a strata building, the body corporate fees (strata) will cover the building insurance, so you just need to ensure you have landlord's insurance in place to cover yourself against internal damage to the property.

STEP 6: MAINTAIN THE PROPERTY

It's important to look after good tenants. If they complain about a leaking tap or that the air conditioner's making a noise, attend to it straight away. Don't just ignore it and think, oh, it's just a whinging tenant. You really need to get onto that and keep them happy. They are paying you for a service, which is a working property. All those repairs and maintenance jobs are tax-deductible anyway.

I also send Christmas cards to my tenants and say, 'Hope you have had a good year and enjoy the summer in Brisbane [or Newcastle or wherever].' Because they only ever hear from the property manager throughout the year, it's good for them to get a personal Christmas card from me, a little human touch and that makes them feel appreciated.

WHO PAYS FOR REPAIRS AND MAINTENANCE?

There's a lot of confusion around who should pay for what when it comes to repairs and maintenance, so it's important for your property manager to be familiar with the current legislation. They should also make your tenant aware of their responsibilities at the beginning of the lease to avoid any confusion and neglect to the property.

The regulations vary from state to state but in New South Wales, for instance, if the property requires general pest control after the tenant has been in the property for more than three months, it's the tenant's responsibility to arrange and pay for this. However, if the tenant just moved in and there's a pest infestation immediately, it's the landlord's responsibility to resolve the problem.

It's so important for your property manager to know the legislation instead of asking you to pay for everything the tenant requests, as this sort of expenditure adds up and will affect your cashflow.

General maintenance of the building, like making sure the roof is in good condition and not leaking, that the windows are all functioning properly, that doors and locks are working and so on, is the landlord's responsibility. Certain fittings and fixtures, such as blinds and air conditioning, are also the responsibility of the landlord to maintain.

As you'd expect, there is a difference between maintenance and repairs for general 'wear and tear' and those clearly resulting from the tenant's negligence. For example, if a tenant was filling up the bathtub and left the tap running, causing the bathroom to flood and water to saturate the carpets, it would be the tenant's responsibility to have the damage fixed.

WATER CHARGES AND SMOKE ALARMS

Once again, this varies among the different states and territories of Australia, so make sure you discuss these items with your property manager.

WATER CHARGES

Water rates service fees are your responsibility, but if your property has a separate water meter you can charge your tenants for water 'usage', which is the amount of water they have used during that period. If you want the property manager to enforce this, your property must comply with any water-efficiency measures mandated by your state or territory.

If it's a dual-occupancy property such as a duplex or a house with a separate granny flat onsite, you'll need to ensure there is a separate water meter for each dwelling; otherwise you can't charge either tenant for the water usage. If there is only one water meter on the property, you can get another one installed by a licensed plumber for the second dwelling so there are two separate meters to read and you can determine the individual usages.

It is definitely better, in my opinion, to have separate water meters for each unit in a multi-unit development so you can charge water usage back to the tenants. If you have built a duplex, you will need separate water meters to have the property subdivided, if your goal is to create equity or to sell the units separately.

SMOKE ALARMS

It is your responsibility as a landlord to ensure that smoke alarms are fitted within the property in accordance with the local regulations.

Make sure you replace the batteries in any smoke alarms before any tenants move in. During the tenancy, it is the tenant's responsibility to replace any 'low' or spent batteries. If the smoke alarm is faulty, however, it is the responsibility of the landlord to have it repaired or replaced.

Some companies specialise in smoke-alarm maintenance, which can be a great solution if you are interstate or abroad. Again, this is something your property manager will take care of for you.

TAX PERKS FOR LANDLORDS

Rent is income, which is why we're buying and creating rental properties. And with income comes tax, but as a landlord you can claim lots of benefits.

We touched on the depreciation claims you can make as a property investor, and there are more tax benefits if you invest in a rental property.

If you're a landlord, these tax benefits can be hugely helpful in offsetting the cost of holding a property.

You'll need to keep records right from the start. These records should include proof of all your expenses so you can claim everything you're entitled to. You'll also need records of the date and costs of buying the property, so you can work out any capital gain (or loss) if and when you sell it.

Table 10.1 lists the kinds of things you'll be able to claim against your rental property. To claim deductions for expenses, your property must include a dwelling that is rented or available for rent — for example, advertised for rent. If you're building a rental dwelling, you can claim deductions for the land *while* you're building.

Table 10.1: what you can claim on your investment rental property and when to claim it

Type	Claimable?	Deductible/depreciable?
Property management fees	Yes	Deductible in year incurred
Maintenance costs (not improvements or enhancements):	Yes	Deductible in year incurred
a. renovations	Yes (partially)	Depreciable as capital works
b. interest	Yes	Deductible in year incurred
Advertising (for tenants)	Yes	Deductible in year incurred
Body corporate fees and charges	Yes	Deductible in year incurred
Council rates	Yes	Deductible in year incurred
Water rates	Yes	Deductible in year incurred
Land tax	Yes	Deductible in year incurred
Cleaning/gardening/ lawnmowing	Yes	Deductible in year incurred
Building and pest inspections, and pest control	Yes	Deductible in year incurred
Insurance	Yes	Deductible in year incurred
Legals/conveyancing	Yes (some)	Deductible in year incurred
Borrowing fees	Yes	Deductible either in year incurred or over the loan term
Depreciating assets	Yes	If under $300, these are deductible in year purchased; if over $300, they can be depreciated over the asset's useful lifetime

CHAPTER 11

THE DREAM TEAM

Get your investment portfolio started right with these key players.

 Buying and developing property involves hiring a team of experts from diverse fields. In this chapter, I'll introduce you to the key players we haven't yet covered, and in what order you need to engage them when building your 'dream team'.

To successfully finance and complete such complex projects as purchasing and developing properties on time and within budget, you need to surround yourself with people you trust. You need a team of professionals who you know will act in your best interests to help you meet the multitude of legal and practical requirements you now have as a property investor. When you find good professionals, you can end up using them over multiple projects spanning many years as you build your investment property portfolio.

I've told you everything you need to know about finding a property manager.

Who else should be on your dream team? The list of professionals I recommend includes:

 a buyer's agent

 a mortgage broker

 a financial planner

 an accountant

 a solicitor/conveyancer

 a building and pest inspector

 a quantity surveyor

 an insurance rep.

Normally, engaging a buyer's agent takes priority, so most of the time clients will come to me as a very first step. They want to buy a property, or they want a strategy to get ahead financially through property investment. I'll set up their dream team by referring them to all the wonderful people who are going to help them along the way.

My service is completely independent and transparent, so my clients don't have to adopt my recommendations; they can go with their own people if they want to — it's totally up to them.

I'll now walk you through the other key players I recommend you hire.

Mortgage broker

You can't start looking at property unless you know how much you can borrow, so the first step with any kind of strategy is to know your finance. Here you've got a choice: either you ask the bank for a mortgage or you go to a mortgage broker, a go-between who deals with banks or other lenders in order to arrange a home loan for you. I recommend mortgage brokers for the reasons outlined in chapter 3, and I suggest my clients talk with a mortgage broker before I do anything with strategy or property-hunting.

As you've learned, a lot of information is required for a loan application. It can take anywhere from a few days to three or four weeks to get financial approval from a bank. It really depends on your individual circumstances and whether you can get all your required information to the bank or broker fast, as they can't proceed with your application if any items are missing. Approval time also sometimes depends on the property you're considering, or even its location.

A good broker will help you put together a successful application. Brokers must conform to a range of compliance laws, so they must make sure they're getting all the right information from you to submit to the banks. Sometimes banks want more information and come back with additional questions, potentially delaying the approval process. Your broker will do all the crosschecks with you to try to avoid such delays.

A good broker will assess your circumstances before making you jump through hoops and lodging your application, which will give you a greater chance of putting in place pre-approval and a higher borrowing capacity. Your broker should ensure you are well-prepared and minimise any delays when you go through the process of purchasing a property.

You have probably heard that it will be difficult to secure a loan if you are employed as a casual, part-timer, contractor, or just started a new job and are still on probation, but a good broker will be able to demonstrate to a lender that there is limited risk for them.

And as an added bonus, some of the specials deals they can get include access to a 10 per cent deposit from a lender or waiving Lender's Mortgage Insurance for specific industries. You might have a lower deposit requirement for first home buyers with either a waiver or discounted Lender's Mortgage Insurance, or a cashback offer on settlement.

Ultimately, the key to getting your loan through is to make sure you're open and honest with your mortgage broker and provide them with all the information they need.

Before meeting with them, check the professional registers on the Australian Securities & Investments Commission (ASIC) website to make sure the broker you choose is licensed to give you credit (loan) advice. If not listed on one of ASIC's three credit licence lists, he or she is operating illegally.

You don't need to pay a mortgage broker directly; their commissions are paid by the bank. And the interest rates on your loan are not necessarily higher simply because the bank is paying the broker a commission. A good broker will still be able to find you a very competitive interest rate.

LLOYD'S STRATEGY

The best way to find someone trustworthy is through word of mouth.

ACCOUNTANTS AND ENTITIES

Businesses engage financial accountants, like Renee, but if you're dealing with property or your income tax, you need a tax accountant. What an accountant charges will depend on how complicated your tax returns are and what type of advice and service you need.

Some people try to do their tax themselves, which is all very well, but if you make mistakes the ATO can impose heavy penalties for misleading or incorrect information. A good accountant will make sure that everything complies with the law and is correct on your tax return so you've got less chance of being audited. Simply using an accountant means you have less chance of being audited, so it's always safer to have a good accountant on your side.

I've had a few accountants over the years and they are interesting people — especially Renee, of course! It's very important to find someone who has experience; not just someone who knows how to do a tax return, but someone who actually knows property accounting laws, because it can get quite complicated, especially when you have a lot of properties and you need to claim a lot of deductions.

It's prudent to consider accountants who have property portfolios themselves. Many don't, in line with their reputation for being risk averse. You will also find that many accountants push the negative-gearing strategy.

Some people are concerned when they feel their accountant is asking them too many questions or isn't getting them a big enough refund, but you really want an accountant who is honest. I've known accountants who bend the rules a bit, seeking out every loophole they can. This is tempting, but you can get into trouble that way. You need to focus on the long game.

An accountant, like your mortgage broker, has to come on board early in the process to advise you on entity structures.

Your *entity* is determined by whether you're going to buy the property in your own name or using a discretionary trust or company structure. You need to get that information *before* you put in an offer on a property. You don't want to buy a property in your name and later decide you want to change entities, because if you do that you'll have to pay double stamp duty.

Sometimes people will decide they're going to find a property and only *then* talk to their accountant about what entity to purchase the property in. Quite often, while they're busy sorting things out with their accountant before they are ready to exchange contracts, the property sells to someone else and they miss out.

So as well as your finance, your buying entity needs to be set up, detailing what you plan to buy in, *before* you go looking at properties. If your accountant has advised you to buy property in a trust, understand that trusts can take a few days to set up.

Always seek advice from an accountant on what entity structures are the best for your circumstances, as everyone's situation is different. The fact that someone you know has bought in a trust does not necessarily mean that this will be the right strategy for you, and vice versa.

UNDERSTANDING TRUSTS

A *trust* allows a person or company to own assets on behalf of someone else or on behalf of a group of people. The *trustee* is the person who owns or controls the asset, while the *beneficiaries* of the trust are the persons for whom the asset, in this case the property, is owned. When you buy property through a trust, you control the asset but you don't actually own it, as it is owned by the trust.

The three main trust structures that property investors use are *unit trusts*, *family discretionary trusts* and *hybrid trusts.*

Under a *unit trust* structure, the assets the trust owns are split up into portions known as units. The trust beneficiaries then own the units, just as shareholders own shares in a company. This means their share of the income and expenses is proportional to the number of units they own. Remember, we are referring here to units of a trust, not apartments.

A *family discretionary trust* is probably the most common type of trust for property investors. Also referred to simply as a family trust or a discretionary trust, this type of structure is usually set up to hold a family's assets. The trustee can use their discretion to distribute the trust's income and assets to the beneficiaries, allowing family members to take advantage of tax benefits.

A *hybrid trust* is a combination of a unit trust and a family discretionary trust. It allows beneficiaries to hold units in the trust while at the same time giving the trustee the power to distribute income as they wish.

The biggest advantage to buying an investment property through a trust structure is *asset protection*. One of the main features of a trust structure is that the investment property is held in the trust's name, not your own, so in most cases the trust's assets are protected from creditors if one of the beneficiaries goes bankrupt or is the subject of legal action. This is ideal if you are in a high-risk job (as a brain surgeon, perhaps), where you might run the risk of getting sued if something goes wrong.

Family trusts allow the trustee to split the income between beneficiaries in the most tax-effective way each year. If the investment property is held by the trust for more than a year, you can also take advantage of the 50 per cent capital gains tax (CGT) discount.

If you are buying a neutral or positively geared property, or it will become positively geared in the short term, it is better to buy in a trust rather than your own name. If it is positively geared it adds to your personal income at tax time. If the property is negatively geared then claiming it in your personal income, therefore having the property in your own name, means you will be able to lower your taxable income and save some tax.

Each trust features a trust deed. This is a document that outlines the rules every trustee must follow and what will happen to each beneficiary's share of the trust's assets upon their death. This simplifies the estate-planning process and can help avoid legal battles over who inherits the assets after a person's death.

There are also some key tax issues to be aware of when you're considering buying property using a trust.

If you own an investment property as an individual and decide to transfer it into a trust, the trust will typically need to pay stamp duty and you will be liable for capital gains tax. When the property was originally bought you would have paid stamp duty on it, so this means you'll be paying stamp duty twice.

Also, if the trust makes a capital loss or a rental loss on an investment property, there's no option to offset that loss. This means there is no option for negative-gearing benefits, if that is part of your strategy.

The different tax implications here are so important that you really need to understand them before buying a property, which is another reason to seek advice from a good accountant and to include them in your investment property portfolio dream team from early on.

LLOYD'S STRATEGY

Often it is more beneficial to buy property in your own name, depending on your strategy. Asset protection and tax implications vary with the different structures so be sure to get good advice, but more importantly, you need to understand that advice and how it fits in with your strategy.

A FINANCIAL PLANNER

Many people use financial planners. A good one can really benefit your dream team. First you need to check that your financial planner has a *financial services licence.*

The last banking royal commission into financial institutions unearthed some dodgy financial planners who were not giving independent advice in relation to some of the banks, such as AMP and CBA, so this can be a tricky area. The key to getting genuinely independent and honest advice is to pay a financial planner a fee for service up front, beyond the services they get paid to recommend.

You also need to find someone whose own finances are well established before taking advice from them. I believe this is very important.

It is worth doing your proper due diligence on them — just as my clients do their research on me and expect me to have a large property portfolio. You're not going to take property advice from someone who has no experience as a property investor. The same goes for your financial planner.

The thing with financial planners is that often they don't like property. They tend to advise people on the sorts of investments they're getting something out of, such as the share market, where the planner can get a commission on the back end.

If you do use a financial planner, remember that their job is to advise on financing only, not the actual property — unless they are qualified in property as well as financial planning, which is pretty rare.

Recently we were about to purchase for a client an established dual-occupancy property in Brisbane with a really high rental yield. The client hired me as the buyer's agent but had their own financial planner.

After I'd suggested this property was exactly what these clients had been looking for, the first thing their financial planner had to say was, 'Well, I'm not qualified in property but I'm just going to advise on it anyway. This property is a bit strange. It's not a duplex and it's not a house; it's a five-bedroom property but there are no five-bedroom houses in the area, and that means there'll be a problem with valuation.'

I almost hit the roof because I was thinking, this guy has admitted he's not qualified to offer advice on property. After reading his email, our deeply concerned clients, who loved the property, called our office.

I respectfully returned the financial planner's email: 'Thank you for your insights here. You are correct that this property is not a duplex or a house. It's actually a dual-occupancy property, which consists of a main dwelling and then an auxiliary dwelling, otherwise known as a granny flat.' I pointed out that it was actually a very common type of property, and it was ideal because it enjoyed really good cashflow.

I quickly sorted it out and the sale went through. The bank's valuation came in on the purchase price so there was no problem there. The financial planner's concerns had been unfounded.

SOLICITORS AND CONVEYANCERS

Conveyancing is the legal process of facilitating the sale of a property. A conveyancer is a licensed professional who specialises in handling the transfer of titles. Conveyancers are not necessarily qualified solicitors and can't give advice on everything a solicitor can.

When I buy property I prefer to use a *property solicitor*, simply because they are more highly qualified and know property law better than conveyancers, which can help if any issues pop up.

I recommend you engage a conveyancer or solicitor whenever you are:

 buying or selling a property

 subdividing land

 updating a title, such as when strata titling or subdividing

 registering, changing or removing an easement.

For the buyer, a conveyancer or property solicitor will be able to perform the following tasks:

 prepare, clarify and lodge legal documents such as the Contract of Sale and Memorandum of Transfer

 research the property and its Certificate of Title, checking for easements, type of title and any other information that needs addressing

 hold the deposit money in a trust account

 calculate the adjustment of rates and taxes

 settle the property on your behalf

 advise when the property is settled

 contact your bank or financial institution when final payments are being made

 represent your interest with a vendor or their agent.

For the seller, a conveyancer or property solicitor will:

 complete legal documents

 represent you in dealings with the buyer, such as title questions and requests to extend dates.

There are three stages in the selling process:

 pre-contract

 pre-completion

 post-completion.

Typically, a conveyancer will do everything necessary to ensure you are prepared for critical dates during the contract process. They are also in regular contact with the other party's lawyers, dealing with issues that arise during the process.

Although you can do this yourself, it is better to use someone qualified and to make that person an essential part of your dream team.

Solicitors and conveyancers may charge anywhere from $1000 to $2500, depending on the scope of the work and the number of title searches that are required in the course of the conveyancing process.

BUILDING AND PEST INSPECTORS

When buying an established property, we need to get it checked out to make sure, first and foremost, that the building is structurally sound, with no evidence of current termite activity.

If serious issues such as these are identified during the inspection, we have the option of either pulling out of the sale or negotiating further on the price of the property based on the cost of repairs. Even without negotiating a lower price, identifying and fixing problems before you buy could save you thousands of dollars down the track.

Always use a licensed building inspector to carry out this inspection. Typically, the fee for this is around $600, so factor this into your budget as it will be money well spent. You may also need to inspect more than one property.

The inspection takes one or two hours, but most companies will need a few days' notice to book it in. The building inspector will prepare a *property inspection report* that must comply with the Australian standards.

QUANTITY SURVEYOR

The specialist quantity surveyor comes in at the end to complete a comprehensive *capital allowances and tax depreciation report* or schedule on your property. Here's where you get lots of money back on tax. Once you have this report, you need to pass it to your accountant so they can work out exactly what deductions you can claim.

Depreciation is a tax deduction available to property investors. The Australian Taxation Office (ATO) allows you to claim for the wear and tear over time on any old or new investment property. Basically, it recognises that the building itself plus its internal fixtures and fittings will become worn over time and will eventually need to be replaced.

A *depreciation schedule* outlines the deductions available for both capital works, and plant and equipment assets, and is used each financial year when preparing tax returns.

There are two types of allowances available.

 ## 1. PLANT AND EQUIPMENT

This refers to mechanical items and/or things that can be relatively easily removed from the property, such as:

- hot-water systems, heaters, solar panels, ovens
- air-conditioning units
- blinds and curtains
- carpets
- light fittings

- swimming-pool filtration and cleaning systems

- security systems.

2. BUILDING ALLOWANCE

This covers the construction costs of the building itself, such as concrete and brickwork, and things that are built in, such as:

- kitchen cupboards

- doors and door furniture (handles, locks etc.)

- sinks, basins, baths and toilet bowls

- clothes lines

- driveways

- fences and retaining walls.

As you can see, there are lots of things you can claim on. It doesn't matter that you may not have paid for them originally; you, as the current owner, can claim deductions as they continue to depreciate. You can depreciate everything up to a period of 40 years (the ATO-specified lifetime of your property), but most of the depreciation happens over the first five to 10 years of the property. This is certainly when you will get the most benefits; after that, the amount you can claim will decrease over the years.

As a property investor you want to make sure you are getting the most from your annual tax return. Claiming depreciation deductions is a significant taxation benefit, and one that many investment property owners don't know enough about.

Depreciation is a *non-cash deduction*, meaning *you do not need to spend any money to claim it*. As with any tax deduction, property depreciation reduces your taxable income. That means thousands more to reinvest in your property portfolio each year.

This is another reason why I love duplexes. Duplexes have two of everything, so you can claim on two of everything. This can mean you receive some seriously exciting money back on your tax. I love it!

You should allow around $500 to get a tax depreciation schedule done, though costs do vary. It will be more for a duplex as they will need to do one for each unit, but you should be able to get a discount on the two schedules.

INSURANCE REP

Now you're an investor, you'll need to take out *landlord's insurance* to cover you for loss of rent, damage to property and so on. You can either go through an insurance broker, who will find you the best insurance, or go directly to an insurance company.

I don't have a preference, but regardless of which you choose, you should get two or three quotes to compare. If you have current policies in place, get quotes from the same companies; they might give you a discount for having multiple policies.

BUYER'S AGENT

Well, here we are at the end of the process!

When I started my buyer's agency Aus Property Professionals, I wore every hat (as business owners often do). It was just me and I was working as a teacher full time as well as managing the business. I never pushed too hard for growth and just let it happen organically.

I now employ 13 people. I have other buyer's agents who I train in my strategies, as well as research analysts, property analysts and admin staff. We have staff based across different states as well so we can easily source and inspect appropriate properties.

Clients come to me for a range of services. While most people engage me as their full-service buyer's agent, including setting their strategy, others might hire me solely to bid on their behalf at auction. Or they may have found a property and want me and my team to carry out a due diligence assessment and advise on whether it is a suitable property to buy given their goals.

Some of our clients come to us to do a single purchase and we can tie things up when they have everything in place. Many others stay with me for the long term as we build up their property portfolio. It all comes down to strategy and what they are looking for.

SUCCESS STORY
Lloyd's thriving portfolio

I have recommended that you do due diligence on me, as on all professionals you work with. Here I'll share with you how well my own portfolio is performing and bringing me and my family so much joy every day.

MY STRATEGY TO BUY A HOLIDAY HOME

I now own a lifestyle property on the NSW South Coast. Buying a holiday home is not a strategy I recommend for people first off. I think you should first build a quality asset base of investment properties to buy and hold. Lifestyle changes will be achievable later.

But since buying our dream home at Lilli Pilli I'm still quite active with my own portfolio. I have used some interesting strategies to pay down my home mortgage and increase my equity so we could purchase a family holiday home.

Most of my property is still 'buy and hold'. I've had Rockdale for over 20 years. A one-bedroom apartment, and a property I paid only about $250 000 for in the first place, Rockdale has ended up working quite well. I've done a fair bit of upkeep, looking after the tenants and maintaining the quality of the property. I've had it painted a few times, and I recently replaced the air conditioner and the dishwasher. After three growth cycles, the building is getting a bit older and it has a few issues. So it might be time to offload it.

(continued)

SUCCESS STORY
Lloyd's thriving portfolio
(*cont'd*)

Despite being an older apartment, Rockdale has still increased a lot in rent in the past few years, like all my properties, and everyone else's. Rental costs have gone up around the country, with the low supply of properties and large demand from people wanting somewhere to live. It makes it harder for people who are looking to rent, but it's certainly a good thing if you're a landlord.

I've sold blocks of land, and I sold another duplex that I'd built in the Newcastle market. But I didn't do any developments in inland regional markets such as Armidale between 2019 and 2024, because there was a large increase in building costs. Some areas where I used to turn a profit did not work so well any more: the numbers did not add up during the boom.

However, I found that building a nice custom-designed property near the water could work really well. So, I developed a lot of bespoke and spec'd-up properties down the South Coast in Ulladulla, which is near Mollymook, and in Merimbula, which is further south on the Sapphire Coast. I did some great projects down there, which were all about what suits the block, what suits the area, what sort of aspect we're going to have, looking at the water or the countryside, how high the ceilings are going to be, where we should have the bedrooms, how we are going to make use of the block if we're building a duplex there, and that kind of thing.

I am also developing a set of six townhouses down in Merimbula, which is a more expensive project than a duplex or a house. The idea will be to sell three of them. I will take the profits to pay down the other three, which will be rented out, and to pay down debt across other areas of the portfolio. I'm working on the build numbers with the builder now. Then I'll do that again, so I'm looking for another block. I've also had great success in the Brisbane market. I own a couple of properties in Brisbane now, including a house, and I'm looking to buy another.

My portfolio has a lot of positively geared properties in it, so in 2022 I treated myself. We bought our very own lifestyle property down on the beach at Mollymook, which is our favourite place to go as a family.

When I bought in Mollymook, I put down a 50 per cent deposit, and borrowed only half the funds for the property. So I've got a smaller mortgage on it. And this is good because, being a holiday home, I'm not renting out all year. We use Airbnb to rent it out eight to 10 times a year. We go down there to see in the New Year, but we've had people staying there over Christmas. The cashflow is good with Airbnb: you can get more per night than you can per week under normal circumstances.

We go down there as much as possible on weekends and holidays. It's just beautiful. The kids absolutely love it there—they are just so at home. And that property is nearly paid off.

MY STRATEGY AROUND FAMILY ASSETS AND GENERATIONAL WEALTH

My lovely mother passed away in 2023 after a long eight years on dialysis. Barbara was my biggest fan and supported me through all my endeavours. Although her health deteriorated in later years, it was the love for her grandchildren Riley and Caelen that kept her going. I think I have a lot of my mother in me, as no matter how hard things got for her she always saw the positives in life. I feel I cope with any of life's struggles well because of my mum's example.

After Mum died, my brother Robert and I inherited the family home in Orange.

The house has been in our family for more than a hundred years. Funny story—it was originally owned by my father's family and was the house my dad grew up in. Dad inherited it from his parents. Then Mum's parents bought her the farm, and Mum and Dad moved out there.

Dad sold his house cheaply to Mum's parents so they could move off the farm into town and retire in Orange. That's how Dad's house ended up becoming Mum's parents' house. When they

(continued)

SUCCESS STORY
Lloyd's thriving portfolio
(*cont'd*)

passed away, the house went to her, and now it's with Robert and me. Things like this happen in the country. So the house has gone through several generations, across two different families, but is back with the Edge family, and we will continue that legacy.

That property is right in the very middle of town, one street over from the main street of Orange. You can't possibly get a better location. The other houses around it are businesses, like hairdressers and surgeries, and it could become a commercial use building.

We cleaned it up and rented it out to a tenant. We may look to turn it into an Airbnb in the future. It recently had a valuation of $1.2 million, which is a decent value for a regional property. Back in the 1970s, when it was changing families, it was worth about $20 000. But the value of that house is not the point. It's a family asset that we'll keep and pass down to the boys along with its importance, because their grandparents and great-grandparents had lived there at one time or another.

The boys will get all the property eventually. I have already mentioned that I want them to grow up balanced. Essentially my parents and Renee's parents had no investment assets, and no properties other than their homes. My dad had his business, which he sold on retirement, so that was an asset. But they had no investment properties, and I want my kids to enjoy a better situation to help them grow wealth to last through future generations.

I won't just be giving them property. I'll teach them how to *buy* property. They will grow up grounded and well educated on the subject. I'll teach my kids how to budget and how to save for the first property they buy. I'll help them with the purchase, of course. I'll teach them how the wealth we create can be used, not for fancy toys or clothes, but for the greater good and to help improve the lives of others in the world. They can then teach their own kids the same values, and so on.

MY EXIT STRATEGY

These are goals I have achieved, and one of the reasons for writing this book in the first place.

My new goal is to focus on an exit strategy, and I'm already in the midst of it (although I still buy as well). What I'm doing now, as well as adding to my portfolio, is using profits to pay down debt, which is the important part of consolidating your portfolio. It comes back to overall strategy. You don't want to carry large amounts of debt forever. And of course I may still decide to retire from investing someday!

So I plan to sell down some properties that have grown in value (some have doubled in value) to pay down the debt on properties I plan to keep, thereby creating more true passive income. An exit strategy can also allow you to buy better, blue-chip properties or to buy your dream home.

My buy-and-hold properties tend to be positively geared from the start now, because these days I put down a larger deposit. If you're buying your first property, you're probably going to have a lower deposit, and it might be slightly negatively geared, but once you build up the equity, you can basically make any deposit and positively gear it from the start. For example, if you put a 10 per cent deposit on the property, and you borrow 90 per cent, then the cashflow is going to be negative. But if you put down a 30 per cent deposit and you're borrowing only 70 per cent, or you put down a 40 per cent deposit, then you're borrowing a lot less and the cashflow is a lot more than your repayments. Of course, this also depends on the interest rate you're paying.

This is how my portfolio has evolved from that little Rockdale apartment to an inventory of blue-chip properties worth millions. It was all through having a strategy and goals in place. I've done it for myself, and for my clients, time and time again. It's real and it can work for you too.

I'd love to help you achieve what I have, to step up and become a property investor or simply to find your family dream home. The choice is yours. I look forward to working with you!

APPENDIX
YOUR PROPERTY INVESTMENT PLAN CHECKLIST

I hope you've enjoyed reading *Positively Geared* and that it has inspired you to realise your own property investment dreams, whether you're saving for that first deposit or leveraging existing investments to start developing your own property trifecta. Remember, knowing where you are will help you know where you're going.

THE PROPERTY TRIFECTA

EQUITY   CASHFLOW   GROWTH

The following checklist has been designed to help you evaluate where you are right now on your own property investing journey, and where you can improve — in short, to help you make a plan that will maximise the returns on your investments.

Give yourself a score of either 1 for 'yes' or Q for 'question against that' for the statements below:

- ☐ I have a clear strategy for the next five years.

- ☐ All my current properties are performing in line with my expectations.

- ☐ I have a great team that includes a buyer's agent, solicitor, accountant and mortgage broker.

☐ I complete an annual review of my portfolio.

☐ I regularly keep up to date with the markets.

☐ I have updated my will to reflect my property portfolio.

☐ I understand how principal and interest (P&I) and interest only (IO) loans will work within my strategy.

☐ I know when to fix rates and when to keep them variable.

☐ I understand the roles of my accountant and solicitor.

☐ I understand the pros and cons of buying in a trust rather than independently.

HOW DID YOU GO?

[0–3] Let's talk about your game plan and where you can improve your property portfolio.

[4–7] There's a lot to like here, but some work to do to reach your full potential and your ultimate goals.

[8–10] You're on fire! Let's talk about how you could become a professional investor.

Are you excited, if a little daunted, by the challenge of getting your goals and strategy on track? I'm here to help. First, contact me and we'll talk through your situation over the phone or by Zoom, or set up a face-to-face meeting. You're under no obligation at this stage. It's important that you feel we are a good fit.

Find me online at:

auspropertyprofessionals.com.au

Send an email to:

lloyd@auspropertyprofessionals.com.au *or*

admin@auspropertyprofessionals.com.au

Listen to our podcasts at:

auspropertyprofessionals.com.au/positivelygeared/podcasts/

or on Apple or Spotify or wherever you get your podcasts

Find me on Instagram at **instagram.com/lloydedge_buyersagent/**

Join our Base Camp Property Club group so you can keep up to date with insights into and news on property markets across Australia and tap into online resources and in-person live courses.

Go to:

facebook.com/groups/basecamppropertyclub

to access free resources and advice from industry experts and successful investors.

FURTHER READING

If you liked *Positively Geared*, you're sure to enjoy the following books that have inspired me:

Rich Dad Poor Dad, by Robert Kiyosaki

Rich Dad's Cashflow Quadrant: Guide to Financial Freedom, by Robert Kiyosaki

Think and Grow Rich, by Napoleon Hill

Midas Touch: Why Some Entrepreneurs Get Rich and Why Most Don't, by Donald Trump and Robert Kiyosaki

From 0 to 130 Properties in 3.5 years, by Steve McKnight

What It Takes, by Mark Bouris

Rich Habits Poor Habits, by Tom Corley and Michael Yardney

The Accidental Entrepreneur, by Janine Allis

Kids Money Habits, by Amy Koit

INDEX